BVB 30,—

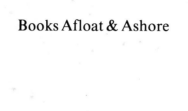

Books Afloat & Ashore

BOOKS AFLOAT & ASHORE

*A history of books, libraries, and reading among
seamen during the age of sail*

by HARRY R. SKALLERUP

ARCHON BOOKS   •   1974

Library of Congress Cataloging in Publication Data

Skallerup, Harry Robert
    Books afloat & ashore.

    Includes bibliographical references.
    1. Libraries, Naval—History.   I. Title.
Z675.N3S54   026.3875   73-15879
ISBN 0-208-01408-X

© 1974 by Harry R. Skallerup
First published 1974 as an Archon Book,
an imprint of The Shoe String Press, Inc.,
Hamden, Connecticut 06514

Printed in the United States of America

In memory of
my great-grandfather
Søren Chr. Nielsen Skallerup
1825-1912
Her er vi endelig!

Contents

Illustrations

Preface

Most of the jewels in the great treasure trove of sea lore have been picked over more than once by writers of maritime history. And in the course of recounting the histories of ships, ports, battles, and commerce and in recording the deeds of famous mariners and their crews, almost every aspect of early nautical existence and experience has been extensively examined, including such prosaic things as the clothing seamen wore, the food they ate, and the songs they sang. Little, however, has been told about the books that seamen read. Yet nestled among the more glittering gems and golden trinkets in the casket of marine riches lies this well-worn coin of the realm, which has been more or less overlooked, perhaps only because it appeared to be too dull or commonplace to inspect more closely.

Indeed, a few nautical researchers have touched upon the topic of books, libraries, and reading among seamen, but the subject has never been fully explored or discussed independently. Neither has it received more than a passing mention in the literature concerned with the history of books and libraries in the United States. It might be thought that everything is already known about the subject, or else that it is too narrow to yield more than a few pages of original comment. Rather the reverse is true. I found this to be so when I prepared to write an article on the origin of American ships' libraries which went a little deeper than present-day knowledge of the subject. One source or clue led to another, and I soon had to confine my research in order to keep it within the reasonable bounds of a book. Although I have been interested in the subject of books at sea for many years, and had accumulated some information from reading the published contemporary accounts of sea voyages (which for every word about books or libraries at sea seem to have paragraphs about sea burials, shipboard divine services, floggings, or seasickness), and from secondary sources, it was only after moving to the Washington, D.C., area that I became aware that what I had been working on was only one part of a larger untold story. The resources of the National Archives and the Library of Congress enabled me to find many of the answers to my questions, and within the library and museum of the United States Naval Academy I discovered an unmined deposit of source materials still remaining from the very beginnings of organized naval libraries in this country.

The history of books among seamen in the days of sail is not unrelated to the cultural history of the world. Social, educational, scientific, literary, military, and religious influences have all played a role in determining the need, choice, or supply of books to seamen at one time or another. Also, the situations in which books and libraries flourished within the martime community were diverse. At the high-water mark of nautical libraries in the United States, there were no less than fifteen different types of libraries for mariners in existence afloat and ashore. And although those libraries aboard ship could not have rivalled in size the fabulous library Jules Verne depicted as the property of the fictional Captain Nemo on his submarine "Nautilus," a few of them were possibly as large and more relevant in content than the combined book holdings of all the missions on the coast of California in the early 1830s. As such, these libraries afloat were a unique manifestation and extension of one of man's oldest cultural institutions.

In the present study I have attempted to trace the origins and development of the several types of shipboard and shoreside libraries for seamen as well as to document the strong tradition of books and reading at sea. The period covered extends from the invention of printing to the beginning of the American Civil War. While emphasis is placed upon the history of books, libraries, and reading in the navy and merchant marine of the United States, the first chapter presents a broad, brief survey of a few examples, international in scope, of the early use of books, and of the precedents for libraries at sea. The second chapter provides some background to the common beginnings of seamen's welfare in Great Britain (the giver and sharer of so many of our social concepts and institutions) and the United States. Each succeeding chapter progresses somewhat chronologically but also concentrates on one or more specific aspects of the American history; and the last chapter is devoted to a consideration of the conditions aboard nineteenth-century sailing ships which fostered or hindered reading at sea. Beyond the mention of certain European influences, no effort was made in this work to include or compare the maritime library history of foreign nations.

I have tried to refrain from slowing or cluttering the text by excluding the listings of books and the contents of libraries. This matter, for the most part, has been collected together in the appendixes where it might also be of value from a comparative standpoint. The facts of life concerning present-day publishing costs have also dictated the extent and form of bibliographic documentation used. Thus, I have followed the example of many other authors of scholarly histories and have presented the more pertinent footnote citations together in the form of "bibliographic notes." It is hoped that this telegraphic indication of sources will nevertheless be useful to others who might wish to explore more fully some of the topics which are introduced here.

During the preparation of this book, there were a number of persons who unhesitatingly extended to me some particular help or kindness, and whom I would like to thank once again. Among them are George M. Ewing, Editor and Publisher of the *Canandaigua Daily Messenger*; A. Blair Cummins, Director, Wood Library; Clyde M. Maffin, Ontario County Historian; Frederic T. Henry, and Helen B. Feenaughty of Canandaigua; Pauline P. Spare, Director, Ontario Cooperative Library System; Adele D. Leonard, Assistant Librarian, State Library of New York; Helen P. Bolman, Librarian, General Society of Mechanics and Tradesmen; W. Noel Clarke, Superintendent Chaplain, British Sailors' Society; William A. Hallen, Executive Director, American Seamen's Friend Society; Raymond H. Shove, Professor, University of Minnesota; John Alden, Keeper of Rare Books, Boston Public Library; J. Thomas Russell, Associate Librarian, U.S. Military Academy Library; Walter B. Greenwood, Librarian, Navy Department Library; Nelson J. Molter, Director, Maryland State Library; Charlotte Fletcher, Librarian, St. John's College; Aloha Smith, Harry Schwartz, Albert Blair, and Joseph B. Ross, all at the National Archives; Howard I. Chapelle, Historian Emeritus (Technology), National Museum of History and Technology; and at the U.S. Naval Academy, Captain Dale Mayberry, USN (Ret.), Director, and James Cheevers, Curator, USNA Museum, James H. Elsdon, Professor, USNA (Ret.), Neville T. Kirk, Professor, and also Theodore de Disse and Lila E. Andreas. Special thanks are due to two others of my associates at the Naval Academy, Patrick F. Clausey, Special Collections Librarian, for his valuable suggestions, and to Professor Wilson L. Heflin, lifelong Melville scholar, who kindly read and criticized portions of the manuscript and generously exchanged information of a mutual interest. Lastly, at home, my wife, Amy Gage, shared with me some of the drudgery and joys of research and editing; while Thomas, Susan, and Janet, each contributed something toward the making of this book.

In acknowledging the aid of the several persons who made my way easier, I must, of course, mention that I am solely responsible for all opinions expressed and conclusions reached, and for whatever errors that may have crept into the text.

H. R. S.

Annapolis, Maryland

Books Afloat & Ashore

Chapter I

Loomings

But the images of men's wits and knowledges remain in books . . . cap-
able of perpetual renovation. . . . If the invention of the ship was
thought so noble, which carrieth riches and commodities from place to
place, and consociateth the most remote regions in participation of their
fruits, how much more are letters to be magnified, which as ships pass
through the vast seas of time, and make ages so distant to participate
of the wisdom, illuminations, and inventions, the one of the other?
—Francis Bacon

Herman Melville introduced and set the nautical mood of *Moby Dick*
with just one word—"Loomings." This old seafaring word stands at the
head of the first chapter of his great work, and it is defined there by the
comments of Ishmael in the sense of a portentous occurrence about
to take shape. Another meaning of loomings, the one used to charac-
terize the present chapter, is taken from the verb "to loom," or to come
into view, especially above the surface of the sea in a distorted or indis-
tinct form, as in a fog. Indeed, much of the very early history of seafaring
appears as a looming shadow, and the story of the reading materials of
the voyager is, of course, no exception. When man first took to the sea,
it was only natural, if not imperative, that he bring with him the necessities needed to sustain life as close as possible to that which he was accustomed to on land. Thus it was inevitable at some point, now lost in the
mists of time, that the phenomena of seafaring and reading came together, and henceforth the enlightened waterborne traveler deciphered
or read, as well as floated. Rather than speculate further about the

setting for this occasion, or attempt the difficult task of tracing the progress of shipboard reading among the ancients, the present study begins with the literate mariner afloat in Renaissance times.

Prior to the Renaissance, both the art of communication by written word and the art of sailing had reached a static plateau of achievement. But with the invention of the printing press, and with the development of the far-ranging sailing ship—spurred on by the desire to explore the world and exploit its riches—the physical obstacles limiting the expansion of knowledge were in some degree reduced. The rapid spread of printing throughout Europe served to quicken the reawakening of learning and to help broaden the base of intellectual inquiry. Printed books became relatively abundant, and books of current translation or authorship in the vernacular displaced the laboriously produced and expensive manuscript texts. By means of the printing press, reading material became accessible to more people, and reading as a skill became easier to acquire.

Out of the fog of these burgeoning times, then, loom a few examples of books, libraries, and reading at sea. They are presented here in an effort to survey the many avenues by which books were introduced into the world of the mariner, and to define the availability and use of books at sea during the fifteenth to the eighteenth centuries. Also, this brief overview is intended to serve as part of the background against which the later American experience can be interpreted; for similar requirements led to the adoption or rediscovery of many of the methods, means, or precedents that had gone before.

As the availability of paper and printed books and the opportunity for literacy spread, and as the sailing vessel roamed farther out of sight of land for longer periods of time, the mariner became more dependent upon books to help him regulate his floating world and to guide it with some degree of certainty upon the ocean. The seafarer, like his land-lubber brother, was also apt to read general books for personal pleasure and knowledge. If he were provident, he might embark with a few books suited to his own taste or needs. Thus books were carried aboard ship for two primary purposes: to help navigate or regulate the vessel, and to entertain or edify the individual. As for the more learned mariner, he needed to take scholarly books to sea with him on voyages of discovery. But if this were not always possible, he usually prepared himself before sailing by consulting appropriate books and libraries ashore. If he were fortunate as well as wise, he did both.

The historic voyages of Christopher Columbus touched off the great age of modern geographic discovery, and books, of course, influenced his idea of world geography. Because scholars have long been interested in the intellectual preparations and activities of Columbus, the nature of his reading has been widely researched. At least some of the titles of the books Columbus owned or studied are known, and hence we have an indication of the possible influence on, or source of, his ideas. Prior to departure on his first voyage, Columbus, over a period of years (1485-1490), spent part of his time poring over ancient and medieval treaties on cosmography or world geography. He owned and read Cardinal Pierre d'Ailly's *Imago mundi,* the *Historia rerum ubique gestarum* by Pope Pius II, the *Book of Ser Marco Polo,* and Pliny's *Natural History.* His copies of these four books which contained geographic knowledge of interest to him have survived (the first three bearing collectively extensive annotations in his or his brother's handwriting), and are preserved in the Biblioteca Colombina at Seville.

While many ordinary mariners who followed in the footsteps of Columbus probably did not care to read about the theoretical concepts of world geography, they were no doubt interested in news and accounts of voyages, and in practical descriptions of the lands that were encountered on them. The news of Columbus's discoveries on his first voyage, as communicated by him to the Spanish authorities in a letter in 1493, was given wide circulation by means of the printing press. In a year's time his letter had been printed as a folio pamphlet in twelve editions in the cities of Barcelona, Rome, Paris, Antwerp, Basel, and Florence; within five years the report appeared in not less than seventeen editions in six countries and four languages. One effect of news and accounts of discovery such as this was to inspire or goad the adventurous into undertaking increasingly distant and prolonged voyages. Antonio Pigafetta, who chronicled Magellan's voyage of circumnavigation, was one of those who was caught up in this spirit of adventure. His comments on how he was motivated to go to sea exemplify the experience of like-minded men of his and later times. It was through reading many books and by meeting "various persons" in Spain in 1509 that the marvels of the "ocean sea" were revealed to him in such a manner that, as he recalled, then and there he resolved to see such marvelous things for himself, and also gain for himself "some renown for later posterity."[1]

As the oral and written accounts of navigators and travelers increased, the value of this corpus of practical geographic knowledge became apparent to a few men who attempted to record, preserve, and otherwise make it known. In Italy, Giovanni Battista Ramusio, a public official with an intense interest in geography, began to gather, in 1523, the accounts of early and contemporary adventurers. Ramusio corresponded with other interested men and combed Spain and Italy for the materials, which he edited and translated when necessary, that he included in his collection of voyages and travels, *Navigationi et viaggi.* This three-volume work was published between the years 1550 and 1559,

about the same time that other scholars began to take a serious interest
in the recording, identification, and description of books and writing
in general. Some thirty years after the first appearance of Ramusio's
work, the English geographer and clergyman, Richard Hakluyt, using
it as a model, produced a carefully compiled and edited collection of
voyages and travels in the English language. Like Antonio Pigafetta,
Hakluyt was first inspired by the romance of discovery through books,
maps, and discourse—in his case, supplied by an older cousin of the
same name whom he visited as a youth. But instead of venturing forth
himself, the younger Hakluyt resolved that he would endeavor to pursue
the study of geography. His countrymen and posterity were rewarded
by the success of his determination, for he ferreted out the archival
materials of many voyages of discovery, and skillfully wove the narratives of adventurers, which he and his cousin assembled over the years,
into an extensive collection of historic and geographic literature, *The
Principall Navigations, Voiages and Discoveries of the English
Nation . . .*, published in 1589 in one volume, and later in 1598–
1600 in three volumes. Today, because of the language in which
it was written, and because of its content—the literal stuff of Elizabethan
maritime history—his work is still read as great literature and history.
In Hakluyt's time, however, the *Voyages* served to supply Englishmen
with practical geographic information on almost every country where
western Europeans had ever journeyed. Copies were furnished to vessels
of the East India Company (formed in 1599, and for which Hakluyt was
a consultant on Eastern problems), and were used with confidence by
their captains. Samuel Purchas, who, after Hakluyt's death in 1616,
continued the work as *Purchas His Pilgrims,* mentioned in it an incident in which £20,000 was saved in expenses by the master of an East
Indiaman who consulted "the Book," *i.e.,* Hakluyt, in time of need,
and happily found a safe harbor.[2] Hakluyt was also selected for shipboard study by scholarly mariners who were not connected with the
company. In 1631, when Captain Thomas James fitted out his vessel
in Bristol for a voyage in search of the Northwest Passage, he purchased "A Chest full of the best and choicest Mathematicall bookes
that could be got for money in England; as likewise Master Hackluite
and Master Purchas, and other books of Journals and Histories."[3]

Captain James's choice of books further defines the professional
literature of his day. Not only did James, a scholar, want to read books
of voyages and travels for whatever geographical value he might derive
from them, but he also carried with him books of a technical nature.
Some of these "Mathematicall bookes" probably were theoretical and
others, no doubt, were practical treatises on navigation and the use of
astronomical instruments. From the time of Columbus, and all the

while Ramusio, Hakluyt, Purchas, and their Dutch counterpart, Théodore de Bry, were recording the results of exploration, other scholars and mariners concerned themselves with the problems inherent in the sailing of ships on transoceanic voyages. The progress that was made in this direction was multifaceted. It involved the application of mathematics and astronomy to the solution of some of the navigational problems which puzzled mariners, as well as the development and perfecting of certain navigational instruments and charts and the introduction of new techniques in seamanship, shipbuilding, and naval hygiene. To be sure, voyages had been made out of sight of land before Columbus. Portuguese navigators, urged on by Prince Henry the Navigator, had sailed long distances in search of India via the African coast, but it remained for others to build upon this experience and change the ancient art of sailing from one known location to another into a science of some precision.

In the process a professional literature, which consisted of certain kinds of printed navigational aids and books written especially for the seafarer, was created. The story of the development of this literature as an important tool of navigation has been told in histories on the subject, and need not be repeated here, except to note and define two important components of the early literature mentioned in some of the examples of technical reading matter aboard ships of the period. In contemporary usage, books of sailing directions (themselves of ancient origin) came to be known generically as "rutters" in English. The word comes from the French "routier"—the name for a book that gave pilot directions or routes to follow at sea, descriptions of certain coasts, and other navigational data. And any book containing both sailing directions and navigational charts was likely to be referred to as a "waggoner," after the Dutch pilot Luke Wagenar's name and work published in 1584. His book, the *Spieghel der Zeevaert,* brought together for the first time in printed form a treatise on navigation, a set of charts, and a collection of sailing directions in detail, which collectively served the mariner as a complete sea atlas.

Navigational works representative of the state of the art at various times during the era of discovery appear to have been acquired as private property by certain seamen who had reached a rank high enough in their calling to be responsible for piloting or navigating a vessel. One of the most illuminating glimpses at the navigational resources of an English navigator is afforded by an inventory of the belongings of one John Aborough, master of the merchant ship *Michael of Barnstaple* in 1533. Among the goods in his two sea chests were a lodestone, two compasses, a sandglass, two charts, other navigational items mentioned by their then-known names, and several books. Three of the books as he de-

scribed them indicate their requisite value to a mariner of the time as
navigational aids, as well as their actual value as items of personal
property. Aborough declared: "Item more in said counter [his chest] a
Rovuttyer in Yenglishe which I John Aborough was a yere and a halfe
of makyng of hyt and a nother Rottier in Castiellan and a Reportory in
portu guyse whiche bokes 1 will not give for xl *s*."[4] As a practicing
navigator, who voyaged to the Levant, Aborough found that he needed
an English rutter, probably for the Biscayan or Spanish coast, and had
accordingly made or copied one himself. He also possessed another
in Spanish. The Portuguese "Reportory" might have been a seaman's
navigational manual such as the *Regimento do estrolabio y do qua-
drante,* the first manual in which certain astronomical tables were combined as one book, and which was in use about 1520.

The possession of practical navigational books and instruments by
John Aborough is significant for it indicates that early navigators owned
certain tools of their trade. Thus, it was not unlikely that ship's officers,
such as he, were required to furnish at least some of the more portable
navigational items, including books, while other articles were probably
part of the ship's property. On the basis of certain records concerning
the building and management of English ships prior to 1519, various
items, such as astrolabes, cross-staffs, and rutters, were never listed
among the purchases of specific shipowners, although compasses,
lodestones, sandglasses, and sounding gear were. This suggests an early
possible division in the responsibility for providing navigational items
between shipowners and ship officers. A proportioning or allotment of
navigational instruments among mariners is also alluded to in the seventh
ordinance of Sebastian Cabot, one of the thirty-three decrees prepared
for the government of an intended voyage to Cathay in 1553. But whatever balance of responsibility was maintained for the provision of essential books over the years, by the eighteenth century in the Royal Navy,
it had come to be placed with the master of a vessel. This officer was
then expected, according to the regulations governing vessels in His
Majesty's Service, to provide himself with "the proper Instruments,
Maps, and Books of Navigation."[5]

While it might be expected that navigators, such as John Aborough,
who were engaged in the day-to-day sailing of prosaic merchantmen in
the course of routine trade would have only a few navigational books at
their disposal, it is not safe to assume that the more daring navigators
on voyages of exploration necessarily carried large collections of books
with them, especially in the form of libraries. The opportunity to purchase suitable books at the expense of the merchants of a seaport or
companies formed for the purpose of fostering overseas exploration was
more or less responded to according to the scholarly inclinations of the

captains of the expeditions. As already noted, in the case of Captain Thomas James, a gentleman and amateur seaman, a chest-full of the best books obtainable was deemed essential for him while at sea in 1631. But by contrast, Captain Luke Foxe, a sea-bred professional mariner, who prepared for a similar voyage in the same year, had little use for book learning. As he contemptuously noted in his book, *The North-West Fox,* published two years after James's account:

> And for Bookes, if I wanted any, I was to blame, being bounti-
> fully furnisht from the Treasurer with money to provide me,
> especially for those of study; there would be no leisure, nor was
> there, for I found work enough; and if the matter it selfe had not
> been in another place when sodaine occasion was present, it
> had bin too late for me (like the Holland Skipper to runne to
> his chest) to looke vpon his Waggoner booke. But those things
> I feare you will say are needlesse (yet give me leave to follow the
> fashion), and good for nothing but to make Courtiers and
> Schollers marvelle at my curiositie, and thinke strange that there
> should be so much adoe about making a Ship take the Sea.

An earlier example, that of Captain Martin Frobisher, falls some-where between the opposing viewpoints of the rivals Foxe and James. For his first voyage in search of the Northwest Passage in 1576, the experienced Captain Frobisher, who admitted to being no scholar, purchased just eight books. Seven of the titles could be considered of professional interest, and these were written in English, French and Spanish. They comprised travel books and cosmographical treatises, and one good practical navigational manual.[6] It is possible that Fro-bisher already owned a few other books personally, and thus did not need to purchase as many books as he could have when outfitting for the expedition. Regardless of the numbers of books that navigators purchased for use on voyages of adventure, the occasions for these voyages at least introduced the precedent, or as Foxe mentioned, "the fashion," of supplying books of such quantity and substance to ships as perhaps would not have otherwise been considered. Yet it appears that the books so purchased may have been primarily or exclusively intended for the use of the chief officer of an expedition, and that they were stored in a chest in his quarters, and were not a ship's library, but more likely a small personal library.

During the period 1500-1640 in England the few occupational groups known to have owned books in any numbers were the clergy, university scholars, and physicians. Further, the amount of books available to seamen, which were of professional interest, was another factor that

probably limited the size of any shipboard collection, personal, or otherwise. Captain John Smith in 1627 addressed himself to the question of
the choice of navigational books and instruments in his own book,
A Sea Grammar, intended as a guide for young mariners. He remarked
that the instruments "fitting for a Sea-man" were compasses, an astro-
labe quadrant, a cross-staff, a backstaff, and a nocturnal. "To learn to
observe the Altitude, Latitude, Longitude," and to acquire about eight
other navigational skills, he advised the reader to "get some" of the
eleven navigational books which he listed by their English titles; yet at
the same time he admonished, "but practice is the best."[7] This appears
to have been more than timely counsel, for a much later edition of his
work, published in 1692, still contained essentially the same list of instruments and books, except that a "waggoner" was deleted.

Another scholarly mariner, Captain Samuel Sturmy, in preparing his
treatise on navigational arts, *The Mariner's Magazine,* published in
1669, mentioned or cited some twenty-seven titles of books that he must
have owned or consulted while he worked on his book in his study
ashore. These titles embraced the subjects of navigation, mathematics,
surveying, astronomy, geography, and a few of the mechanic arts. Most
of the books were written in English, with just a few in Latin. The 1684
edition of *The Mariner's Magazine* also contained a bonus in the form
of a list of "Mathematical and Sea Books" printed and sold by four
London booksellers (fig. 1). From this and other advertisements which
also appeared in similar contemporary works additional information
can be obtained on the kinds of books offered to mariners. The number
of books selected for inclusion in these booksellers' lists appears never
to have exceeded thirty-six or so titles, which consisted mostly of pilot
books, treatises on mathematics and navigation, and a sprinkling of
books on seamanship and related practical topics. Although prices
were not mentioned, many of the current books of Sturmy's and Frobisher's day could be bought for just a few shillings. Perhaps recognizing
that not every worthy mariner could afford his book at fourteen
shillings, Captain Sturmy, in an arrangement with St. George's
Church in Bristol made a copy of *The Mariner's Magazine* available
there. It was "chained too and locked in ye deosk" at the church, but
was to be loaned to anyone able to put up security in the value of £3.
For this kindness, the minister of the church promised to preach a
sermon on Sturmy's birthday every year.[8] Such was the value of his
book.

Aboard ship, in addition to whatever professional books the navigator
thought might be useful, there was another kind of essential literature
provided. It was for the internal regulation of the vessel, and although
not extensive in numbers of printed books, this written matter insured

MATHEMATICAL and SEA BOOKS, Printed for and fold by William Fifher, *at the* Poftern-Gate *near* Tower-Hill; Thomas Paffenger *at the* Three Bibles *on* London Bridge, Robert Boulter, *at the* Turks-Head, *and* Ralph Smith, *at the* Bible *in* Cornhil *near the* Royal Exchange. *viz.*

THE Mariners Magazine; containing the Art of Navigation, Surveying, Gaging, Gunnery, Aftronomy, Dyalling, Fortification: By Capt. *Sam. Sturmey.*

The Coafting-Pilot; with new Sand-draughts; by *J. Sellers.*

The Mariners new Kalender; by *Nathaniel Colfon.*

The Sea-mans Kalender; by *Henry Philips.*

The Sea-mans Practice; by *Richard Norwood.*

Norwood's Doctrine of Triangles with Logarithms, exactly corrected, and much enlarged by the Author.

A Practical Navigation, being an Introduction to the whole Art; the fifth Edition, carefully Corrected by *J. Sellers.*

The Sea-mans Dictionary, or the Expofition and Demonftration of all the parts and things belonging to a Ship; by Sir *Henry Manwaring.*

The Sea-mans Glafs, fhewing the ufe of the Plain-Scale in Navigation, Aftronomy, and Dyalling: with the ufe of Inftruments in Navigation.

The Sea-mans Companion, teaching Arithmetick, Geometry, Trigonometry, Navigation, and Aftronomy: by *Matthew Norwood.*

The Compleat Cannoneer fhewing the Principles and Ground of the Art of Gunnery; as alfo feveral Fire-works for Sea and Land.

The Safeguard of Sailers, and Pilots Sea-Mirror; defcribing the Sea-Coafts of *England, Scotland, Ireland, Holland, Denmark, Norway* according to the neweft Waggoner, with new Sea-Charts; a Book very ufeful.

The Compleat Modelift, fhewing how to raife the Model of any Ship or Veffel, either in Proportion or out of Proportion, and to find the length and bignefs of every Rope in all Veffels exactly, with the weight of their Anchors and Cables.

The Boatfwains Art, or Compleat Boatfwain, fhewing the Mafting, Yarding, and Rigging of any Ship, by *Henry Bond.*

The Compleat Ship-wright, teaching the Propofitions ufed by experienced Shipwrights, according to their cuftom of building; with the drawing of a draught, the making and marking a bend of Moulds, both by Arithmetick and Geometry; by *Ed. Buffnel.*

The Geometrical Sea-man, fhewing three kinds of Sailing; by the true *Sea Chart,* Mercator's *Chart,* and by a Great Circle; with two Traverfe Tables added by *H. Philips.*

Norwood's Epitome applied to plain and *Mercator's* Sailing, with ufeful Tables in Navigation.

The Mariners Compafs rectified; A Book furnifhed with Tables of Hours and Azimuths, ufeful in Navigation, Calculated from oo deg. to 60 deg. of Latitude: With the ufe of all Inftruments in Navigation: by *Andr. Wakely.*

A Mathematical Manual, by Mr. *Philips,* of Navigation, Gunnery, Dialling, Surveying, Gaging; with a Table of Logarithms, to 1000.

The Mirror of Architecture, or the Ground Rules of the Art of Building: by *Vincent Seamozzi,* Mafter Builder of *Venice;* with the ufe of a Joynt-Rule for Roofs, by *John Brown:* to which is added the Elements of Architecture by Sir *Henry Wooten,* Kt.

There are alfo fold all forts of Mathematical or Sea-Books in *Englifh,* or Books of any other Subject, as Divinity, Hiftory, Poetry, &c. Wagoners and Sea Charts, for all Parts of the World, all forts of Paper and Paper Books, at the cheapeft rate; alfo Bibles or any other Books new Bound and Clafped, and the beft Writing-Ink, Pens, Wax, Wafers, Pencils, &c.

1. Booksellers' listing of nautical books included in Captain Sturmy's *Mariner's Magazine,* 1684.

that a vessel was governed according to the authority that provided for its existence. An early example of one form of regulatory matter (which was usually promulgated prior to the commencement of a voyage) survives in the ordinances of Sebastian Cabot, previously mentioned. The third article of the ordinances gives a clear picture of the place of the regulatory material itself. It provided:

> . . . furthermore every mariner or passenger in his shippe hath given like othe to be obedient to the Captaine generall, and to every Captaine and master of his ship, for the observation of these present orders contained in this booke, and all other which hereafter shall be made . . . therefore it is convenient that this present booke shall once every weeke (by the discretion of the Captaine) be read to saide companie, to the intent that every man the better remember his othe, conscience, duetie and charge.

The reading aloud of the ordinances insured that those who were otherwise unable to read became informed of the regulations that governed the voyage. This provision for the periodic reading of such material has persisted in codes of naval regulations through recent times.

Also in force among merchant vessels of the time were the Laws of Oléron, codified in 1266. This compilation defined the legality of many maritime occurrences (and in doing so, had occasion to refer to the ancient Roman laws of the sea), and also regulated the rights and duties of masters, seamen, and shipowners. Whether these parties in times predating the printing press had ready access to copies of the laws is open to question, but some printed rutters are known to have contained them. A latter-day master or pilot owning a copy of Pierre Garcie's *Le grand routier* (first published in French in 1520, and in English translation in 1528 and subsequent editions) would also have been able to read the laws in this practical pilot book of the French and English coasts.

Religious observances, as an important part of shipboard routine, also placed emphasis on the need for the Bible and psalm books to be among the regulatory literature of a ship. In Columbus's day, a public prayer would be recited almost every half hour on shipboard. Prayers were said and hymns were sung in the hope that divine protection would thus be gained, while the religious offerings also served the double purpose of marking various changes in the routine of the vessel as the day wore on. Cabot's ordinances of 1553 called for morning and evening prayers, and the reading of the Bible or paraphrases of it to the crew "devoutly and Christianly to Gods honour." The place of piety in the routine of the ship was mentioned by Captain John Smith in 1627, and although Captain Luke Foxe had little use for professional books, he recognized the need for religious guidance, for he began and ended his eight "Orders and Articles for Civill Government" for his voyage with a reference to public prayers, and took note of their proper place in the routine of the ship.

The Bible as the repository and symbol of religious authority was no doubt carried aboard most English ships from an early date. Depending upon the religious and political temper of the times, the printed authorized version of the Bible then in vogue was likely to have been specified on vessels that came under official notice. In 1533, John Aborough, master of the merchantman *Michael of Barnstaple,* listed the "gospell and Pistell" along with the previously mentioned rutters and navigational instruments in his possession. The work was one of the two "Greate Bokes in Castelyan" that he valued at ten shillings. In this circumstance it might have also served as the *Barnstaple's* Bible. But a well-financed and fully outfitted expedition such as Captain Frobisher's probably could afford to purchase a more impressive ship's Bible. Frobisher paid £1 for a "greate" English Bible, and it was one of the eight books that he is known to have taken with him in 1576.

Aside from fulfilling the practical or imperative navigational and regulatory needs of the ship, books, of course, were uniquely suited to serve the recreational needs of the individuals who were aboard the ship. Voyagers from earliest times to the present have relied on certain ubiquitous objects of recreation and amusement to help them pass their time while engaged in one of the modes of land, sea, air, or space travel. The pilgrim Felix Fabri, in 1483, mentioned many of the ancient shipboard pastimes in his account of a sea passage from Venice to Palestine aboard a galley. He noted that wine, dice, playing cards, chess, and musical instruments were used by his fellow pilgrims to help reduce the tedium of the voyage. The more thoughtful voyagers, he observed, discussed worldly matters or read books. Some prayed with beads and some sat and looked at the passing scene, or wrote about their experiences.

Dice, cards, and gambling were often regulated against aboard ship, but seemed to be indulged in nevertheless. Attempts at controlling reading were unsuccessful also. During the sixteenth century, despite efforts by the crown and church of Spain to forbid the shipment of prohibited books to the New World, these materials were successfully imported by sea and were often read openly en route by voyagers aboard transatlantic Spanish galleons. Some idea of the kinds of books that were read aboard ship at this time is gained from the records of the Inquisition authorities who inspected the ships at the ports of arrival in the colonies.

Books of devotion, such as prayer books and pietistic tracts, were almost universally found among passengers and crew; but profane or lay literature was also plentiful. The latter consisted of "chivalries and histories," poetry, travel, and other works, some clearly prohibited, but only noted and seemingly not confiscated by the inspectors. The genre of literature, popular in that day, known as romances of chivalry, was especially common and widely read, as was later the best seller, *Don Quixote*. Thus, current, popular literature representative of this and other periods was apt to be found aboard ships just as it was usually to be found wherever else the literate public might dwell, notwithstanding authoritative disapproval. On the other hand, possession of books aboard ship which were recognized as religiously orthodox might in some instances help an early mariner's reputation. A barber-surgeon aboard one of Her Majesty's ships in 1588 was able to clear himself of charges of suspected "papacy" by proving that he "had many good books, as the New Testament, the Book of Common Prayer, [and] the Book of Psalms, which he daily sang with the company."

Mariners who engaged in foreign trade were also exposed to the literature of many languages, and usually had some opportunity to acquire or read such materials. The bilingual John Aborough listed among his possessions the romance of chivalry, *Renaldos de Montalban,* and spelled it "Renod of Monttalvay," thereby betraying also some acquaintance with French. It was the second of the two large Spanish books which he claimed to own aboard the English merchantman *Michael of Barnstaple.* His copy (if indeed it was in Castilian) was probably published in Spain between 1523 and 1533. Thus, this remarkable mariner had among his effects an example of each type of reading matter that was likely to be found aboard ship.

It is quite possible that Aborough had obtained some of his books for the sole purpose of reselling them. Mariners as individuals had traditionally engaged in their own private trading operations in order to supplement their wages, and in Medieval times were even allowed free cargo space aboard ship to convey their own merchandise for sale. Although this practice of "portage" seems to have become obsolete by the early sixteenth century, sailors of later periods still were able to find room for items aboard ship that they could resell. Books, by virtue of their intrinsic and physical properties, were ideal goods to trade in. One Edward Barlow, an English seaman, mentioned in his journal the reselling in London at a profit of a dozen Bibles that he brought with him from Amsterdam in 1675. This sale, together with his wages, enabled him to stay ashore just long enough to recover from his arduous voyage of over three years' duration.[9]

At a higher level, books were also given as gifts by commanders of expeditions who followed the ancient custom of bestowing presents on the dignitaries of the places that they visited. Books, especially those illustrated with maps and pictorial matter, were considered among the more valuable gifts to be presented by mariners, for they could instruct as well as impress both the savage chief and the sophisticated head of state. Hakluyt's advice to two voyagers about to depart for Cathay in 1580 mentions the advantages that could be derived from using certain books for gifts or display. He suggested that they take with them maps of England and London, and "Ortelius booke of mappes . . . for it would be to a Prince of marvelous account." He also believed that "The booke of the attire of all nations" would be much esteemed as a gift. Further, Hakluyt recommended to the voyagers that "If any man will lend you the new Herball, and such bookes as make show of herbes, plantes, trees, fishes, fowles and beastes of these regions, it may much delight the great Cam, and the nobilitie, and also theyr merchants to have the view of them."[10]

In addition to the books that were brought aboard ship to satisfy the purely recreational needs of individual passengers and crew members, or possibly as items of barter, other books of an instructional or reference nature were also taken to sea for the personal edification of their owners. Most of these books probably found their way on board in much the same manner as recreational books, and were read by individuals for any of a number of reasons; however, still other books were likely to have been introduced on certain vessels in connection with a few specialized occupations among the crew which required their use. Four of these occupational "landsmen's" billets—surgeon, chaplain, schoolmaster, and scientist—were adapted to suit nautical conditions and were ideally best filled by men of some learning who had previously acquired or practiced their specialties ashore. Books have been written about the rise and progress of the sea surgeon and the chaplain (whose presence aboard ship can be traced to ancient times), and about their contributions toward the amelioration of life at sea through the practice of their professions among seamen. The doctor afloat needed materia medica and surgical instruments to perform his duties, and he needed books for reference. His experience at sea also led to the development of a specialized literature for this branch of medicine. Before 1617, apprentice surgeons had only general medical texts available for study, but in that year a book written in English for surgeons serving in East Indiamen appeared. This work, *The Surgions Mate,* by John Woodall, undoubtedly was thereafter referred to at sea by English sea surgeons until superseded, as were later materials such as the guides to the medicine chests with which the United Netherlands East India Company provided its surgeons in 1645 and subsequently.

The chaplain, entrusted with the keeping and reading of the Bible, was required to offer up prayers, to preach, and to provide counsel to his seagoing or shoreside congregation. At times he was also called upon to teach not only religious doctrine but also diverse elementary and technical subjects to various designated classes of young officers and seamen. The more conscientious members of the chaplain corps played a major role in the provision of reading materials to seamen and in the elevation of the moral climate aboard ship.

Eventually, the schoolmaster also went to sea. He was to employ his time, according to the early regulations and instructions relating to His Majesty's Service at sea, "in instructing the Voluntiers in Writing, Arithmetick, and the Study of Navigation, and in whatsoever may contribute to render them Artists in that Science," and "likewise to teach the other Youths of the Ship . . . with Regard to their several capacities, whether in Reading, Writing, or otherwise."[11] In fulfilling these requirements, books on navigation were needed by the midshipmen, or "voluntiers," and spelling, arithmetic, and composition books were wanted by schoolmasters and chaplains in order to teach the boys, or "other youths of the ship," the rudiments of education. More will be said concerning the activities of chaplains and schoolmasters in the pages that follow, for these two parties, being closely involved with attempts at education in the maritime environment, had much to do and say about books.

While the book requirements of the seagoing clergy, medical men, and pedagogues and their pupils were more or less limited to helping fulfill the specialized duties of these occupations aboard ship, the book needs of the seaborne scientist were more universal in scope and in scholarly application. The advent of the scientist among the crews of certain vessels of exploration was fostered by an increased interest in scientific discovery by the scholarly community. Although there had always been and there continued to be a few mariners whose scientific outlook matched or was ahead of the spirit of their times, other men of more specialized scientific attainments also sought the opportunity to explore personally, and to collect specimens, in the unknown regions of the earth accessible to them only by ship. Toward the end of the seventeenth century, learned societies such as the Royal Society of London and the Académie des sciences of Paris began to influence the course of maritime discovery by proposing to their respective governments various voyages of scientific import.[12]

The first voyage for purely scientific reasons under British auspices occurred in 1698, when the astronomer Edmond Halley set sail in HMS *Paramour* in order to make certain observations in terrestrial magnetism. It is of interest to note that on this voyage Halley, a civilian, was in actual command of the ship, a rare occurrence in the history of any navy; however, in subsequent voyages this precedent was abandoned and any scientist who accompanied a naval ship on a voyage of discovery generally went out in the capacity of a supernumerary.[13]

The participation of scholars in the planning and outfitting of scientific expeditions not only insured that the proper scientific apparatus was procured but also that books which would aid in the identification and description of natural history specimens, and which would help interpret other scientific phenomena likely to be encountered, were also carried aboard ship. This requirement on the part of shipboard scientists provided certain vessels with perhaps the first substantial collections of books which could be considered as libraries in the true sense of the word. Contemporary recognition of the existence of these libraries and of the influence of scientists on the proper outfitting of exploratory expeditions is documented in the remarks of a Fellow of the Royal Society who, when writing to Carl von Linné, commented on the preparations made for anticipated research on HMS *Endeavour* in 1768. He observed: "No people ever went to sea better fitted out for the purpose of Natural History. They have got a fine library of Natural History; they have all sorts of machines for catching and preserving insects; all kinds of nets, trawls, drags and hooks for coral fishing . . . in short . . . this expedition would cost Mr. Banks £10,000."

Joseph Banks, then a young gentleman-scientist, underwrote the expenses of equipping the scientific needs of the *Endeavour* expedition. Throughout the remainder of his life he continued to subsidize and influence naturalists, artists, and explorers, and to make his collections and library available to all. In 1818, two years before Banks died, the navigator William E. Parry of the Royal Navy used his valuable library ashore prior to departing on his first voyage to the Arctic.

Banks and an entourage of scientists, artists, and servants, as well as the astronomer royal, accompanied Captain James Cook on the *Endeavour*. This was the first of Cook's historic voyages, and it occurred near the beginning of the second great round of exploration, or the "golden age" of discovery by the world's maritime powers. The voyage was a success in many respects. The skill of Captain Cook and the talents of the civilians with him brought it about, but the patronage of the king and the Royal Society, together with the solicitude of some of the lords of the Admiralty made the prospects for success all the more auspicious. An example for future mutual effort by naval and scientific personnel in the planning and execution of exploring expeditions had been well set.[14]

A good look at the contents of a ship's scientific library of this period is afforded in an account of a similar voyage of discovery begun seventeen years after that of the *Endeavour*. The ill-fated expedition of France's Comte de la Pérouse was furnished with a large collection of books at its outset in 1785. Over 119 entries appeared in the catalog of the library which was intended on the voyage "for the use of the officers and men of science embarked" under the command of La Pérouse. The traditional mariner's choice of accounts of voyages, including "Hawkesworth's Voyages, and Cooks three Voyages, in French and in English" headed the catalog and comprised twenty-five titles. Next came the other category of books of interest to mariners—astronomy and navigation, which numbered nineteen treatises, not counting "all the usual books of navigation." For the scientists, eight titles in physics were listed along with sixty-five in natural history, a category that contained works on science in general, botany, zoology, chemistry, languages, and the *Mémoires de l'Académie des sciences.*[15]

The example of La Pérouse's library furnishes also one last observation concerning the early provision of books to seamen, which is rather self-evident. Libraries and book collections at sea, no matter what their content or intended usage, were exposed to an additional destructive hazard not shared by similar collections ashore—shipwreck. La Pérouse and his ships, as Carlyle wrote, "vanished trackless into blue immensity," and so did his books. The library at sea, often formed to serve some temporary expedient, could and did perish even before its fleeting mission was fulfilled. But if the library did survive a long voyage, often the volumes composing it, like the men composing the crew of the ship, might be disbanded and lost sight of forever at journey's end, or might be recruited again for further service.

Chapter II

Religious Influences

Darkness has covered our ships, and gross darkness our sailors. They have been without Christ, strangers from the covenant of promise, having no hope, and without God in the world. A man of war has been proverbial for every kind of wickedness, and a sailor but another name for a lawless being, neglected by man, and apparently abandoned by God,—given up to his own heart's lusts, to work all uncleanliness with greediness, his places of resort on shore have been infinitely more fatal than winds, or seas, or storms; for in these, thousands, and tens of thousands, have made shipwreck of body and soul; whence they have been hurried unprepared to meet an angry God.

—Annual Report of the Port of
New York Society, 1821.

Just as man took to sea the physical necessities of life, he also brought his religious beliefs with him to provide spiritual sustenance. Religion and the sea have been closely linked since ancient times, and some of the vestiges of pagan religious practices connected with the sea still remain today. In early Christian times, the church fathers referred to the spiritual church as the Ship of Salvation, comparing it to Noah's Ark, and a portion of the physical church came to be called the nave, from *navis,* or "ship," in Latin. Evidences of the kinship of the sea with Christian religion are manifold in the Bible, while the Bible itself occupied an important place in early shipboard routine and in seafaring life.

Holy men were also traditionally carried aboard ship. During Saxon times priests began to serve as chaplains on the English vessels that guarded against seaborne raids by the Danes. By the Middle Ages, chaplains were regarded as "a link with divine providence as well as guardians of the moral standards and spiritual needs of the ships' companies." Chaplains accompanied Frobisher and Sir Francis Drake on their exploring expeditions to the new world. They were also aboard early East Indiamen. In the British navy, the custom started by Queen Elizabeth of appointing chaplains to her larger vessels was well established by the time of Charles I.[1]

Toward the end of the seventeenth century, religiously inclined individuals and groups ashore, as well as the chaplaincy afloat, began to take more of an active interest in the spiritual condition of seamen. The attitude toward religion aboard ship slowly shifted from that of regarding it as a kind of protective shield employed to propitiate the gods, or as a means to support discipline and routine, to that of one concerned with the religious salvation and education of the individual seaman.

Outstanding among those who attempted to bring religion to seamen and to others of this period was a book-conscious clergyman by the name of Thomas Bray. About the same time that Edmond Halley was sailing aboard the *Paramour* on his second voyage of scientific endeavor for the British crown in 1699, the Reverend Thomas Bray embarked on the ship *Adventure,* bound for the colony of Maryland on a mission of importance to the Anglican Church. Dr. Bray, who was the Commissary, or superintendent, of the Church of England for the province of Maryland, was going overseas to insure personally the establishment of the Church there. He had already taken steps to help propagate religion abroad by sending various libraries to the colonies, for he had a penchant for starting libraries wherever he thought they might do some good. Because some of Bray's early efforts also included the provision of books and libraries to members of the seafaring population, his activities are of particular interest to this study and provide a convenient point from which to begin to trace the course of book-related missionary work among seamen in America.

Thomas Bray was born in 1658 at Marton, in Shropshire, England. As a young man he studied divinity and eventually entered holy orders. Later in life, Bray's notable activities and abilities so impressed the Bishop of London that he was selected, in 1696, as Commissary for Maryland. As part of his duties in organizing the life of the Church overseas, Bray had to recruit clergymen for the distant parishes. He found that the only ministers interested in leaving their homeland to take these positions were so poor they could not afford to purchase books. Without proper books, Bray reasoned, the missionaries would stagnate in the outposts, and the mission of the Church would fail. Upon receiving approval to form libraries in the colonies, Bray developed a detailed plan for furnishing the clergy and laity with various libraries to meet specific needs. The first and largest library that he sent abroad was to Annapolis, Maryland, in 1697. This "Annopolitan Library" was intended to serve as the central library of the province, but like many other colonial libraries, it and Bray's smaller libraries did not become permanent. Today a portion of the 1,095 volumes in the original collection still exists at St. John's College in Annapolis.[2]

Bray was also concerned that young clergymen en route to their foreign posts should be supplied with reading matter and a suitable place to study when they were detained in port due to the vagaries of sea transportation. He observed that a library would provide the proper atmosphere for missionaries, sea-chaplains, and others in these circumstances, for here they could better occupy their time in self-improvement and good companionship. Using the library would "prevent also the expenses and scandalls to which they would be too much exposed, by saunting away whole hours together in Coffee Houses, or may be less sober places." Characteristically, Bray took the opportunity to establish a library in each of three English ports where his ship touched—Gravesend, Deal, and Plymouth—when he embarked on his trip to Maryland in December of 1699. He believed that once the foundations of these libraries were laid, they would be kept up by "the benefactions of the sea-officers, who are usually generous enough, as well as from other gentlemen . . ."[3]

Bray also had navy chaplains and seamen in mind as direct or indirect users of certain of the libraries which he sent to the colonies. His "Directions for the use and preservation of the Library sent with his Excellency the Earl of Bellamont to New York in America," drawn up in 1697, state: "First the Chief Design of this Library is for the Use of the Church of England Ministers belonging to the Fort, and City of New York, and for the Chaplains of His Majesty's Ships during their Residence in that Port." The library was to be kept in an accessible place, such as a public room of the fort, or the vestry of the church of Trinity parish. It contained some 157 titles, numbering 220 volumes, and represented mostly standard works of the period of use to clergymen. Other smaller book collections comprising multiple copies of about thirty-five or forty titles, known as "laymen's libraries," were also sent to the colonies beginning in 1700. The minister in charge of a laymen's library could use his discretion in either lending or giving books from the collection to his parishioners.[4] Inasmuch as these libraries usually contained ten copies each of *The Seaman's Monitor* (a book of religious admonitions written by the Reverend Josiah Woodward specifically for seamen), it is probable that the work was intended to be made available to mariners ashore, as well as through their chaplains. A more likely place where seamen and others perhaps came in contact with religious reading matter was in certain public houses. At least in New York, two packets of small books on the subject of the Reformation were intended to be placed in these establishments.[5] As it has been observed, "The good doctor thought of everything except the difficulty of getting people to read to good purpose the books provided,"—a difficulty, one might add, that has not diminished with the passage of time or with a substantial increase in the availability of secular literature.

From 1706 until 1730, when he died, Bray was rector of St. Botolph Without, Aldgate, London. In his later years, he became interested in the education of the Negro in the American colonies, and in the improvement of British prisons. Out of his efforts to encourage educational and missionary activities grew the Society for Promoting Christian Knowledge (S.P.C.K.—formed, 1698), and the Society for the Propagation of the Gospel in Foreign Parts (S.P.G.—founded, 1701) which still flourish today. The early concern of the S.P.C.K., as reflected in its publishing activities, was directed toward certain isolated classes in society who were in need of special pastoral care or enlightenment—colonists, seamen, soldiers, servants, and farmers. In its early years the S.P.C.K. especially concentrated on the distribution of religious materials among seamen in the Royal Navy. Thousands of tracts were given out by naval chaplains, under the authority of Vice Admiral John Benbow and others, and Dr. Bray himself was reported to have derived satisfaction from preparing a kind of lending library for the fleet.[6]

As early as 1708-1712, the S.P.C.K. had supplied religious and educational materials to the captain of the fourth rate *Norwich* to be used in a school for boys aboard his ship. Instruction in reading and writing and the Church catechism was offered to the young crew members, as well as some instruction in navigation. It was hoped by the S.P.C.K. at the time that this example would be followed by other naval commanders. In later years, William Bligh and Horatio Nelson were among the officers of the Royal Navy who requested supplies of religious books from this source. When in command of the *Director,* Bligh indicated to the society that the books furnished his ship would be used constantly, and Nelson was inclined to ask for supplies of religious books whenever he took command of a ship. In 1793 Nelson had received a quantity of religious tracts and Books of Common Prayer when he was aboard the *Agamemnon.* He also requested as many Bibles and prayer books as the society would allow for the *Vanguard* in 1798. His subsequent duty aboard the *San Josef,* and later the *Victory,* led him to repeat the requests, for he believed that a respect for religion by seamen resulted in the ultimate good for king and country.[7]

In the late eighteenth century the spiritual plight of the seaman also became the concern of other religious and philanthropic organizations and individuals working within the general matrix of the advancing Protestant missionary and reform movements. Seamen as a class of society, after centuries of near ostracism and neglect by landsmen, began to receive the same kind and degree of missionary attention as the natives of some heathen land. The moral and religious condition of the seaman was now regarded as deplorable, and his salvation was considered imperative. His moral views were to be raised, and he was to be led "to a course of life, by which he might be prepared for greater usefulness in this world, and for a crown of glory in the world to come." Negroes, Indians, settlers, and others considered in need of religion also claimed the missionary's attention, but seamen presented an especially rewarding challenge. Inspired by the association of Jesus with the fishermen of Galilee, and by other appropriate scriptural texts, the missionary regarded seamen as sons of the tribe of Zebulun—"the Mariner's Tribe" in Israel—and sought to help them to see again "a great light."

One way of redeeming the so-thought benighted and profligate seaman was through the distribution of Bibles and religious literature, usually in the form of tracts and books published by interdenominational organizations or denominational churches. Several accounts of life in British and American naval and merchant ships of the nineteenth century mention the work of tract and Bible societies, missionaries, chaplains, colporteurs, temperance workers, ship owners, and proselytizing crew members as agents in distributing printed religious materials aboard ship. Also, the official reports of societies and the activities of individuals as recorded in the contemporary religious press and elsewhere furnish abundant evidence concerning the zealous exertions of those concerned with spreading the Protestant Word among the infidels, Jews, Catholics, and the otherwise unenlightened inhabitants of the world. A few examples of the manifold and overlapping religious efforts that were directed toward seamen will be presented in the following pages. These examples are intended to illustrate how ships and men were supplied with reading matter from this collective source, which proved to be, in general, the largest and most enduring of the groups to espouse the cause of books and libraries among seamen. Other significant religious influences relating to maritime libraries and shipboard reading will be discussed as they occur either chronologically or topically later in this study.

Although the S.P.C.K. had pioneered in the circulation of religious materials in Great Britain and abroad, its activities, confined to operating within the doctrine of the Church of England, were not exclusively devoted to the distribution of tracts and books, or Bibles. During the latter part of the eighteenth century organizations which were mostly concerned with the printing, translation, and distribution of the Bible and tracts began to flourish. In Great Britain the Bible Society, founded in 1780 and later revived as the Naval and Military Bible Society in 1804, was the first to initiate systematic efforts to promote the Bible among soldiers and seamen. The ill-fated *Royal George,* accidentally sunk in August, 1782, at Spithead, was the first vessel of the Royal Navy to be supplied by the society. Other Bible societies were subsequently founded in Europe and in the United States, the first in this country being in Philadelphia in 1808. By 1816, when the American Bible Society was established, there were 128 Bible societies in the United States. The following year the Marine Bible Society of New York was formed and added as the eighty-fourth auxiliary of the new national organization. Its constitution stated that the sole object of the society was "to encourage the circulation of the Holy Scriptures, without comment among seamen." The only copies of the Bible in the English language to be circulated by the Society were to be "of the version in common use." This specialized mission did not prevent the parent organization from donating Bibles to ships, for in November of that year, the American Bible Society made its first presentation of Bibles to a U.S. naval vessel, when it put sixty-five copies aboard the small frigate *John Adams* for the use of her crew. The next month, it gave 250 Bibles to the Marine Bible Society "for the supply of seamen from all quarters frequenting the neighbouring ports."[8]

The topic of literacy among seamen was incidentally touched upon in early reports of the Merchant Seamen's Bible Society. During an unspecified period in 1819, the society's agent, stationed at Gravesend, England, visited 1,681 ships having a total complement of 24,765 men, "of which number 21,671 were stated to be able to read." He also found that 2,200 copies of the Scriptures were already on board the vessels, but "owing to the paucity of pecuniary means possessed by the seamen," he was only able to sell an additional 390 Bibles and 207 Testaments for the sum of £89 4s. 10d. Another 590 ships having 6,149 men on board, "of whom 5,490 were said to be able to read, would have proceeded to sea without a single copy of the Holy Scriptures had it not been for the seasonable bounty of this Society." Besides the number sold aboard merchant vessels, the agent gratuitously distributed 1,705 Bibles and 4,068 Testaments for use by the ships' crews. Being a methodical man, the agent kept exact records of each transaction and made it a point to inquire into the result of these benefactions upon the return to port of any ship so supplied. Of course, he was happy to report that the effects on the moral and religious interests of the men had generally been satisfactory. However, no indication was given on how he determined or defined "ability to read," or how thoroughly his census was conducted, but the findings, such as they were, in three determinations place the illiteracy rate of the seamen between 10 and 18 percent. Another noteworthy fact brought out in the report was that the Bibles which were already aboard certain ships had been placed there "by well-disposed owners for the use of seamen, or were the private property of sailors."[9]

The cost of carrying out a vigorous program of Bible distribution was revealed in a brief 1819 report on the operating expenses of the Naval and Military Bible Society on the occasion of its thirty-ninth anniversary. Although the society had received some £2,000 in contributions, its disbursements exceeded receipts by £980 in the course of distributing 6,500 copies of the Scriptures to the military and 2,600 to the Royal Navy. Many other requests for Bibles and Testaments could not be fulfilled, it was reported, despite "testimonies of the happy influence of the Scriptures" which had been received from several quarters.

Three years earlier a widely read and more lasting tribute to the efficacy of Bible reading aboard ship had appeared in a book by a former lieutenant in the Royal Navy. Writing under the pseudonym, "Aliquis," Richard Marks told in one of the chapters of *The Retrospect, or Review of Providential Mercies,* how he had obtained sixty-four Bibles from the Naval and Military Bible Society when his ship, HMS *Conqueror,* went into port in order to pay her crew. The Bibles, "together with some hundreds of good little tracts," were distributed so that each mess was provided with a copy of the Scriptures. Through an earlier suggestion of his to have religious services performed in the ship, Marks was permitted by his sympathetic captain to take the lead in these ceremonies. As a result of the introduction of Bible reading, prayer meetings, psalm singing, and regular worship, Marks claimed that many of the crew responded and became reformed in their ways. Unfortunately for the author, this condition did not prevail very long, for with a change of captain, coupled with the enmity of the senior lieutenant, worship aboard the *Conqueror* was suppressed and a relapse took place among many of the crew. Not long after this, Marks quit the navy in 1810. He subsequently became a clergyman of the Church of England and continued to take an active and influential part in the cause of promoting the spiritual welfare of seamen.

While still aboard the *Conqueror,* Marks also initiated a subscription library of religious books for the crew. He obtained permission to form it soon after his success with the Bibles. Some 150 members of the 640 man crew subscribed four shillings apiece to purchase 200 or more "volumes of pious evangelical works." The books were kept in a chest under the care of the purser's steward. Each subscriber was entitled to exchange one book from the library as often as he pleased, and it was

claimed that two-thirds of the collection was always in circulation. A
subscriber upon leaving the ship was allowed to take one or two volumes
with him.[10]

In all probability, most of the religious books in the *Conqueror's*
library, as well as the "hundreds of good little tracts," had been obtained
from one or more tract societies. These societies, like the Bible societies,
increased in number and activity beginning in the early nineteenth century. They had as their purpose the distribution of brief popular religious treatises, or tracts, among a wider audience than that reached by
the church. Religious tracts have a long history, extending back to
Martin Luther's ninety-five theses of 1517, but those of Marks's time
attempted to present the evangelist's sectarian viewpoint on social and
religious topics and were intended to counteract the antireligious, or
otherwise unacceptable, secular literature of the day. While most tracts
were generally small, cheap, ephemeral pamphlets, other religious
materials published by tract societies were of substantial size and of
lasting quality.

The ancestry of the many general and specialized tract societies
formed in the United States can be traced to the Religious Tract Society
(established in London in 1799), which itself was preceded in organization by the S.P.C.K.'s tract activities and by the popular efforts of
Hannah More, with her "Cheap Repository Tracts," and the Reverend
George Burder (a founder of the Religious Tract Society) with his
"Village Tracts." By 1824, the Religious Tract Society had distributed
over sixty million tracts in the cause of evangelization. American tract
societies, closely patterned after it, date from 1803. In 1825 the two
largest, the New England Tract Society and the New York Religious
Tract Society, merged to become the American Tract Society. At the
time of their union they had together distributed over six million tracts.[11]
From an extract of the 1816 report of the New York Religious Tract
Society, given in the *Christian Herald*, some insight can be gained concerning the distribution activities of a general tract society, for, in its
report, the society accounted for the 85,576 tracts it dispersed that year.[12]
These went to foreign countries, to various states of the Union, and to the
several counties of New York State, and lastly to "various parts of Long
Island, 2,982 [tracts, and] on board of the Steam Boats during the year,
4,170." In addition, the society presented nine other nearby tract societies with materials to be disseminated by their members. Finally, the
remainder of tracts was distributed in New York City to "the Alms-
House, the Hospital, the Bridewell, among Charitable Institutions, in
the Markets, on board of Vessels, and among the inhabitants of the
city."

Thirteen new tracts were also printed by the society that year in quantities of 5,000 to 10,000 copies each. One of these titles was intended expressly for the mariner's edification. It was tract no. 16 in the society's series, and was entitled, *Covey, or Anecdotes of a Sailor*. The four-page pamphlet told a story that was presented repeatedly in tracts and religious magazines—that of the tearful conversion of an ignorant and blasphemous sinner, who hoped on his deathbed that his fellow wicked neighbors might also find mercy before it was too late. "James Covey," the redeemed English sailor in this tract, lost his legs in battle, but found his soul at church, and thus, it was thought, provided an anecdote of courageous fortitude and a powerful testimony in favor of religion. The titles of some of the other tracts mentioned in the report are indicative of the moral concern of the American and British tract societies who printed and reprinted such pamphlets as *Sin, No Trifle, The Converted Negro, The Importance of Sobriety*, and *The Swearer's Prayer* (fig. 2).

In 1817 the successful activities of the Liverpool Religious Tract Society as they related to the distribution of tracts afloat were thought to be deserving of attention by similar institutions in this country. The society, in addition to distributing its wares in the borough jail and among the homeless seamen about the docks, had placed sets of its tracts, bound in six volumes, in the cabins of the Dublin and Newry packets, in the Mersey steamers, and in the Wigan Canal boats. These tract collections appear to have been intended to be used as "libraries," for the captains of the Dublin packets also engaged in the circulation of single tracts among their passengers.

Oftentimes ships' officers and pious crew members aboard deep water vessels were also willing and active participants in the dissemination of tracts and Bibles abroad as well as on shipboard. Because of their unique advantage in traveling about the earth, it was hoped by many religious groups that merchant and naval seamen could be enlisted in the cause of spreading the Gospel. Many articles on this subject appeared in the religious press, and inspirational examples illustrating the good work that could be achieved by God's seafaring messengers in foreign lands were also abundantly recorded. When the ship *Comet* departed for Le Havre in 1819, to cite just one instance, her captain had aboard 1,500 French tracts furnished by the New York Religious Tract Society for distribution.

The presence of missionaries on their way to distant lands introduced a religious element into many a ship's routine. Not content with the passive distribution of tracts among the crew, many missionaries began or continued their evangelical labors while at sea. Prayer meetings and

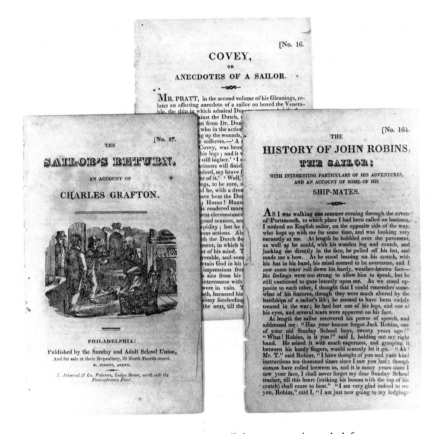

2. Examples of nineteenth century religious tracts intended for seamen.
Author's collection

religious services were performed with a captain's permission, or certain amenable crew members were sought out and proselytized. Pages of testimony to the joyous conversion of seamen, and of emigrants, soldiers, and convicts being transported overseas aboard ships on which missionaries had taken passage, were dispatched homeward in letters and reports to missionary societies by their agents. Had Samuel Johnson lived to gain the view of maritime life that is offered in the early nineteenth century reports of Bible, tract, and missionary societies, he might well have added to his observation: "No man will be a sailor who has contrivance enough to get himself into a jail; for being in a ship is being in a jail with the chance of being drowned"—*or being converted!*

Other forms of religious endeavor directed toward mariners afloat were reported during the period of the War of 1812. Various landsmen in Great Britain corresponded with religiously inclined officers and seamen on nearly eighty warships of the Royal Navy in all parts of the world, assisting them to seek salvation, while the Chaplain-General of the fleet requested £1,500 from the Admiralty for purchase of religious books.[13] And as for the seaman loitering ashore, or attached to some ship in a harbor, another front was opened in the campaign to bring religion into his life. At this time, efforts were begun to provide seamen in port with a living ministry, "the great instrument of usefulness to sinful men."

A prayer meeting held aboard the brig *Friendship,* anchored on the Thames River in 1814, developed into a regular occurrence whenever the ship was in port. Two years later, the practice was extended to other vessels, mostly colliers on the Thames. These services were attended by seamen in general, rather than by the crew of just one ship. The Reverend George C. Smith, himself a former sailor and ship's officer, after attending one of the gatherings in 1817 devoted his efforts to establishing a floating chapel for seamen in London, in which regular religious services could be held. This goal was realized concurrently with the formation of the Port of London Society for Promoting Religion Among Seamen, in 1818. An old ship of 380 tons was converted into the first floating chapel, the "Ark," and she was moored in the Thames near the London docks in order to be close to the greatest concentration of seamen. The Port of London Society initially received contributions from the East India Company, the Parliamentary Commissioners for the better regulation of the River Thames, and from others who recognized the utility of the floating chapel and the society, or who incidentally might have stood to benefit, themselves, from an improvement in the moral standards of the maritime community. Services aboard the "Ark" were termed a success. As many as 800 seamen were worshiping on board every Sunday in 1819, but estimated thousands of others

were still not being reached. It was apparent at this time that another
society was needed to promote itinerant prayer meetings from ship to
ship in the river, and also to establish them in other domestic and
foreign ports. The British and Foreign Bethel Union Society was formed
to provide for this want on an organized basis. Among the provisions
of the society were the conduct of interdenominational services afloat,
the publication of a periodical, the *Sailor's Magazine and Naval Miscellany,* to foster its aims, and the use of a special flag, the "Bethel Flag,"
as a signal for divine worship aboard ship. Also, the distribution of
Bibles and tracts was to be an important part of its program in bringing
religion to the seaman in his own element. Within a year's time the
bethel flag was hoisted aboard ships in the many ports in Great Britain
which established similar societies. By 1824, there were sixty-seven
bethel unions established in different parts of the world, and fifteen
floating chapels and churches for sailors had also come into being.

   The idea to promote regular divine services for seamen also in the
harbors of the United States appears to have been initiated with the
founding of the short-lived Boston Society for the Religious and Moral
Improvement of Seamen in 1812. Besides providing for shipboard
preaching, another goal of the society was the selection, purchase, and
distribution of books among seamen which would "engage their notice,
to leave upon their minds the most useful impressions, and to advance
their virtue and happiness." The society seems to have ceased to exist
around 1817, when its eleventh or last numbered publication was published.[14] Almost simultaneously with both its demise and with the
inception of prayer meetings overseas on the River Thames, the idea to
provide a house of worship was conceived in New York. Here, it was
decided from the start to build a permanent Mariner's Church on land.
The church was not dedicated until 1820, but in the intervening years,
The Society for the Promotion of Gospel Among Seamen in the Port
of New York, formed in May, 1818, supported a minister for seamen
while it raised money to build the church. In December, 1818, the
society, whose object was "to supply seamen with the means of intellectual and religious instruction," opened a temporary place of worship
on Cherry Street. Services were held there on Sundays and at other
times. The church was reported to have been well attended by seamen
and their families, and ministers of different denominations occasionally
were guest preachers.

   During his first year at this location, the Reverend Ward Stafford
was visited by some 800 seamen. He distributed to them, and aboard
various ships as well as in his church, about 600 Bibles, 130 Testaments,
100 to 200 copies of the Book of Common Prayer and about 5,000
tracts. He had obtained these materials from various sources—the

Bibles and Testaments from "the Marine and other Bible societies"; the prayer books from the Auxiliary New York Bible and Common Prayer Book Society; and the tracts from the New York Religious Tract Society, and from benevolent individuals. Although a more personal and active approach to bringing religion to seamen had begun with the establishment of a church for them, its minister still relied on "those silent preachers"—tracts—and on Bibles to reinforce his efforts. This literature was the staple of the seaman's churches, chapels, bethels, and missions throughout the world.

Bibles were distributed at the new Mariner's Church on Roosevelt Street from the first day of its opening. Seamen attending the commencement services were able to receive a Bible from an officer of the Marine Bible Society for the asking.[15] On that day of June 4, 1820, the plain brick church, built to accommodate 1,000 persons, was filled to overflowing. Secretary of the Navy Smith Thompson, Captain Samuel Evans, and other naval officers, as well as merchant ship captains and a detachment of U.S. Marines, were among those whose presence dignified the occasion. A year later, the Port of New York Society imported the bethel plan of shipboard prayer meetings from London, and during the decade a proliferation of bethel unions, seamen's friend societies, and mariners' churches followed in the sea- and inland ports of North America.

Provision for the seaman's physical wants, as well as for his spiritual needs, gradually evolved out of the evangelist's concern for his salvation. It would take almost one hundred years before the merchant seaman's welfare became more dominantly a secular than a religious acitivity, but the seeds of the idea for material assistance were to germinate early.[16] Some of the first steps taken to provide for the seaman's well-being were linked to the plans for his moral reform. These advances were mostly involved with the sailor's shoreside environment. Christian boardinghouses, savings banks, registries of seamen, and various kinds of schools were provided by religious groups primarily to improve the seaman's moral habits and conduct.

All along it had been thought that seamen could be influenced for the better through reading the Bible and religious literature if these materials were sold or given to them. Now the time and opportunity had arrived to enlist another resource of the greatest elevating potential to help achieve this goal—libraries.

The early organized efforts to supply libraries to seamen came from a number of sources, some of them interrelated, much as had the earlier efforts to supply tracts and Bibles. Indeed, some of the early seamen's libraries were nothing more than small collections of tracts. Whether the maritime worker was employed on inland waters, on coastwise

craft, or on deep-water vessels, there was a society that endeavored to
bring religion to him, and even to his family. Many of these religious
sailors' friend groups sooner or later turned to the provision of some
kind of shoreside or shipboard libraries. The type of library service that
was formed in each case was influenced by local circumstances. These
conditions in turn helped introduce a spirit of innovation into the overall effort. The resulting implementation produced some variations and
blending among the kinds of libraries that were proposed or established;
however, the actual number of possible types was obviously limited by
concept. For purposes of description, examples of the religiously sponsored seamen's libraries may be grouped into four major. types: (1)
sailors' boardinghouse libraries and reading rooms, (2) church libraries,
(3) shipboard libraries, (4) institutional libraries and reading rooms.

SAILORS' BOARDINGHOUSE LIBRARIES. The sailor when
ashore was apt to be victimized in any number of situations by members of a waterfront milieu who thrived at his expense. Prominent
among the long-standing snares that contributed to the perpetual dis-
soluteness and poverty of the sailor's life was the boardinghouse for
seamen. Here the hapless seafarer was often separated from his hard-
earned wages by means of readily available wine, women, and song, or
by outright theft. The vicious cycle then began over again with the sailor
facing the prospect of immediately finding another job or ship, begging,
getting into debt, or going to jail. Often he became indebted to the
boardinghouse master, who, if he found the sailor another berth, would
receive an advance on the sailor's future wages. If, however, a sailor was
to take lodgings at one of the selected houses sponsored by a bethel
society, such as the Liverpool Bethel Union in 1822, he could expect
fair treatment, along with a reminder on the Sabbath to attend church.
Here, also, a library was provided for his use. It consisted of only a
Bible, a Testament, and a volume or so of tracts. The initial total of
volumes in the Liverpool boardinghouse libraries was determined by
the number of men in a house, at a ratio of one book to one man.

In late 1822, the New York Bethel Union had not yet started its boardinghouse libraries. It was thought that little had been done in the way of
distributing suitable books like *The Seaman's Devotional Assistant* to
sailors, but that it and similar books and tracts should be furnished for
its proposed libraries. Meanwhile, the Charleston Bethel Union, in
South Carolina, was gathering donated books and tracts for cabin (*i.e.,*
ship) and boardinghouse libraries. It considered the establishment of
boardinghouse libraries an object of vital importance in its operations,
for even though a man might room in a Christian house, he still needed
to be shielded from temptation. In its second annual report, for the year

1823, the governing board of the bethel union summed up the evangelist's reasons for establishing libraries in boardinghouses: "We deem it
utterly impossible to induce seamen to sit down quietly and soberly at
a boardinghouse, unless some means are furnished for their entertainment. But supply them with books, the periodical journals of the day,
and interesting tracts, and we believe the best method is taken to draw
them from the haunts of vice which can be adopted. Indeed we believe
this to be the only method of inducing them to abandon such places,
from inclination, and therefore the only one which will prove effectual."
Just how effective these libraries actually were in changing the moral
habits of seamen ashore is open to question; however, the boardinghouse library appears to have been the one which the reformer believed
would accomplish the most good, and it was likely to be explicitly
specified among the goals of the various societies. The American Seamen's Friend Society, which emerged as the major institution in the
country concerned with the seaman's spiritual welfare, called for these
libraries in the first of six of its aims, as circularized in November, 1825:

> I. The establishment of reputable and orderly boarding houses
> in the several sea-port towns of our country, where special
> attention will be paid as well to the morals as to the protection
> of the property and civil rights of seamen. Each of the houses,
> when practicable, to be furnished with a reading room, and a
> small library of suitable books, and to be under the general
> superintending care of a committee.

CHURCH LIBRARIES. The early libraries formed in floating chapels,
religious meeting rooms, and mariners' churches were similar in purpose
to those set up in sailors' boardinghouses but differed to the extent that
the families of sailors had access to them and that books were more
likely to circulate from the collections. These libraries also tended to
be larger than those in lodging houses. The library of the floating
chapel at Hull consisted of more than 200 volumes in 1827, when it was
reported to have been eagerly used by the wives and families of seamen,
as well as by the seamen themselves when ashore. The collection was
thought to be insufficient to meet an increasing demand in usage, and
donations of books were solicited to augment it the following year. A
similar lending library of 439 volumes was provided aboard the floating
chapel of the Port of Dublin Society in 1827. Here a sailor attending the
chapel could borrow one book. The books so chosen apparently were in
constant circulation, for that year seven of them were noted as lost,
"owing to the perpetual changes and chances of a sailor's life." Books
from the library, which were all numbered and marked with the society's

ownership stamp, were also loaned to a few ships, in the care of their captains. Through a similar arrangement aboard the floating chapel at London, it was stated in 1828 that 1,715 volumes, 212 pamphlets, and thousands of tracts had been issued, "many of which had been returned with expressions of the liveliest gratitude."

The library operations of yet another group, the Thames Rivermen's Society, were somewhat decentralized. This society, in 1824, maintained five stations along the river where religious meetings were held, and from which books were made available to barge and rivermen and their families. The books included in the libraries were supposedly selected with care, so that the readers "might be led to the Scriptures as the standard of truth." It was also hoped that the libraries would be a source of "rational entertainment" and a beneficial means of keeping the rivermen at home at night, thereby preventing "much domestic misery." In this regard, the Port of Dublin Society thought that a useful library "might afford a safe and profitable occupation for those leisure hours" of sailors which it was feared were then not employed to best advantage. Books, tracts, and the Scriptures were also made available in an adult school and in the Sunday school which was conducted by the society. In New York, in 1823, steps had been taken to collect a "Circulating Library" for the use of the children of seamen and others who attended the already established Sunday school at the Mariner's Church. Although a few books in this library had been selected and purchased from donated funds by the minister, the rest of the collection was made up of books given to the church, as was usual for most of the seamen's libraries.

In attempting to set up their own libraries, the seamen's pastors no doubt followed the examples which existed in regular situations ashore. At this time Sunday school libraries were becoming popular in established churches, and the benefits to be derived from libraries for the use of congregations and ministers were being commented upon in articles in the religious press. The interest expressed in these libraries appears as part of a larger contemporaneous movement toward the establishment of libraries in general for various social and occupational groups in the United States and Great Britain.

SHIPBOARD LIBRARIES. Many of the same societies that furnished libraries for seamen in shoreside locations also made attempts to circulate books among them by means of libraries put aboard ship. Although religiously inclined groups had taken the lead in forming boardinghouse libraries, they were not alone in the field of providing libraries to ships. As early as 1821 benevolent individuals, shipowners, and ships' crews (whose contributions in this direction will be discussed in the next two chapters) had already sponsored libraries, mostly of secular content, aboard ships sailing from New York. But in 1823, the New York Bethel Union recommended that a small and well-selected library (probably a standard collection available from a religious book supplier) costing no more than ten dollars, be considered for purchase by ship owners as part of the necessary outfit for every vessel.

That same year the Reverend George C. Smith, of Penzance, addressing the Port of Hull Society for religious instruction to seamen on the occasion of its second anniversary, brought to its attention an item about ship libraries, which, at the time, may have been news to the society. He reported that "some of the ladies of the church of England" had recently adopted a successful plan, which he termed "portable libraries" for ships proceeding on long voyages. These libraries each consisted of a box of books which was loaned to a vessel for the duration of a voyage and which was to be returned when the ship arrived back home. That the Reverend Smith commented on these portable libraries, at this time, would seem to indicate that at least the "lending" aspect of the idea was relatively new. As editor of the *Sailor's Magazine and Naval Miscellany,* and through his travels in connection with his various activities, Smith was probably aware of the many advances which were made in all aspects of bringing religion to seamen. His remarks about the advent of "portable" libraries may thus date the organized beginnings of lending libraries on ships.

By 1827 the Port of Hull Society itself had adopted the plan of portable libraries and had thirty-one of them in circulation. Some of its boxes of books were put aboard the famous Hull whalers that voyaged to Greenland and the Davis Straits. One box had already traveled to the East Indies and back. The books in these collections had been donated by individuals and by the Society of Friends of Hull. Each box contained sixteen to eighteen volumes. The books, of course, were termed "suitable" and "valuable" for seamen, and it was reported that they seemed to have been generally read. The following year the total inventory of available portable libraries had increased to forty-six in number.

Religious books appear to have been selected for these shipboard libraries almost exclusively. The Guernsey Seamen's Friend Society, which had nine sets of portable libraries for use of vessels belonging to the port in 1827, noted that their contents consisted of a Bible, a Testament, and other religious books. In return for the privilege of borrowing one of these libraries, a ship's master was expected to give an account of the use that was made of it while under his care. This was more or less a common request or requirement attached to libraries of this type. Among other things, these reports must have given the sponsors some satisfaction to learn of the progress of their cause on the high seas.

The Port of Dublin Society's early attempts to supply ships' libraries indicate that this type of library might have been adapted or developed from a floating chapel's lending library. It appears that in 1827 the Dublin Society made little distinction between lending a book to a sailor for his personal use on a voyage, or lending a box of books to a captain of an outward bound vessel for the use of his crew. The four boxes of books that were circulated that year contained copies of the Scriptures and a selection of books and tracts. Individual books were usually taken for one voyage and could be exchanged for others when the ship returned. The boxes of books or libraries could remain in a vessel "as long as they were found to answer the purposes intended by the Society."

If the choice of religious reading materials to be found in a portable library was not wholly to the mariner's liking, at least the box or case in which it came suited his predilection for neatness and compactness aboard ship. A collection of books in a box nicely fitted the stowage requirements of nautical life, and the box itself lent some substance and dignity to the word "library," for it was a quasi-official collection of books in the custody of a ship's officer, rather than just a handful of isolated volumes scattered about the ship. The library box was also likely, at least in the very beginning, to be in the respected company of the ship's supply of medicines, which on merchant ships was kept in a small wooden medicine chest, usually stored in the captain's cabin. The boxed library at sea paralleled in some respects the longer development of the portable wooden medicine chest, whose outward form became commercially standardized during the nineteenth century. According to law medicine chests were required aboard American merchant ships above a certain tonnage and complement as early as 1790.[17] Although it never achieved the distinction of being required by law, the boxed lending library aboard ship was also to earn its rightful place among those few items of a well-founded vessel that made life at sea more tolerable.

The practice of boxing up books into collections or libraries, although uniquely suited to nautical needs, was already prevalent on land. The early (ca. 1705) small parochial libraries of the S.P.C.K., for example, were fitted with wooden cabinets or cupboards, which were really pieces of finished furniture.[18] In 1828, when portable ships' libraries were becoming popular, the *New Sailor's Magazine,* in pointing out the valuable influence of the Book Society for Promoting Religious Knowledge Among the Poor as a source of cheap, but select, and pious publications, also mentioned that the society had "for sale neat cases, containing a copy of each of its books, in whole or half binding, admirably adapted for Sunday School or Village Lending Libraries." This kind of religious book collection, as well as later commercial publishers' "libraries," notably "Harper's Family Library," were well adapted to this and subsequent library developments among seamen.

Apart from the fortuitous qualities of the box for sending books to sea, the very nature of the kind of library operation undertaken—a lending library—made the use of a container imperative if the library was to be kept intact aboard ship and to be returned. Although the initial investment by some of the various societies in a lending library operation to ships consisted only of the provision of the boxes (the books being mostly donated in these instances), the societies nevertheless wanted the collections returned, or accounted for after each voyage. The libraries usually were not intended to be donated or given away. Further, each port only supplied libraries to those vessels that sailed from it as a home port. The natural desire to help one's own, coupled with the example of shoreside library practices and a limited operating fund, probably contributed to the provincial nature of the early libraries. Moreover, the opportunity to extend the influence of a society or church to sailors aboard ship could be better realized by lending rather than giving books to ships.

INSTITUTIONAL LIBRARIES AND READING ROOMS. It was inevitable, in view of the vigor of the seamen's spiritual cause, that out of the many local efforts put forth a few societies would emerge encompassing all of the goals of the movement and serving as national organizations. Among the many benefits derived from such a development would be increased and better organized library services. Also, the creation of a headquarters office and staff would provide the opportunity to extend libraries into new situations at home and abroad. For want of a better term, these libraries will be grouped together and referred to here as institutional libraries, for they were administered by a society in its secular headquarters, offices, or stations, or were otherwise made available in shoreside facilities not already described.

By the beginning of the 1830s, the combined goals and experience of three dominant societies (two in London and one in New York) had provided the basic plan which would be followed in future library operations to seamen on a national scale. Of the three societies, the one founded by the Reverend George C. Smith in 1825 as the Mariner's Church Society appears to have been the first to establish a secular headquarters from which its business was transacted on a full-time basis. In 1827, the society was operating from its "Mariner's House" offices in London's Wellclose Square, and it had just acquired the long four-part appellation of the British and Foreign Seamen's Friend Society, and London Mariners' and Rivermen's Bethel Union. A bookshop, called the "Sea-Book Depository," which sold religious books, maga-

zines, and tracts of marine interest was located on the premises of the
Mariner's House. The shop also contained the society's "Mariners'
Lending Library." Here, from such titles as the *Evangelical Magazine,*
and *Observations on Afflictions,* and from parcels of books and tracts
which were copiously donated to it, the society's recording secretary
and librarian received and circulated books for ships' libraries. The
agent who served in this full-time position received a salary of £50 a year
for his services. Inasmuch as the society claimed that the Sea-Book Depository was the first of its kind connected with religion in the kingdom,
this claim probably could have been extended to the position of its
librarian as well.

The society in May, 1828, had developed ambitious plans for a
"Mariners' and Rivermen's Library" which was to be opened in a new
dock area in London. The plans envisioned a combined seamen's library
and ships' lending library facility, a museum, and a room in which
writing materials were to be made available to seamen. The proposed
content of the library was remarkable, for it was expected that a well-
rounded book collection would be assembled from donations of
reading materials sent from all parts of the kingdom. However, the
original scheme was not fully realized. Instead, the library was set up
in a second house rented by the society on Wellclose Square. In this
house, two separate reading rooms were prepared, one for ships' officers which was to include a library, and one for seamen. The Mariner's
Lending Library was moved to the new location due to crowded conditions at the Mariner's House, and the new quarters were referred to as
the "Sailor's Loan Library House." This library appears to have been
the first of its kind to be established for seamen in quarters intended
chiefly for library purposes.

The society located at Wellclose Square had been formed by Smith
after he had a falling out with certain members of the Port of London
Society over matters concerning the *Sailor's Magazine.* Although his dynamic support and leadership were withdrawn from it when he established
the Mariner's Church Society as a rival organization, the older and
original Port of London Society continued steady on its course. In 1827
the Port of London Society united with the Bethel Union Society and
was then known for a few years as the Port of London and Bethel Union
Society for Promoting Religion Among British and Foreign Seamen.
Another name change took place in 1833, when it reorganized as the
British and Foreign Sailors' Society. At this time the society had as many
as eighty ship libraries, consisting of twenty to forty volumes each,
available for loan.[19] Three thousand books had been put into circulation before 1835, and during that year, 1,125 bound volumes, 1,500 religious pamphlets, and thousands of tracts were distributed.

The society also extended the idea of supplying libraries to another isolated segment of the maritime community, the coast guard stations of Great Britain. Life saving services for ships and crews in distress had begun to be provided on more than a local basis in Great Britain, France, and the United States by 1789, just slightly predating the landsman's intensified and organized interest in his seafaring brother's soul. In 1835 the British and Foreign Sailors' Society estimated that there were some 500 of these stations along the British coast, and that the men, women and children at the locations were in need of libraries. Some aid was begun at the time, but it was contemplated that 25,000 volumes would be needed to supply all of the stations. In addition to this concern for new shore-based libraries on a national scale, the society also furnished books for distribution in foreign ports, and it exhibited other attributes of a national society, such as the continued publication of a magazine through which the sailors' cause was promoted and the partial support of agents in outlying areas. It was this society, the original Port of London Society, which was to endure. As the British and Foreign Sailors' Society, it continued into the twentieth century and was succeeded by the British Sailors' Society of today.

In New York the American Seamen's Friend Society, as already noted, was founded as a national organization in October, 1825. Although a constitution was adopted and officers appointed in 1826, the society existed in name only, being kept alive mostly by the enthusiasm of its agent, the Reverend John Truair, until May 5, 1828. At this time a reorganization occurred, and a determination to make the society prosper became evident.[20] The wording of the new constitution did not limit the society's library activities to just boardinghouse libraries as the resolution of 1825 had. Instead, it called for the promotion in every port of libraries in general, as well as reading rooms and museums, among its general aims to aid the seaman. One of the first communications made to its *Sailor's Magazine and Naval Journal* mentioned looking forward to the day when every vessel would be "regularly supplied with Bibles and tracts and little libraries of useful books as with compass and charts and ballast." This was a hope also expressed by others, such as the friends of seamen in New Haven, who in 1829 had resolved to furnish every vessel that sailed from that port with a suitable library. But it was to be some years before the American Seamen's Friend Society was to furnish libraries to ships in an organized manner. It did, however, encourage and support libraries and reading rooms in foreign ports at an early date. In response to a request for donations of books to be supplied to four libraries for American and British seamen which were established in France by a minister, the society in 1829 began its long career of supplying books to seamen. Collections of 150 volumes each were sent to Marseilles, Bordeaux, Le Havre, and Honfleur. The contents of the collections consisted of a set of publications of the American Tract Society; one French, one Spanish, and two English Bibles; two sets of the *Sailor's Magazine*; thirty volumes from the American Sunday School Union publications; and other "choice" books.

This initial venture stimulated the executive committee of the society to offer to furnish a small select library in every foreign port frequented by American seamen, when the proper assurances could be made that the library would be received, used, and preserved. In order to accomplish this aim, the society hoped to enlist the services of the foreign consuls of the United States. The original library formed in Marseilles served as a model to follow, for it had received the protection and help of the American and British consuls, and was more than a mere reading room. Its collection was reported to have been composed with great care and to have contained books on history, voyages, travels, science, and the arts, as well as religious works. In order to provide similarly well-rounded libraries for its new program, the society, to its credit, solicited donations of books on many subjects at this time.

The rise of the American Seamen's Friend Society did not obviate the need for local societies. To be sure, they continued to flourish either independently or as affiliates of the society. The success of the national body provided encouragement for the formation of even additional local seamen's friend societies; other local groups such as Sunday school, female aid, and juvenile societies also took up the seamen's cause. As it is beyond the scope of this study to follow the eventual course of the seamen's religious movement on a worldwide basis, even as it relates to libraries, the subsequent developments in this phase of libraries for seamen will not be pursued further in a general manner.[21] Rather, the more significant or representative library activities of the American Seamen's Friend Society will be presented in relation to other secular library developments in chapter V.

Before taking leave of the general topic, some mention should be made of the notice or reception given to religion by the seafaring community which stood to benefit from the uplifting promotions made in its behalf. Seamen, for the most part, appeared to take these ministrations in stride along with the other accustomed aspects of their life at sea and ashore. But against the array of articles and reports which testified to the successful effectiveness and acceptance of the evangelist's endeavors, there were a few recorded utterances by mariners to the contrary. In bulk they hardly begin to balance the view presented by the religious reformer, but in substance they add an element of candor to an otherwise distorted perspective.

From the remarks of the famed Arctic voyager, Captain William E. Parry, in 1826, it is evident that there was less than unanimous agreement at the officer and administrative level of the Royal Navy concerning the good effects of religious teaching aboard ship. After professing his positive beliefs on this topic and other religious matters before the Naval and Military Bible Society, Parry observed that his speech had been "talked of very sneeringly" at the Admiralty.[22] And in the U.S. Navy, Nathaniel Ames, a Harvard man with several years' experience at sea, had enough contact with religious tracts aboard ship in the 1820s to observe that they were supplied by landsmen who "have volunteered a feeble crusade against the vices and sins of seamen and have accordingly stuffed ships full of tracts which have entirely defeated their own object . . . ," and that sailors paying little or no attention to the "'serious calls' of these 'gospel trumpeters' . . . have quietly handed over to the cook [for the galley fire] all the tracts which a blind sectarian zeal had intruded upon their notice."[23] Herman Melville, some years later, surveyed the entire maritime religious scene with a jaundiced eye. He wrote in *Redburn* (1849) that despite the floating chapels, the clever tracts, the harangues of clergymen ashore and the sermons of naval chaplains afloat, the provision of evangelical boardinghouses on land, and the attempts to achieve temperance at sea, "notwithstanding all these things, and many more, the relative condition of the great bulk of sailors to the rest of mankind, seems to remain pretty much where it was, a century ago."

Although the reformer held the seaman's moral life in low esteem and criticized his spendthrift ways, he was not above taking advantage of these weaknesses in order to receive support for his religious causes. Often the distribution of Bibles and tracts was based upon their sale. If possible, they were to be sold at cost. Otherwise the price was reduced, or as a last resort the literature was given away. At seamen's chapel, bethel, prayer and church meetings, collections were usually solicited from the transient congregations. Whether the seaman cared or believed, he was asked to contribute money to help support the local religious activities in ports wherever he might sail. For example, in 1827, the crews of over thirty-eight ships subscribed $11,124 to the Mariner's Church of Philadelphia. Subscription-books for noting individual donations were placed aboard these ships, so that their masters could record in them the pledges against the crews' wages to raise money for the church. At the Norfolk Navy Yard in 1828 every vessel arriving there was boarded, and with her commander's permission, the crew was asked to contribute to the bethel union of that city when they received their wages for the completed cruise. Opportunistically it was observed:

"It is believed that if this practice should become general in our country, seamen would comply with it with great cheerfulness." The seaman was made to help pay for his elevating literature and his moral improvement whether he took advantage of the local situation or not, and, as it was thought, if the land sharks could be deprived of some of the sailor's money in the process, so much the better for the seaman and for the seamen's cause.

As the Reverend Thomas Bray observed in 1699, mariners were generous men. The literature abounds with examples of individual and collective generosity on the part of seamen. On one American frigate alone (the *Potomac*), it was reported that $4,997.25 had been collected for various benevolent purposes while off on a cruise during the years 1831-1834. Thus, it is no wonder that seamen in general proved to be passively cooperative toward a religious revival at sea and willingly or unwittingly gave money for its support.

If the seaman patiently bore with the reformer's determination to impose uplifting literature upon him, the reformer, on the other hand, was sensitive about his own right to distribute tracts on shipboard. This privilege was threatened in a brief episode of censorship by the Royal Navy in 1827. On May 28 of that year an order from the Lord High Admiral was given that no religious tracts were to be distributed in the navy, except by authority of the naval chaplains, and that all tracts were first to be submitted to the Reverend Samuel Cole, Chaplain of Greenwich Hospital, who was to superintend the issue of religious books to the fleet. This action created a furor among the dissenting clergy who likened the act of prohibition and censorship to that of their common enemy, the papal church. They were particularly incensed at the thought of the navy allowing "songs and plays and obscene and infidel books" to be distributed as usual, while their worthwhile endeavors were checked. The following year, King George IV was petitioned to abrogate the order of his impetuous brother, the Duke of Clarence, Lord High Admiral, and the incident was ended.[24]

The perseverance in a cause which was fervently believed to be righteous offset whatever obstacles the evangelist encountered in furthering the seaman's redemption. Motivated by a sincere and often selfless desire to elevate the moral condition of seamen, the evangelist also laid the foundations for the seaman's social welfare. Some of the immediate direct results, as we have seen, were manifested in the creation of libraries afloat and ashore. The tradition and example of the early disseminators of religious literature were to influence the secular library efforts of benevolent, philanthropic, and governmental groups for years to come.

Chapter III

An Eventful Summer

I hear America singing, the varied carols I hear,
Those of mechanics, each one singing his as it should be blithe and
*   strong . . .*

* * *

The boatman singing what belongs to him in his boat, the deckhand
*   singing on the steamboat deck . . .*

* * *

Singing with open mouths their strong melodious songs.

—Walt Whitman

As ripples of the maritime religious movement began to wash the shores of America, a secular "plan" to provide books to seamen was made known in New York City in the summer of 1821; and like the effects of a pebble cast into the harbor, the idea radiated rapidly over the surrounding waters of the metropolis. Although the introduction of this plan was an event which made 1821 an *annus mirabilis* in the history of seamen's libraries, the year itself was not one of great moment in the history of the world or the nation. But it belonged to that group of post-War-of-1812 years which has been described as "the era of good feelings." The major powers of the world were at peace. It was a time of growth and development in the United States and of the awakening American nationalism. President James Monroe enunciated his famous Doctrine in 1823, which was to allow the Western Hemisphere to work out its own political future relatively free from foreign intervention. Six new

states were admitted to the Union between 1816 and 1821, and the first
of the many-to-be frontiers of America—that of western New York
state—was being settled. The *Savannah,* in 1819, had demonstrated the
feasibility of using steam power in ocean navigation, even as the golden
age of American sail was dawning, and another engineering feat, the Erie
Canal, 363 miles and nine years a-building, was completed in 1825.
New York City began to emerge as the leading seaport and publishing
center of the nation, and its destiny as the wealthiest and most populous
American city was apparent. It was also a time for reviving and founding
social organizations and for concerned action by benevolent men in
behalf of many worthy causes.

One of these benevolent men was John Pintard, a merchant who had
spent most of his life (1759–1844) in New York City. He was interested
in, or had been associated with, at least twenty associations which provided for the physical well-being or moral enlightenment of the poor.
Pintard had founded the New York Historical Society and also was
active in many intellectual endeavors. Fortunately, he wrote about the
many local activities he and his contemporaries were involved in. The
spirit of the times was captured by Pintard in his many detailed letters
sent to his daughter in New Orleans over the years 1816–1833.[1] Through
these letters we also learn what this man with his sense of history and
social responsibility thought of the events that took place about him.
Some of the formal and informal societies mentioned by Pintard that
began, flourished, or foundered within this time-span were concerned
with such affairs as prison discipline, relief of the destitute, support of
poor widows, the encouragement of faithful domestic servants, the pre-
vention of pauperism, fuel saving for the poor, the reformation of juvenile delinquents, and the support of an orphan asylum. As Thomas
Babington Macaulay, also distinctly a man of the period, remarked
about the number and diversity of societies in England, "This is an age
of Societies." There was scarcely one Englishman in ten, he guessed, who
had "not belonged to some association for distributing books, or for
prosecuting them; for sending invalids to the hospital, or beggars to the
treadmill; for giving plate to the rich, or blankets to the poor."

Seamen, as already discussed in chapter II, were not entirely forgotten
by those who were concerned with the moral and physical condition of
their fellow man. Pintard commented upon some of the groups directly
or indirectly involved with sailors. A few of these he was personally associated with, despite his low opinion of seamen as a "thoughtless, im-
provident set" who had to be forced to save for a rainy day, and whose
officers were little more than splendid beggars. Neither was the support
of libraries forgotten by philanthropic individuals, such as Pintard.
There had always been interest in the organization of libraries and read-

ing rooms in New York, since the first library started there in 1698 by the Reverend Thomas Bray at Trinity Parish. Over the years unsuccessful attempts had been made to provide reading materials through commercial circulating libraries and reading rooms, or by subscriptions in common. One of these attempts, in 1809, was fostered by John Pintard, DeWitt Clinton, Washington Irving, Gulian C. Verplanck, and others who had hoped to support a reading room in the Government House for their interests.

In the early months of 1820, the library of prominence in the city was the New York Society Library, although other smaller libraries (such as those maintained incidentally by a church, or those related to some specialized society) were also in existence. The New York Society Library had been founded in 1754 and was for the use of those persons who could afford to own shares in it. But concerned individuals in New York were soon to bestir themselves in projects which would make libraries available to the working classes, also.

Those who supported worthy causes, the businessmen, professional people, and the independently wealthy, had frequent business and social contacts, and were apt to meet in literary or political groups, bookstores, clubs, and in private homes. Another meeting place, which has been described as the birthplace of famous charities, banks, and corporations in New York, was the Tontine Coffee House, which was built in 1794 and housed the city's Merchants' Exchange until 1825. From a proposal made there in November, 1820, to found a library for the benefit of merchants' clerks, blossomed forth a new kind of library in the city, the New York Mercantile Library Association. It was one of the many libraries for workingmen that was founded in the United States and Great Britain in the early part of the century. These libraries were intended to provide the means whereby young mercantile clerks, mechanics, and mechanics' apprentices could utilize their leisure time constructively, and supposedly educate themselves in the process.

Several months after the founding of the New York mercantile library, a few men met under like circumstances and formed themselves into yet another group for a specific philanthropic action. This association (which was so informal that none of the old chroniclers of the contemporary scene, including Pintard, who might have been present at the meeting, bothered to list its membership or note its activities) decided to extend the idea of libraries for workingmen to seamen also. The "Committee for the Distribution of Books to Seamen," as it was sometimes referred to, applied the same methods of solicitation and book procurement to the formation of libraries for seamen as were commonly employed in starting workingmen's libraries. One of the first things that the members did was to advertise their intentions in two local news-

papers, and to ask for donations of books. During the period of June 27
through July 6, 1821, the *New York American* and the *Commercial
Advertiser* carried this notice:

> *TO THE FRIENDS OF SEAMEN*
>   LADIES & GENTLEMEN.
> It is the intention of some individuals to procure, by gift, for
> the exclusive use of SEAMEN, a LIBRARY, of 20 to 25 vols.
> for every ship belonging to the port. To effect which purpose,
> it is requested that all persons, friendly to this idea, who have
> new, old, or even odd volumes to spare, will please send them
> to this office, as soon as possible. They shall be distributed in
> a faithful manner, and with due discretion, under the care of
> the captain of each ship. The owners of the Liverpool line of
> ships have, in accordance with the plan, given each of their
> vessels a similar Library.

The appearance of the announcement came at an opportune time. It
sparked interest among several ship owners who were anxious to attract
attention to their ships, and who were receptive to any innovations
which they could employ to give them an advantage over their competi-
tors in the eye of the public. In New York there was a rivalry among sailing packets to win over passengers and lucrative light cargoes. This was
the time when ships began to sail on schedule without regard for weather
or a fully loaded hold. It was the beginnings of the ocean liner—a ship
belonging to a line of ships which regularly serviced two or more ports.
New York and Liverpool on either side of the Atlantic became the chief
maritime centers for this activity, and steam was yet to begin to compete
with the fast packets which developed in the transatlantic trade.[2]
    The spirit of competition brought about rapid improvements in
service and accommodations among the packets. Such luxuries as a
bathing room (a house on deck where the bather could sluice water over
his body from a bucket) and private staterooms were soon to be introduced. Ship owners quickly realized that libraries would be as desirable
for their passengers as for their crews. A library in the passenger cabin
would help ameliorate the long and often boring ocean voyage and
would be another service which could be advertised. Some owners
simultaneously provided libraries for both passengers and crew, while
others apparently left it up to the newly formed committee to furnish
crews' libraries to their ships. The basic idea of libraries for seamen and
the derivative idea for passenger libraries spread rapidly on the New
York waterfront within two months.
    As each new adoption of the plan for shipboard libraries took place,

it was reported by the press, beginning with an inevitable claim of a "first" in priority, which may or may not have been true. In reporting maritime news, the local editors usually provided favorable and enthusiastic accounts of the activities of the packets, for they relied on them for overseas news; and the editors were not about to risk losing their valuable contacts with the Continent by ignoring or offending the packet owners and their captains. The new plan for libraries on shipboard thus received some notice in the newspapers. Its progress from situation to situation can be best described by quoting the brief newspaper articles themselves, for they contain perhaps the only information that remains about the libraries. Within two days of the first appearance of the advertisement by the committee there was a notice in the June 29 *New York Evening Post* which confirmed the presence of a library on at least one of the "Liverpool Line's" packets, the *Albion.* It reported:

> Yesterday Gov. Clinton, at the request of the owners of the Liverpool Line of Packets, paid a visit to their superb ship, the Albion. After viewing her admirable accommodations, and the *Seaman's Library,* which the owners have presented to the Albion, her commander gave to his Excellency and friends an excellent lunch, consisting of every delicacy of the season. We understand they have it in contemplation shortly to furnish a library for the cabin, for the benefit and amusement of the passengers.

The *Albion* had many claims to fame, and was a likely candidate for the first library. She was the first ship built as a packet (1819) for the famous Black Ball Line (the first Liverpool packet line), which had inaugurated scheduled sailings in 1818. At the time that the seamen's library was shipped aboard the *Albion,* she was considered one of the fastest and finest ships afloat, and well worthy of a visit by the governor of New York. Her captain and host on this occasion was an able mariner, whose name, albeit probably misappropriated, still lives on today as "Kicking Jack Williams" in the well-known sea shanty "Blow the Man Down." Within a few days of the excellent luncheon *à la Albion,* it was reported in the *Mercantile Advertiser* on July 11 that prior to the packet's departure libraries had been placed in both the cabin for the use of the passengers, and in the forecastle, where books would be available to the crew; and the claim was made that the *Albion* was "the first merchant vessel that has ever sailed from this port with a library." The fact that the statement was qualified with the words "from this port" would indicate that perhaps other libraries were known to the editor, or else that he was hoping to avoid an anticipated counterclaim. A similar statement, in the same vein, about the library being the first to perish at sea in a packet can be made today, for the *Albion* was lost in a storm off the Irish coast in April, 1822, just nine months afterward. With her sinking, the *Albion* again set a record—this time for the loss of life— which stood until another more disastrous packet wreck occurred in 1847.

According to the July 11, 1821, article about the *Albion*, two other vessels in port, the *Hercules,* and the *Rockingham,* were to be furnished with libraries in the same manner as the Black Ball packet before they sailed to Liverpool, and several other vessels were "following this good example." No further comment was made in the *Advertiser* regarding the libraries aboard the *Hercules* and *Rockingham* from the above date until they cleared port on July 15 and 29, respectively. The *Hercules,* described as having "most elegant furnished accommodations" in an advertisement in the *Advertiser* of July 3, was owned by Byrnes, Trimble and Company (who formed the second Liverpool packet line, the Red Star Line in 1822), and was likely to have been provided with libraries by the company. The *Rockingham,* on the other hand, was apparently a regular trader of the day, and in typical tramp-ship fashion departed nineteen days after the date she was advertised to sail. If she had acquired a library during her stay in port, it was probably only through the efforts of the committee for libraries.

The owners of a new steamship, the *Robert Fulton,* which had been featured in the news even before her maiden voyage out of New York in April of 1820, were also eager to tell the public about their intentions of putting a library in her cabin. As the first steam vessel to be especially constructed for ocean service, the *Robert Fulton* was then an object of technological curiosity. She offered speed, innovation, and luxury in travel, and was "an elegant steam ship," built to ply between New York and New Orleans, "touching at Charleston, and Havana." It was only fitting that this modern vessel, which excited so much popular attention, should have a library or two on board. By July 7, a seamen's library consisting of "25 volumes of voyages, travels, Geography and Navigation" had been selected by Davis Dunham and Company, the owners, according to the *Daily Advertiser* and the *National Advocate.* Three days later it was reported in the *Mercantile Advertiser* that this library had been augmented by a gift of "several volumes of valuable books" through the generosity of two city book firms, those of Peter A. Mesier, and Collins and Hannay, and that the books would be "carefully disposed of to meet the views of the donors." Booksellers of that day, because of their occupation, often figured as participants in the donation and collection of books for worthwhile causes and incipient benevolently sponsored libraries. They were likely to be public spirited men, whose shops, while fulfilling the varied aspects of the stationery and book business (*e.g.,* the printing, publishing, importing, stocking, and selling of books and pamphlets) under one roof, also served as informal places where like-minded friends might meet incidentally, while keeping up with the latest in the literary world. Peter Mesier was a former alderman, and was an old, established book dealer. He had sold books to the New York Society Library as early as 1810, and would be one of the venerable standard bearers for the booksellers and stationers in the parade that celebrated the opening of the Erie Canal. What he contributed to the *Robert Fulton's* forecastle library is not known, but it is possible that the firm of Collins and Hannay included copies of their recent editions of Hugh Blair's *Lectures on Rhetoric,* or a copy of *A Critical Pronouncing Dictionary,* by John Walker.

Not to be outdone by the oceangoing sailing ships and steamers, the local Long Island Sound and Hudson River passenger steamers also began to carry libraries. Under the caption, "Elegant Improvement in Traveling," the *New York Evening Post* of August 3, 1821 reported:

> The Steam Boats *Connecticut* and *Fulton,* on the Sound, have on board, a well chosen *Library of Five Hundred Latest Publications,* for the use of their Passengers. This excellent arrangement will render it unnecessary for Gentlemen or Ladies to take volumes in their trunks. We learn the *North River* steam boats intend to follow this example.

It is hard to imagine where the relatively large libraries for these two early Long Island Sound vessels were placed, for they were described as not having any staterooms, saloons, or hurricane decks. Much of their interior space was given over, of necessity, to the storage of wood for firing the boilers, and as a result only a small quantity of freight could be carried. Their passengers did not fare too well, either. Once the engines, which were of Robert Fulton's design, were set in motion, they made noise sufficient enough "to destroy the peace and comfort" of those taking passage aboard the steamers. But at least there was ample time to read, if the distractions of sights and sounds allowed it. The newer *Connecticut* (built, 1818) left New York for New Haven at 6 A.M. every Monday, Wednesday, and Friday, and met the older *Fulton* (built, 1813), which operated out of New London, at the port of New Haven. Each ship then departed for her home port at 6 P.M., so it was possible to make a through-trip from New York to New London in about a day's time. Compared with the alternative method of traveling by stagecoach, the steamer offered a faster and less tedious journey. No doubt, a library aboard ship made the passage more enjoyable for some,

especially if "all of the latest publications" were added to it weekly, as
was claimed by the Sound Line in the *National Advocate* of August 4.

The cabin library, once it was introduced, became a permanent
feature on well-appointed vessels which catered to the passenger trade.
As long as there would be discriminating voyagers to please, ship owners
could not afford to neglect to furnish their vessels with libraries for the
use of travelers aboard them. Numerous references to the presence, size,
or content of these libraries have occurred in the literature of sea travel
from their inception to the present day. By contrast, seamen's libraries
of a mostly secular character, such as the one described as having been
provided to the *Robert Fulton,* apparently had a short existence on
American merchant ships sailing out of New York. Some twenty-one
libraries of this kind were shipped by the committee before it faded
away, and doubtless others had been provided by individual ship owners.
The plan for furnishing these libraries in an organized manner was
apparently discontinued after its short flurry of success. In 1825, an
article in the *National Advocate* of March 14, which described the London
packet, *York,* made no mention of a forecastle library, although it
praised the richly bound 150-volume passenger library aboard her. The
Black Ball Line's *Nestor* still had a seamen's library in 1822, which her
mate believed was used to good advantage by the crew.

It was also about this time that the Charleston Bethel Union was
collecting donated books for seamen's shipboard libraries, and the Reverend George C. Smith was making known the "portable" library plan
in Hull, while the New York Bethel Union was urging ship owners to
purchase small "well selected" libraries for their ships. A year previously,
coincident with the introduction of the seamen's libraries plan by the
philanthropic New York committee, the New York Bethel Union had
begun its activities—in fact, just a few days before the library committee's newspaper advertisement was printed. This bethel group was formed
for the purpose of conducting prayer meetings aboard ship, as was already being done in London on the Thames River. In aid of the Society
for Promoting the Gospel Among Seamen in the Port of New York
(or the Port Society, as it was commonly known), the Bethel Union held
its first meeting aboard the merchant ship *Cadmus,* lying at the Pine
Street wharf. On Friday, June 22, 1821, the bethel flag, a gift of the London Bethel Union, was hoisted to the masthead of the *Cadmus*; and as
seamen crowded aboard or listened from the pier, the opening meeting
was presented. The objects and plans of the society were stated and "the
Mariner's psalm was sung with great animation and feeling." After
prayer and other exercises it was reported that "tracts were distributed
among the seamen, who received them with gratitude."

A similar scene took place soon after aboard the United States warship *Franklin,* on August 21, 1821. This vessel was one of the newer and more heavily armed ships of the navy. She was then preparing for a three years' cruise and was about to depart for the eastern Pacific Ocean. Apparently the bethel meeting on board the *Franklin* was a success in the eyes of the bethel's board, the reverend clergy, and the local citizens who attended it. A congregation of about 800 persons, most of whom were seamen, was claimed to have been in attendance. The *Mercantile Advertiser* of August 23 reported this historic evening divine service as "Hope for Sailors," and attributed the favorable outcome of it to the "cheerfulness with which the overture of the [bethel] committee was received by Commodore Stewart as well as the promptness and civility of Lt. Hunter and all officers of the ship for the regularity and accommodations of this meeting."[3]

Commodore Charles Stewart and his officers and men were indeed in a receptive mood. Earlier in the month they had also accepted the overtures of the committee for the distribution of books to seamen, and thus participated in another historic incident—that of receiving what was claimed to be the first seamen's library aboard an American naval vessel. Not only did they accept the small library that was donated to the *Franklin,* but they authorized the committee to purchase a larger library, for which they collectively paid some $600. In doing so, they started a custom in the navy which was followed by other vessels for a number of years.

No mention was made in the official logbook of the *Franklin* of either the bethel meeting or the receipt or purchase of a library, although a few items of note appear amid the daily loggings of inspections, sick reports, drills, punishments, and other routine matters which occurred while in port. The circumstances involving the prayer meetings on both the *Franklin* and the *Cadmus* were later recounted with veneration by the American Seamen's Friend Society, which regarded the occurrences as momentous occasions in the "great enterprise of converting the maritime world to the service of Jesus Christ." The story of the *Franklin's* library was also given more lasting notice some twenty years after the fact, when the navy's own leading critic of the day summed it up in about 260 words. It was mentioned in the third of a series of articles written by one "H. B." in the *Southern Literary Messenger* of December, 1840. "Harry Bluff," as it soon became known, was the pen name of Matthew Fontaine Maury, a lieutenant in the navy who later gained enduring recognition for his pioneering contributions to the science of oceanography.

Several of Maury's criticisms in the *Messenger* focused on the training of young men for the naval profession, which in those days was formally carried out in a limited and desultory manner either ashore or aboard the larger vessels of the navy. In concluding his negative observations on the subject, Maury stated that the furnishing of libraries to men-of-war was the only effective step that had ever been taken toward education in the navy; and he then told how it came to pass that the *Franklin* was the first vessel in the navy to acquire a library. He ended the sketch about the *Franklin's* library by declaring that its success and the actions of its originator, a William Wood of Canandaigua, New York, induced the Navy Department to provide every vessel with a small library.

Maury's brief account of the *Franklin's* library and its alleged far-reaching results has served as virtually the only record of the occurrences which may have contributed to the official establishment of libraries aboard American naval vessels, and for 133 years it has been accepted as he wrote it. The sequence of events concerning the library on the *Franklin* as recorded by Maury appears essentially correct, yet the acount is not quite true; and his assumption that the example of the *Franklin's* library and actions of William Wood were directly responsible for the authorization of libraries by the navy is false. Although Maury, judging from his articles, was quite familiar with the everyday happenings in the navy, he probably did not have complete or reliable information on the subject of naval libraries available to him at the time that he wrote. The details which correct and add flesh to Maury's skeleton history are found among the correspondence of the Navy Department, and in newspaper accounts and other contemporary records. When this evidence is examined, a different, and, of course, expanded history of the establishment of seamen's libraries in the navy emerges. Prominent in the beginning of this history is the story of the *Franklin's* library. This story is essentially complete in itself, and is told in the following chapter. Closely linked with the *Franklin's* library, and a few other naval libraries, is the name of William Wood (fig. 3), a man who is credited with starting various libraries for workingmen during the first quarter of the century, but about whom practically nothing of an evaluative nature has ever been written. Inasmuch as he figures conspicuously in the history of early naval libraries, his biography is included at this point, for it helps put into perspective the contemporary scene involving the beginnings of seamen's libraries, as well as tells something about his character and about how he accomplished his aims.

When Lieutenant Maury mentioned William Wood in his *Messenger* article as the "landsman" who introduced libraries to the navy, Wood's deeds were probably still fresh in both the public's mind and in his own. At this time William Wood was enjoying a lingering reputation for being a philanthropist, especially where libraries were concerned. He had been active in several worthwhile causes in the recent past, and

3. William Wood, 1777–1857.
Wood Library, Canandaigua, N.Y.

many of his contemporaries regarded him as the originator of the idea
to provide libraries to workers in the mechanic and mercantile trades.
Yet today the remembrance of his good works has almost escaped mankind's cluttered memory. Wood rates just a mention by name in the
general histories of American libraries; and in the larger scheme of
American history, his name is misspelled in an eminent historian's
introduction to the diary of Philip Hone. Even the very libraries that
Wood was said to have founded have, for the most part, vanished and
are themselves forgotten. One day in 1828 John Pintard promised that
he would write everything he knew about his "extraordinary eccentric,
modest" friend, Wood, and his benevolent activities. He then likened
Wood to the "Man of Ross"—John Kyrle, the Herefordshire benefac-
tor made famous by the poems of Pope and Coleridge, and commented
on by Samuel Johnson—no doubt because both Kyrle and Wood
supposedly did astonishing things for the public welfare by successfully
soliciting the aid of the wealthy in their charitable causes. But if later
Pintard did write something more about William Wood, his words are
not now readily evident.[4]

There have been several men of importance by the name of William
Wood, among them the more famed British zoologist and surgeon
whose life began three years before and ended the same year as his contemporary in America. The latter William Wood, a merchant, was born
on Bunker Hill in Charlestown, Massachusetts, in 1777, the son of a
distinguished resident of the town, Colonel David Wood. As a young
man, William Wood was apprenticed to a firm of glassware and crockery
dealers in Boston, where he also was educated. When he was twenty
years old, he went to Liverpool as a clerk in a mercantile house. After
a brief stay, he returned to Boston where he and his brother carried on
a successful business. In 1818, the first notice of his public generosity
is recorded in connection with the giving of cash prizes for the construction of the best casks made by apprentice coopers. Wood probably was
interested in improving casks if he was still in the crockery trade when
he anonymously made his offer. The following year he personally gave
a larger amount of money for the best produced casks and hats. The
exhibiting of artisans' wares and the auctioning off of these items for
the benefit of the Massachusetts Charitable Mechanic Association
became, more or less, a regular event in Boston. About the same time
that Wood fostered the concept of exhibitions for the association, he
conceived the idea of establishing a library for apprentices in the mechanic trades of Boston. The execution of this idea, whether it was
original with Wood or not, brought him moderate fame and set him on
a lifelong hobby of promoting libraries.

One account of Wood's founding of the Mechanic Apprentices' Library

Association mentions that in 1818 he began soliciting for books through the newspapers and by means of circulars, and in a few months he had accumulated several hundred books. These were put in a room of the town hall of Boston. He then appealed to the Massachusetts Charitable Mechanic Association to form a library for apprentices. On February 9, 1820, the officers of the association accepted this trust with appropriate ceremonies. Wood, like most givers of gifts for the common good, attached a few conditions to be lived up to by the recipients; and his terms appeared to spell out the operating policies of the new library. In presenting the keys to the library to the president of the association, Wood repeated the pledge that he had given to most of the donors of the books, and which, in turn, the association was to honor: That the books and library be forever "opened for the use of the mechanics and all needy apprentices, gratis; that a room [shall be provided] containing the Cyclopedia, and where all large works shall be placed, which room shall be opened twice in the week for information and use of all apprentices who are mechanics of twenty years of age, and if convenient to those of nineteen years of age." The association agreed to take on the management of the 1,480-volume library on condition that it would not be charged for its incidental expenses. The library did not flourish long on public subscriptions as a free institution for apprentices, and after a few years it had to close its doors for lack of support. It was re-organized in 1828. At this time, a qualified apprentice could become a member by paying one dollar per year to the association for his library privileges.

Even though a mechanics' library was already in operation in Bristol, Connecticut, in 1818, Wood was remembered by his contemporaries for founding the first mechanics' apprentices library. Actually, his plan was nothing new. It was another version of the early social library—a library supported by subscription or through the ownership of shares by its members or its supporting patrons. Social libraries date back in this country to 1731, when Benjamin Franklin organized the Library Company of Philadelphia; and similar social libraries were in existence in England several years before Franklin's. By the 1820s the time was ripe for the idea to be applied to a group of the population newly aware of its identity, the emerging middle-class workers.[5] In fact, within a month of the founding date of the mechanic apprentices' library in Boston the merchant clerks of that city held a meeting to form a library association of their own, and on April 4, 1820, formally opened their subscription library, the Mercantile Library Association. Wood claimed to have originated this library, also. If he did, by 1850 its membership had forgotten his part, for he was not mentioned as one of its founders in a résumé of the library's history printed at that time.

Wood, no doubt, did take part in the founding of several other libraries for workers. Henry Lord Brougham, who in his long political career was involved in improving social conditions in Britain, and who helped found the Society for the Diffusion of Useful Knowledge in 1826, was responsible for publicizing William Wood's activities in this regard. In an address printed for the benefit of the London Mechanics' Institution in 1825, he attached a footnote about Wood to a paragraph tracing the history of the Mechanics' and Apprentices' Library at Liverpool. Apparently unmindful of the history of early libraries in Great Britain, he stated that the Liverpool library was formed on the plans of the Library Company of Philadelphia and in the footnote explained:

> Although the remote origin of these institutions may be traced to Franklin, Mr. W. Wood has the high merit of establishing them on their present plan and adapting them peculiarly to the instruction of mechanics and apprentices. He founded the first at Boston in 1820; he has had the satisfaction of seeing the plan adopted in New York, Philadelphia, Albany, and other towns; and I have now before me a letter in which he says that he has succeeded in forming one at New Orleans, where he was called on business. His plan is to obtain loans or gifts of books which almost every one has beyond his own wants; and he reckons 30,000 volumes thus obtained in different towns, and as many readers.

The citing of Wood as the originator of mechanics' and apprentices' libraries by Lord Brougham has either been alluded to, or has been partially quoted without source of publication in accounts of Wood's activities, including two valuable works on the enumeration of libraries in mid-nineteenth century America. The distinguished librarian of the Smithsonian Institution, Charles C. Jewett in 1850, and William J. Rhees in 1859, quoted a few lines of Lord Brougham's tribute to Wood in their descriptions of the Mechanic Apprentices' Library of Boston, thus helping to spread or perpetuate Wood's fame. But if Lord Brougham was perhaps correct in ascribing to William Wood the honor of originating libraries for mechanics and apprentices in America, the editor of the *Mechanics' Magazine* did not agree with Brougham's account of the founding of the London Mechanics' Institution in his own country. The editor maintained that Brougham in his address of 1825, and on other occasions, had credited the wrong person with being the founder. The true founder, so he claimed, was himself, Joseph C. Robertson, and not Dr. George Birkbeck, as Lord Brougham allegedly often repeated. Robertson apparently became so exasperated with his neglected status that in 1835 he presented his case in the pages of his *Magazine* by generating, and then publishing, correspondence with Brougham on the subject. After writing two letters, Lord Brougham terminated his part of the controversy by stating that the question was a matter of opinion, and that he too had a right to express it.[6]

In the long run, Robertson failed to win his argument. His biographical sketch in *The Dictionary of National Biography* does not mention his early connection with the rise of mechanics' institutions in England, whereas Dr. Birkbeck is cited as "the founder of the mechanics' institutions." From his vain tempest in a teapot, Robertson probably learned what others before him and since have had to ruefully accept— that it is difficult to change certain popularly attributed "facts," whether they be right or wrong, and that the honor of being called *the* founder of something that others were also involved in establishing is an elusive glory for many. While William Wood had no apparent contender to fend off or fight with over his laurels during his lifetime, he did nevertheless from time to time remind persons of influence, such as Lord Brougham, DeWitt Clinton, various secretaries of the navy, and others, about his role as the modern-day originator of libraries for mechanics and clerks and for seamen.

A challenge to one of his claims did come some years later. When William Wood died in 1857, certain members of the General Society of Mechanics and Tradesmen of the City of New York who thought that he was responsible for founding their apprentices' library wanted to offer some expression of thankfulness for the services rendered by him years before. In order to determine just what role Wood had played in the establishment of the library, the library committee of the society was appointed to look into the record and report on the details of Wood's early connection with the library. The committee found that the idea of establishing a library had occurred to at least three members of the society as early as January, 1820, and that in a letter dated March 4, 1820, Wood was asked how to go about setting up a library. Also, a few days earlier, it can now be added, the February 28 issue of the *Mercantile Advertiser* had noted that a plan to establish an apprentices' library in New York City was afoot.

Wood complied with the committee's request for information by going to New York in person. At a later date he managed to transmit a memorandum written on the original letter of request, and it somehow found its way into the files of the association. The memo is of interest for it describes Wood's *modus operandi,* and incidentally shows how he liked to assert, whether true or not, that he was the sole founder of certain libraries. Wood wrote:

> Memo.—After receiving this letter, went to New-York to
> assist the work of effecting a Mechanics' Apprentices' Library;
> gave three or four months to the object; induced all persons I
> knew, (was introduced to many,) also, to give either old or
> new books; wrote in many papers in favor of the scheme; and
> deposited the same at Kirk & Mercein's book store, Wall-
> street; received from Thomas R. Mercein one thousand
> printed certificates, and went in person to nearly as many
> mechanics' shops and manufactories, and induced the "boss,"
> then and there, to sign them, inserting the names of the appren-
> tices; had but one refusal—that by Mr. C———, in Pearl-
> street; 740 lads drew volumes on the opening of the library,
> 25th November, 1820. I then founded the Merchants' Clerks'
> Library, Clinton Hall; called the first meeting at Tontine
> Coffee House, and gave the first volume; workd at that insti-
> tution some four to six months previous. I had the sole honor
> to found and originate the Merchants' Clerks' and Mechan-
> ics' Apprentices' Libraries in Boston; those in New-York came
> next, and so on, to New-Orleans, to Montreal.

It appears that only one letter was written to a newspaper at the time
"in favor of the scheme" to establish the New York library. A notice
suggesting that donations be given to the "Library for use of Mechanics,"
appeared in the *Mercantile Advertiser* of April 13, 1820, and was signed,
"A. Mason." Later, the committee advertised in the *American,* on November 29, and asked for donations of books. The donors were then
requested to inscribe their names in any of the books that they gave.

In addition to unearthing the convenient memorandum, the committee presented other information concerning Wood's biography and
correspondence with the association, but had to conclude that Wood
was not the founder of its library. The committee further proposed
several resolutions, one of them recognizing Wood as the originator of
the first mechanics' library in the country (in Boston), and another
which noted that he had earned the respect and honor of all good men
throughout the country for his promotion of the moral and mental
improvement of young apprentices.

Wood's decision to journey to New York in order to help the General
Society of Mechanics and Tradesmen establish a library provided him
with another opportunity to promote libraries, this time for the seafaring segment of the working population. Apparently within a year
after gathering books and pledges for the support of the General Society's library, Wood became involved in supplying books to ships and
seamen in the port of New York.[7] His interest in this cause extended

over a period of twelve or more years, it being revived now and again by events that brought the navy to his attention. The few notices about his life which mention his contacts with the navy ignore or compress this time-span, so that it appears that Wood was directly responsible for having libraries put aboard naval vessels. Wood's contributions to this achievement will be told more fully as part of the story about the *Franklin* and the odyssey of her library, which follows in the next chapter.

Other distortions in sequence of time and in fact, some contributed by Wood himself, are encountered in the brief sketches of his life. These sketches include a few glimpses of his personality and eccentricities which lend an air of almost sinister mystery to an otherwise benign character. According to most accounts, in 1826 Wood went to live in Canandaigua, New York, after apparently having done most of his active library founding. His brother-in-law, Nathaniel Gorham, Jr., had settled there as one of the pioneers of the early western frontier and had acquired large holdings of land in the Genesee country by the time he died. At some time, Wood helped influence the planning of Canandaigua, for he was given credit for advising that broad avenues be laid out and shade trees be planted along them. He was also remembered there for his many acts of kindness and benevolence toward the young, the sick, and the poor of the community; and a poem written in his honor kept alive the memory of his durable deeds. In it his name was connected forever with that of his adopted residence, for the poem concluded, "She'd scarce be Canandaigua if stripped of her Wood."

An old friend reminiscing about Wood's activities in the village wrote, "He affected peculiarities in appearance, quaint ways of living, and odd means for the accomplishment of his many objects." At times Wood, who never married, was said to disappear from his strangely furnished room in his widowed sister's home on some project of philanthropy. Later, news of his good deeds supposedly would filter back to the village and account for his absence. "He never did things as other men," stated the friend, "if there was any *outré* way of accomplishing his object he was sure to adopt it, and [he] claimed his reward by his secret enjoyment of the surprise and mystification of beholders." In addition to his local philanthropies, Wood did take part in two benevolent causes on a national scale, which another old friend claimed that Wood was responsible for originating.[8] However, it again appears that Wood was given credit for something in which he had only a minor role. He was reported to have helped obtain funds for the cause of the Greeks during their war of independence from Turkey. In a detailed account of the distribution of American aid to the Greeks in 1827–1828, Wood's donation is listed as: "From the ladies of Canandaigua 3 boxes of clothing &c. by William Wood, $375.00." This was against a total sum collected for the cause of $46,321.61. Wood was also cited as being instrumental in helping the Polish refugees of 1834 establish a colony in the United States. Whatever his contribution was in this regard, it was not too obvious, for an extensive work on the Polish exiles of 1831 does not mention him. However, the author did state that it is difficult to identify the originator of this unsuccessful plan to settle the Polish exiles on a governmental grant of land in America.[9]

William Wood mostly contributed his time and efforts to the initial stages of worthwhile projects. Not being a wealthy man himself, he induced others to donate money or materials to worthy causes, although he did modestly contribute to them, also. In soliciting for these good causes, it appears that Wood followed Benjamin Franklin's recommendations on how best to succeed. Franklin mentioned in his autobiography that he soon learned when soliciting for his library to propose it as a scheme of a number of friends, rather than his own idea, for those solicited were less likely to contribute if they believed that some one person's reputation would be advanced in the slightest by the success of the idea. Wood may have originally sought anonymity in his good deeds, as Franklin advised, but later he did claim the merit for many of them. Today he probably would be called a fund-raiser rather than a philanthropist, but on the day of his death, August 5, 1857, many people who then knew the extent of his good works, mourned the passing of a kindly man who had devoted his life to helping others have a more bearable or worthwhile existence.

Chapter IV

The *Franklin,* 74

As Franklin drew lightning from Heaven,
May prayers from the Franklin *arise;*
And Covenant blessings be given,
Descending to us from the skies.

May the thunder Columbia pours,
Be such as pure Justice decrees;
The God of Thunder be ours,
To give us success on the seas.

—Hymn to the Franklin

Beginning in the year 1818, the United States established a cruising
station in the eastern Pacific Ocean so that American interests could be
protected by naval forces in these waters. Both the Spanish blockade
of Valparaiso and the activities of the Peruvian Patriot forces that were
rebelling against Spain threatened the rights of neutral commerce. By
1820 it was thought that American representation there would be more
effective if a capital ship were present, as was the case in the British and
French squadrons assigned to this duty. When the time came to relieve
the frigate *Constellation* on the Pacific station, it was decided to send
the ship-of-the-line *Franklin.*[1] This vessel, the third in the U.S. Navy
to be named after Benjamin Franklin, was built in Philadelphia in 1815.
She was designated as a 74-gun ship and was in the class of the most
heavily armed vessels in the navy. The *Franklin* had been the flagship
of Commodore Charles Stewart in the Mediterranean Sea from late
1817 to early 1820 when she returned to the United States. While in the

Mediterranean, the *Franklin's* design was much admired by foreign
visitors, and she acquired a fair reputation for her sailing qualities. In
short, she was a splendid ship to represent the United States in any
waters. Because of the *Franklin's* large size, the schooner *Dolphin* was
assigned to accompany her and to do most of the active cruising when
on station. The two ships made up the first true Pacific Squadron of
the U.S. Navy, and Commodore Stewart was given command.

Charles Stewart, then forty-three years old, was a renowned and experienced naval officer. He had gone to sea in the merchant marine as a
poor boy at age thirteen. After becoming an officer in the navy, he rose
to the highest commissioned rank at that time—captain. He also retained
the title of commodore from his previous command of the Mediterranean
Squadron. By custom in the U.S. Navy, once a man had commanded a
squadron as commodore, he was thereafter addressed by this title as a
courtesy. Stewart's career in the navy spanned the years from the
Quasi-War with France in 1798 to the beginning of the Civil War. It is
said that he remembered John Paul Jones, having seen him just before
Jones left for Russia, and that he had drunk wine with Washington and
dined with every succeeding president except Harrison and Tyler, who
died before he was afforded the opportunity. He was further described
as having a broad and vigorous mentality and possessing coolness and
courage in times of stress. He lived to the ripe old age of ninety-one,
retiring from the navy in 1862 with the rank of rear admiral.

As early as May, 1821, Commodore Stewart and Secretary of the Navy
Smith Thompson were corresponding about the contemplated cruise of
the *Franklin*. On June 9, the secretary gave permission for Stewart to
take his wife aboard the *Franklin* for the voyage, stating that it was in
compliance with the current rules and regulations of the navy.[2] Stewart
also corresponded with the Board of Navy Commissioners about more
specific details concerning his ship and her equipment and stores. Being
intimately acquainted with the *Franklin* from his previous voyage in her,
he early asked that a "light half poop" be constructed "as a further accommodation and well calculated for the Pacific." This request to alter
his ship was granted on July 13, provided that the expense did not exceed
$500. By adding, in effect, another short deck above the quarter deck at
the extreme after end of the ship, another cabin could be created in the
enclosure. Such a cabin was well situated to receive the benefits of natural light and ventilation, and could be occupied by either the ship's
commanding officer or a commodore, depending upon the elaborate-
ness of its construction and furnishings (fig. 4). The building of the light
poop on the *Franklin* probably affected the eventual location of the
crew's library. Maury's article, and a later newspaper account, placed
it "in an apartment set apart," or in the captain's cabin, respectively.

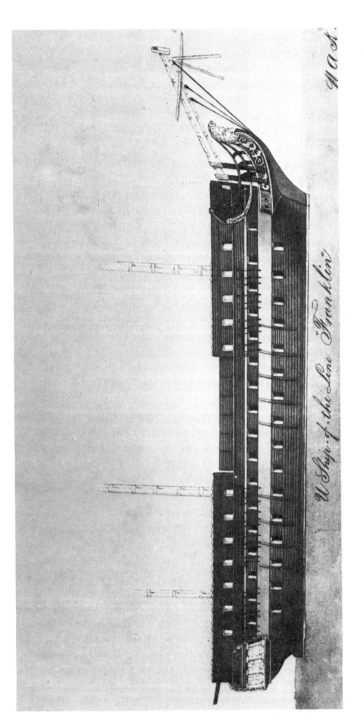

U. Ship. of the Line "Franklin"

U.S.A.

4. The hull of the *Franklin*, 74, as depicted by the contemporary artist W. A. K. Martin. The location of the captain's cabin is indicated by the starboard quarter gallery (Q). Commodore Stewart's "light half poop" would have been constructed above this cabin in the area (P) between the quarterdeck bulwarks (B) and abaft the mizzenmast (M).

National Archives

One of the first small items Stewart requested from the Board of Navy Commissioners was a book, Jacobsen's *Sea Laws,* and a copy of it was sent to him from their office in Washington. He also forwarded, in July, a short list of educational materials that his schoolmaster, Oliver Smith, required in his department. The list included "1 — Set of Globes (13 inch), 1 — Set of Instruments, 1 — Sextant, 1 — Quadrant, Maps and Charts, 1 — Telescope belonging to the Navy department, 1 — Gunter's Scale," and one copy each of several books. The requested books were listed by short English titles and their authors' last names. Editions of these works were then probably available as: Nathaniel Bowditch's *New American Practical Navigator* (fifth ed., 1821), Charles Hutton's *Course of Mathematics* (rev. ed., New York, 1812), William Enfield's *Institutes of Natural Philosophy* (third American ed., 1820), Georges Cuvier's *Le règne animal* (1817), C. H. Persoon's *Synopsis plantarum* (Paris, 1805-07), Parker Cleaveland's *Elementary Treatise on Mineralogy and Geology* (1816), Emmerich de Vattel's *Law of Nations* (1820), and the British Admiralty's *Nautical Almanac* for the years 1821, -22, and -23.

Only half of the meager list was approved for purchase. The navigational items—the globes, mathematical instruments, sextant, quadrant, Bowditch, the nautical almanacs and the Gunter's scale—and a copy of Vattel's *Law of Nations* were authorized for purchase only if they were not already in the sailingmaster's department aboard the *Franklin.* Concerning the remainder, the commisioners reported (July 13), "The other articles cannot be supplied at public expense. It is presumed that the young officers requiring them will provide themselves." The early navy was one of economic operation and strict accountability of stores and equipment. As will be discussed later, midshipmen and others had always been required to provide their own books for study; but this attitude toward books in the service was about to become a little more generous within the next six years. In the meantime, the scientifically inclined schoolmaster of the *Franklin* was faced with the prospect of attempting to teach up to forty midshipmen without having even one copy of the books he thought necessary furnished to him by the government.

Either from past knowledge, or by more direct communication, Commodore Stewart was led to believe that the *Columbus,* 74, just recently returned from the Mediterranean station, had some charts of the Pacific Ocean aboard her. He wrote to the Board of Navy Commissioners and requested that these charts and some books of voyages be transferred to his ship. Subsequently, Commodore John Rodgers, the president of the board was notified by Commodore William Bainbridge in Boston, on August 29, that he had arranged for eighteen volumes from the *Columbus* to be packed and forwarded to the *Franklin.* The books that the commodore sent comprised four different sets of voyages, which he listed in a cursory manner, but yet noted the number of volumes in each set. It is almost a certainty that the editions of the works that Bainbridge sent to the *Franklin* via the Boston navy agent were: *A Collection of Voyages Round the World . . . Containing a Complete Historical Account of Captain Cook's . . . Voyages,* edited by John Hogg (London, 1790), Vancouver's *Voyage of Discovery to the North Pacific Ocean* (London, 1798), *Voyage de la Pérouse autour du monde* (Paris, 1797), and John Hawkesworth's *Account of the Voyages . . . in the Southern Hemisphere* (London, 1773).

This request, and the response to it, illustrates another standard practice concerning navigational books in the early navy. A maximum amount of use was derived from a limited number of books and charts by means of transferring them from one vessel to another. Only when a transfer could not be made were navigational materials authorized for purchase. Thus, in this instance, Stewart, Rodgers, and Bainbridge made use of the books on the *Columbus,* which was then being placed in ordinary. "Ordinary" was a condition of inactive service for a naval vessel. Usually her crew was reduced to a small custodial force and her stores and other valuable equipment of a portable nature were removed, and she then came under the custody of the commandant of the navy yard where she was berthed. The *Franklin* had also been ordered to be put in ordinary on August 16, 1820, after her return from the Mediterranean. However, it is unlikely that Commodore Stewart allowed any books which he had aboard her as government property to get away from him. To these he added Jacobsen's *Sea Laws* and the items from the *Columbus,* thus rounding out the *Franklin's* collection of reference volumes.

Other preparations for the voyage were being taken care of by the *Franklin's* first lieutenant, William Augustus Weaver. In the course of his duties, he became directly involved with the group of men who were then putting libraries aboard some of the merchant ships in New York harbor. Through a letter of his, printed in the *New York Evening Post* of August 2, and other local newspapers, we are provided with the first installment of the true account of how the *Franklin's* seamen's library came into being. Lieutenant Weaver wrote:

> U.S. Ship Franklin
> July 31st, 1821
>
> Gentlemen of the Committee for the
>   distribution of books to seamen—
>   I have the honor to acknowledge the reception of the present
> of books* you have been pleased to make to the seamen of the

Franklin. Allow me to return my thanks with those of the crew for your generous kindness.

The sailors of this ship could not witness your exertions for the diffusion of knowledge among them unmoved. When your letter was read to them, they requested unanimously that one dollar might be appropriated from the pay of each, towards the increase of the Seamen's Library on board. This fund I will take an early opportunity of placing at the disposal of the Committee, from whose philanthropy originated the laudable design, tending so much to ameliorate the condition of seamen.

*One hundred and fifty volumes of Voyages, Travels, History, Geography and Navigation.

Perhaps if Lieutenant Weaver had made the voyage in the *Franklin,* he later might have been able to tell more about the use and contents of the library, for he seemed to be interested in literary matters. It appears that Commodore Stewart had promised Weaver the berth of first lieutenant on the cruise, but instead the position was given to the more senior Lieutenant William M. Hunter by the Navy Department. What followed as a result of Weaver's not going on the *Franklin* is a long story that was a *cause célèbre* in 1824. Lieutenant Weaver either naively, or with full knowledge, on August 24, 1821, entered into a contract with several speculators to accompany the merchant ship *America* loaded with flour to Peru. His presence aboard her as a naval officer was to give the appearance that the vessel was a storeship for the *Franklin* and thus permit her to pass through a blockade if challenged. The *America* successfully ran the blockade, and the speculators received a high price for their flour; however, Lieutenant Weaver did not think he received a fair share of the profits, so he sued the other parties to the contract. This was a mistake on his part, for instead of gaining more, he lost everything including his commission in the navy. The chancellor who reviewed his case decided that the contract was illegal because of Weaver's conflict of interest, and ruled against him. Further, he took Weaver to task for allegedly accepting a bribe to do his duty, among other things. Weaver exonerated Stewart from any involvement in the scheme, but was unsuccessful in defending himself in a subsequent court-martial. He was cashiered from the service and his reputation was all but ruined.[3]

It is perhaps of interest to note that while this incident in the voyage of the *Franklin* was the undoing of Lieutenant Weaver's career, a similar one in reverse order, which occurred almost simultaneously, served to enhance the career of Midshipman Charles Wilkes. When the American merchant ship *O'Cain* arrived in Valparaiso in need of a captain to take her back to the United States, Commodore Stewart, then on station with the *Franklin,* recommended Charles Wilkes for the command, and assured him that he would remain on the navy rolls while he undertook his new duty. Stewart designated the *O'Cain* as a storeship of the *Franklin,* and as such she was allowed to pass safely through the blockade. Midshipman Wilkes distinguished himself by bringing the *O'Cain* around Cape Horn and back to Boston in an eventful, but successful, passage. For carrying out this assignment and delivering a profitable cargo, the owners of the *O'Cain* paid Wilkes $8,000.[4]

Weaver, left to ponder the bitter inconsistencies of fate, later anonymously published a book of poems, many of them having explanatory and autobiographical notes. In the poem "Engagement between the *Chesapeake* and the *Shannon,*" details of this famous battle can be found. Weaver had been wounded repelling boarders from the *Shannon* and was present when were uttered, "The dying words from Lawrence' lip . . . 'brave lads, don't give up the ship.' "[5] After leaving the navy, he found employment in the State Department. In 1834 he was commissioner to Mexico, and later was superintendent of the sixth census of 1840. He died in 1846. Paullin, in his comments on early naval officers' contributions to literature, does not mention Weaver's indifferent poems, although he did notice the poor ones published by Midshipman William Leggett in 1825.[6] Unfortunately for Weaver, if he was remembered at all, it was for his indiscretion and not for his heroism or his poetical ability.

But Lieutenant Weaver was not forgotten by one of the "Gentlemen of the Committee for the distribution of books to seamen," even ten years after the *Franklin* had sailed for the Pacific. A letter written by Weaver to William Wood on December 2, 1831, at the latter's request, furnishes the second installment in the story of the *Franklin's* library. The beginning portion of this letter, which Wood somehow got Weaver to write (so that he could forward it to the secretary of the navy the following day), is quoted below out of chronological sequence. It provides the details on how the money to purchase the library was raised, and definitely links Wood to the committee. The concluding portion of the letter will be presented later in connection with the final disposition of the library, which took place a few years after the letter was written. Weaver wrote:

> In reply to yours of Dec. 1st requesting a statement of facts relating to the Seamen's Library, which belonged to the crew of the Franklin 74, & which had been purchased by you at their request, previous to her sailing for the Pacific Ocean, under the command of Commodore Stewart.
> Although some of my recollections of the Navy of the United

States are of a particularly painful nature, & you will acknowl-
edge the justness of my unwillingness to revive them, yet with
reference to the Seaman's Library, I have reason to feel a laudable pride, that I then had it in my power to second your
philanthropic views, for the benefit of a class of men, with
whom I have been associated for twenty years, & than whom
none are more worthy of the Pity and the Admiration of the
people of this Country. In recalling to mind that event of by-
gone years, you will remember the promptitude with which I
accepted on behalf of the seamen the donation of some 200
volumes, with which private liberality endowed them. That
Donation was the nucleus of the subsequent library—After the
reception of those volumes, with the approbation of my superior, The crew of the Franklin were called upon the Quarter
deck, & informed of their present & of the kind and friendly
motives which had produced it & the suggestion was made to
them, that if they wished to add to their store of books, a
small voluntary subscription on their part would be accepted &
devoted to the purchase of books, by the same gentleman, who
had been chiefly instrumental in procuring the donation before
them. They were directed to consult among themselves & return
an answer through the Petty officers—The reply was that each
man would willingly give a dollar & they authorized the Purser
to pay & charge to their Accts. respectively $1. each. This sum
of $600 thus raised, originally placed in my hands, as their
agent, and by me transferred to you, was the money employed
for the purchase of the "Seamen's Library of the Franklin . . .

The purchase of the library was heralded in the *New York National
Advocate* of August 7, 1821, as "A noble deed and worthy of our brave
Tars"; other newspapers referred to the incident in similar terms. A few
days later, an account in the *Evening Post,* and an anonymous letter to
the editor of the *Mercantile Advertiser* on August 13, provided the third
and last group of details about the library. Both told how on August 11,
the library was put aboard the *Franklin* with ceremony that today is
reminiscent of a Gilbert and Sullivan operetta. The letter described the
spectacle as it was seen by a bystander, but it betrayed more than a casual
knowledge of the incident by the writer. It was signed "A. Mechanic,"
and might have been one of William Wood's communications to the
press written to further the cause of libraries:

In common with thousands of my fellow citizens I was (on
Saturday,) highly gratified with the procession of the seamen of

the Franklin ship of war, from their boats to Wiley & Halstead's book store, for the purpose of receiving the Books, which the crew had directed to be purchased for a Forecastle Library, amounting to more than 1,000 volumes, consisting principally of abridgements of Voyages, Travels, Naval Actions, History of America, &c. The procession consisted of about 100 well dressed fine looking Tars, preceded by the elegant band of the Franklin. They formed opposite the Book Store, and the Books tied up in bundles of about 10 each, were then delivered to them by the committee, in addition to which they were furnished with a pair of Globes, and a variety of Charts and Nautical Instruments.

The pride and pleasure manifested by the sailors, on receiving their books, were a sure indication that they duly appreciated their value, & that they would not leave them unread.

The balance of the letter, which exceeded in length the portion quoted above, pointed out that exemplary exertions were under way to produce a moral and intellectual reformation in almost all classes of society, and that the sailor, being a defender of his country, was not to be neglected in this regard, for only good could come of his being educated. The writer also hoped that the example of the *Franklin's* library would be followed, and . . . "That no vessel will be permitted to depart from our shores without an attempt to furnish them with an assortment of moral and interesting books." From an account in the *Evening Post* of August 11, and in a correction to it which appeared two days later, it was additionally stated that the sailors marched up Wall Street, "two and two, dressed in white short jackets and trousers . . . ," to Wiley & Halsted's bookstore, no. 3 Wall Street, "the Repository of the 'Sailor's Floating Library.' " The article added that from this place twenty-one vessels had been supplied with books, and that donations for the same laudable purpose would continue to be received.

No doubt, the committee that was formed to supply libraries to seamen in June of 1821 was brought together by William Wood. Dr. John W. Francis in his reminiscences of old New York City, published in 1858, mentioned how "Pintard . . . and the excellent William Wood began to think of the Apprentices' Library, and to suggest the Mariners' Library for ships at sea." But as already noted, Wood was the originator of the Boston apprentices' library, and not the one in New York, although he took an active part in its founding. Francis, writing some thirty years after the fact, had this detail wrong. He may have been wrong about Pintard thinking up, with Wood, the "Mariners' Library" plan, too, for Pintard gave Wood all the credit. In one of his letters, dated October,

1823, he identified Wood as "the author & founder of Apprentices & Naval Libraries, and eminently distinguished for every good work."[7] Finally, Wood himself also made the claim of originating the seamen's libraries a few years after, and repeated it on other occasions. Inasmuch as it is not likely that there was any other secular group in New York which was engaged in supplying donated books to ships in the harbor at this time, the "Repository of the Sailor's Floating Library" must have been the name that the committee gave to its book collection point or headquarters.

Sometime during the summer the committee had moved its original places of deposit for donated books from the offices of the *American* and the *Commercial Advertiser* to Wiley & Halsted's bookstore. This was in keeping with Wood's actions of a year before in soliciting for the apprentices' library, when he had used Kirk & Mercein's bookstore on Wall Street as his depot for donated books. Although the advertisements for donations appeared in the two New York newspapers, nothing further followed in them in the way of news about the seamen's libraries. The politically oriented *American* was one of those newspapers of the period that did not ordinarily comment on local news, and the *Commercial Advertiser* devoted itself mostly to the events of the mercantile world, although it did occasionally report city happenings. The editors of these newspapers, though, were men who were themselves involved in, or at least aware of, the local social and literary causes of the day, and may have personally supported the library plan. Until May 12, 1821, the *American's* office had been located at 20 Wall Street. One of its neighbors and constant advertisers in its columns was Wiley's bookstore. As Wiley's bookshop was a rendezvous "for bookish people," and became increasingly so during the early 1820s, it probably served as a better location to receive donated books for the seamen's libraries than the newspaper offices.[8]

Charles Wiley had been a bookseller at no. 3 Wall Street for a number of years. In March of 1820, he dissolved his firm of C. Wiley & Co. and went into partnership with his cousin Oliver Halsted. Almost immediately, they announced themselves as successors to Stephen Gould, a specialist dealer in law books. By May, they had moved Gould's stock to their store and united it with the miscellaneous books they had for sale there. Wiley, at this time, had begun to lay the foundations of a publishing firm which would survive to the present day. He had the true publisher's instinct for recognizing authors of promise, for he had already published on his own Constantine Rafinesque's translation of Claude C. Robin's *Florula Ludoviciana* in 1817, and Henry Schoolcraft's *A View of the Lead Mines of Missouri* in 1819. From his firm of Wiley & Halsted, during the eventful year of 1821, he published James Fenimore Cooper's novel, *The Spy,* thus helping to launch Cooper on his literary career. Cooper, in turn, was to immortalize Wiley's bookshop by participating in an informal literary club that met in the back room, or "Den," of the store.

It is likely that Wiley had a personal as well as commercial interest in the success of the committee for seamen's libraries for he seems to have been acquainted with people having diverse interests. No doubt William Wood paid him an early visit of solicitation, and might have, in addition to obtaining permission to use the premises of the store for his project, extracted a donation of books similar to that given by the firms of Mesier, and Collins and Hannay to the *Robert Fulton.* But as far as the $600 purchase of books for the *Franklin* was concerned, it appears that Wood bought the books for the library from more than one dealer, for in a later year he mentioned that he gave "the booksellers no quarter as to prices."[9]

The purchase of a library by the crew of the *Franklin* provided Wood with a variation on his plan which could be used more successfully in supplying libraries to naval vessels. Up to this time, his committee seems to have either made initial donations of libraries to merchant ships only, and then asked the owners of these ships to provide additional books, or else might have proposed that the owners supply the entire libraries. Once the idea was broached, it is possible that some owners decided to supply books to their ships on their own accord without solicitation from the committee. In the case of the *Franklin,* no owners were available to be importuned. After the first gift of 150 volumes was presented, it must have been obvious that a library of this size, while better than nothing, was hardly adequate for the use of some 600 men. Perhaps it was Wood, as he later claimed, who suggested that the crew purchase the additional books. The custom of clubbing together by crew members for common causes and the taking of "tarpaulin musters" was already quite prevalent at sea, so the idea of pooling a crew's donations for the purpose of purchasing a library could have easily occurred to anyone. In any event, the suggestion at this time probably introduced into the U.S. Navy this variation on the subscription plan that Lieutenant Richard Marks had employed on HMS *Conqueror* some years before. As "A. Mechanic" had observed, more than 1,000 volumes on various subjects were thus obtained, along with a pair of globes and some nautical instruments. The inclusion of the latter items would seem to indicate that, perhaps after all, the schoolmaster also received those few books for his use that had been previously denied him by the Navy Department.

The *Franklin* finally departed New York on October 9, 1821, and arrived at Valparaiso in early February of the following year. As reported in *Niles' Weekly Register* of June 22, she excited the astonishment of Chilean visitors who boarded her in crowds throughout the day and night. They apparently found many things to admire, including of course, the seamen's library. One of the visitors (or perhaps one of the crew) took the trouble to write to the *British Luminary* about it, describing it as . . . "consisting of about a thousand volumes. The Captain has 700 volumes in his cabin, which is exquisitely fitted up and beautifully furnished." The correspondent also observed that "here we see what was never before seen or heard of, and what will never be seen or heard of, except on board a ship manned by freemen—a library of books for the men; an arrangement utterly incompatible with a crew composed of pressed men, or men who have entered from fear of the pressgang." This critical comparison was directed against the notorious, but by now abandoned, method that the Royal Navy had employed in recruiting crews for its ships, and which was anything but voluntary. Further, the editors of the *Liverpool Mercury,* which copied the article, added insult to injury by commenting that this American navy that George Canning, the British statesman, had liked to sneer at and joke about was also protecting British merchant ships from pirates while his "big red lion" was asleep.[10]

Even the presence of Mrs. Delia Tudor Stewart was considered an asset to the ship. The commodore's wife was praised as an accomplished, handsome, educated woman, who could play the harp and speak fluent French, Spanish, and Italian. Such was the impression that the *Franklin* made upon arrival. By the time she left, however, the Peruvian government had complained officially to Washington about Commodore Stewart, and American consular officials had communicated criticisms of his conduct while in command of the Pacific Squadron. Stewart was subsequently tried on four charges brought against him in a court-martial which was convened in Washington in 1825. He was acquitted on all charges by a court of illustrious fellow officers, who also concluded that, in fact, he had performed his duty with distinction while in command.

The frigate *United States* and sloop-of-war *Peacock* were sent to relieve the *Franklin* in 1824, and to bring out new officers for the *Dolphin* which remained in the Pacific. Not everyone returned in the *Franklin* who went out with her, for several of her crew were to die through accident or sickness. Two losses occurred just after arriving in, and just before leaving Valparaiso. Seven officers, including Lieutenant James Alexander Perry, brother of Commodore Oliver H. Perry, and three seamen died when one of the *Franklin's* boats was overwhelmed in the surf near Valparaiso; and at least two men died when smallpox began spreading through the ship, infecting among others, Commodore Stewart's children. Three men died in accidents on the passage out; and in 1824, eleven men were injured and two died in an explosion that took place in a boat fitted out from the ship to search for pirates. Others of the crew deserted, and some, like Oliver Smith the schoolmaster, transferred to the *Constellation* at Valparaiso in 1822, and did not stay with the *Franklin* very long. Many of the seamen who successfully completed the voyage were last seen in New York enjoying their hard earned wages by making themselves conspicuous in hired horse carriages on the streets where three years earlier some had marched with books in hand.[11]

What had happened to those books? One person remembered to inquire. "A Landsman," writing to the *Evening Post,* on October 1, 1824, identified himself as one of the several private donors of the library. He suggested that some account of the utility of the library during the late voyage be made and asked what had happened to the library, or experiment, now that the *Franklin* had returned and her crew was paid off. Was it still aboard, or was it to be transferred to another man-of-war? Unfortunately no reply to this letter is apparent in the New York newspapers, and we are thus deprived of a fresh, first-hand account of the library's effectiveness aboard ship. But the library was still secured on the *Franklin*. This William Wood soon found out, and he lost no time in writing a letter to Secretary of the Navy Samuel Southard about it. It was a rambling, unpunctuated letter typical of those he dashed off and signed with his own name and was not at all like the smooth and coherent ones sent to the *Mercantile Advertiser* by "A. Mechanic" and "A. Landsman." But then, perhaps these had been written or edited in behalf of Wood's committee by one of his fellow members. Nevertheless, the letter to Secretary Southard tells something about Wood's point of view regarding the seamen as subscribers as well as about his plans for the library. He wrote from New York on October 6, 1824:

> The writer who had the pleasure of presenting you with a Glass of Champagne at Canandaigua N.Y. while on your late Tour had also the pleasure /pure, and deep/ of selecting the Seamans' Library on board the Franklin Com^dr Stewart who is now at Washington, and he requests the secretary will use his influence to allow the same to be transferred to the care of the Revd. Cave Jones Chaplain of the Navy Yard for the purpose of forming a Naval Library there we have laid a foundation already and the Cm^drs of the U. States & Erie, who allowed the writer to select Libraries for their Ships will follow the same plan,—the seamen who in fact pay nearly all the money for the Books care nothing for them & in addition a number of them promised to give up all rights & title provided

they were transferred to the N. Yard as a Free Library which plan will be followed allowing any petty officer to draw the same amount of Books therefrom when, he embarks on a voyage as he gave previous.

I leave the matter at the feet of the Secretary praying him to receive the honour, of presenting to the Navy Yard the first, Seamans' Library which ever floated on board a National Ship.

Secretary Southard apparently did not reply directly to William Wood's letter but forwarded it to Commodore Stewart with the recommendation that Wood's views of forming a library at the Navy Yard be accepted as long as Stewart did not have any insurmountable objections to them. The commodore saw Wood personally about the subject and then gave Lieutenant Hunter directions which were to carry out Wood's wishes concerning the library.[12] The books were landed but they were still in storage when Commodore Isaac Chauncey took command of the navy yard in December of 1824. Early the next year, the Reverend Cave Jones, chaplain of the navy yard, brought the books to Chauncey's attention, specifically mentioning that if someone was not appointed to take charge of them, they would probably be lost. Accordingly, Chaplain Jones was directed to look after the books, and they were placed in a small vestry room of the chapel. Here they remained until December, 1831, when William Wood again became concerned about them. He thought that "the residue of the Franklin's Library lay mouldering away in a dark room at the Navy Yard," as he explained in a letter to a new secretary of the navy, Levi Woodbury. Along with this letter, dated December 3, 1831, Wood enclosed Weaver's letter or statement, already quoted in part. Wood introduced here the idea that the *Franklin's* library had always been intended by the entire crew to be transferred to the navy yard when the ship returned, and Weaver repeated it in concluding his letter:

. . . I have always understood that on the return of the ship, the books were intended for the foundation of a library at the Navy Yard for the use of the Seamen & men employed in the service generally.—To which object if my original agency gives me any control I should wish to see them destined.—I cannot quit this interesting subject, without mentioning the pleasure I have frequently experienced in hearing from various sources from both officers & men of that ship how much your labours in their behalf had tended to lighten the many tedious

hours of a three years cruize.—The books were read and re-
read. Can good books be read without advantage?

Upon receiving Wood's and Weaver's letters, Secretary Woodbury
directed Commodore Chauncey, who was still in command of the navy
yard, to inquire into the matter and report his findings to him, and wrote
Wood to that effect.[13] This prompted Wood to write still another letter
to Woodbury on December 10, 1831, in which he now stated that the
library he planned would have a good effect on the marines and "men
of all work" at the station. He thought that the marines in particular
were in need of the library, for that "class of men have much time to use
which is usually spent in an unseemly way," and further mentioned that
Colonel John M. Gamble of the U.S. Marine Corps had volunteered
his services "to take charge of the volumes and use his influence among
the marines etc to read them." Also, he indicated that friends of the navy
living in the city were ready to present "many valuable volumes" to the
library. It is possible that Wood feared, no doubt from past experience
with Chauncey, that the commodore would return a negative report,
and so tried to make his new appeal on behalf of the marines.

On December 12, Commodore Chauncey made his report to the
secretary. He accounted for the library during the period of time it was
in the yard, and presented all the facts about it that he could determine.
His appraisal of the situation was fair and realistic, although he was
not entirely convinced about Wood's claim. Inasmuch as the library
did not belong to the navy but was really private property, Chauncey,
no doubt, would have liked to give it back to Wood or any other rightful owner, if they would only ask for it. Nevertheless, he explained that
the books had been well taken care of and were in a good state of preservation. He also mentioned that he had no knowledge of any agreement
between Wood and the crew of the *Franklin* as to the ultimate disposition
of the library, and if he had, he had received no authority from the Navy
Department to form a library for the use of the seamen and marines at
the station. Further, he had inquired among some of the officers and
seamen who had gone out in the *Franklin* in 1821 about the alleged agreement and they had no recollection of it. In fact, he found that the crew
viewed the books at the time of the voyage as their own personal property
to be divided or disposed of as they deemed best at the termination of
the cruise: "That many acting upon this belief took books with them,
when the Ship was paid off,—and this is evident from the small number
remaining, and those composed of broken sets and odd volumes. . . ."
Chauncey estimated this remainder to be worth not more than $150. He
suggested that the secretary ask Commodore Stewart, Captain Hunter,

and other officers and men who had sailed with the library if they remembered any terms of agreement, for although William Weaver's
supporting letter was precise as far as it went, he maintained that Weaver
could not have known what disposition the crew made or intended to
make because he did not go to sea in the *Franklin*.

Apparently, Secretary Woodbury did not bother to inquire further
among the *Franklin's* former officers about the library, but approved a
recommendation which Chauncey proposed. The commodore believed
that the best disposition that could be then made of the books was to
place them aboard the receiving ship in the yard. They would be in charge
of an officer for the use of the personnel who from time to time would be
attached to that ship. The books would remain there until otherwise
ordered by their owners.[14] Whether they were put aboard the receiving
ship is not clear, because Wood again, on September 18, 1833, brought
up the matter of their being "locked up in a room next to the Chapel,
mouldering and useless to those who might receive benefit from [them]."
This time he mentioned that there were some 600 or 700 books remaining. He also stated again that if these books could be used as the foundation of a "Naval Library in the Yard," large additions from the friends
of the navy would be made from people in the city, "and the creation of
such a noble establishment would give additional glory to the service."
This prediction did begin to come true with the founding of the U.S.
Naval Lyceum by a group of naval officers at the yard later that year.
However, in answer to Wood, Secretary Woodbury assured him, on
September 26, that the books were being used aboard the receiving ship
as per Chauncey's suggestion and his own decision of December, 1831,
but also added that if his order had not been complied with he would investigate the subject further.

Within two months of this exchange of letters, a happy ending to the
story of the *Franklin's* library was provided. The remaining books of
the seamen's library were donated, in the name of the ship, to the U.S.
Naval Lyceum, to become part of the newly-formed association's library.
Although William Wood had claimed that there was a residue of 600 or
700 books in the library, only 250 to 265 volumes, comprising 149 titles,
were actually turned over to the Naval Lyceum in 1834. The smaller
figure is calculated from information contained in a unique manuscript
record which today survives the Naval Lyceum. This source, its "Donor's
Book," lists all of the items which were given to the Naval Lyceum's library and museum over a considerable period of time.[15] Under the
heading, "Franklin, U.S. Ship," the short titles of the books were entered in the record book along with the number of volumes for each
listing.

It appears that Commodore Chauncey's estimate of the library's condition in 1831 was accurate. What remained were broken sets, odd volumes, and some not too appealing titles. Religious books and those on voyages and travels accounted for the two largest groupings among the ten or so general categories represented. Other books composing appreciable amounts of the collection were in the fields of history, biography, and belles lettres. Only a few science books were evident and just one book on navigation remained.

Lieutenant Weaver in 1821 had described the initial gift of 150 volumes from Wood's seamen's library committee as consisting of voyages, travels, history, geography, and navigation; and "A. Mechanic" had noted that "the more than 1,000" volumes that the crew of the *Franklin* subscribed for were principally voyages, travels, naval actions, history, etc. He also had hoped that each ship would carry an assortment of moral and interesting books. The original character of the library as mentioned by these two sources was still evident in 1834. If what Commodore Chauncey had said was correct about the crew members taking books from the library as their supposed rightful shares when they quit the ship, then the remaining books could be considered the least desirable in the library. However, it is also likely that over a period of thirteen years aboard ship and in the vestry room at the navy yard, some fate other than rejection alone had determined which books were to be left as remnants of the original seamen's library.

Today many of the titles can be identified with some certainty because they were listed and bibliographically described in another surviving record, a manuscript library catalog of the Naval Lyceum, dated 1841.[16] About two dozen of the titles in the 1834 "Donor's Book" exactly match the volume numbering given in the 1841 library catalog, leaving little doubt that these titles became part of the Naval Lyceum's library. This library was eventually acquired by the U.S. Naval Academy, and among those books retained by it were a few volumes that may have been in the *Franklin's* library. Happily, of these, three works remain that unquestionably were in the seamen's library, for they bear inscriptions testifying to their provenance. In volume two of Isaac Weld's *Travels Through the States of North America,* is written: "For the use of the U.S. ship Franklin during her cruise to the pacific, by John Reid. At the expiration of the voyage to be at the disposal of Dr. Du Puy." Had the promise to deliver up the book been otherwise fulfilled some 149 years ago, this last bit of direct evidence would also have been lost. The message penned in John Reid's book verifies that certain books, such as this one, were donated to the *Franklin's* library. It also casts doubt upon Wood's assertion that all the books were intended to be placed in a naval library ashore when the *Franklin* returned. So does a bookplate found in the second remaining work (Cook's *Voyages,* vol. 1) which is worded: "PRESENTED   BY

THE CREW, TO THEIR SHIP FRANKLIN, Com. Stewart, 1821."

One other book still exists from this early shipboard library, its title perhaps having served it as a talisman over the years: *The Life of Dr. Benjamin Franklin.* On its flyleaf, in what appears to be William Wood's hand, is written, "No. 20, U.S. Franklin. Seamans Library." How fitting that this copy of Franklin's autobiography should have survived! It remains like the engraved cornerstone of some ancient temple of learning, imbedded, as it were, in the outlines of a barely discernible foundation—the other ruins of the structure long since scattered, destroyed, or forgotten. No less remarkable is the connection of Benjamin Franklin's name and influence to other aspects of this story. He was the namesake of the *Franklin,* and his likeness, in the form of a figurehead, adorned her prow. William Wood had followed Franklin's example in the solicitation of donations for libraries and had extended his concept of social libraries to the navy. If it was inevitable that subscription libraries were to be placed aboard American naval vessels, what better way to initiate them than in the name and spirit of Ben Franklin?

Chapter V

Seamen's Libraries

Seamen need a good library on board ship. They have mental as well as bodily wants. They have not only the bone and sinew of other men, they have also, in proportion to their cultivation, the same intellectual powers and the same capacity of mental elevation and enjoyment. They must be taught as other men, and the same importance attaches to the proper culture of their minds as is plead so wisely and successfully for the merchants, farmers, mechanics and daylaborers of their native land.
—Wants of Seamen

SUBSCRIPTION LIBRARIES. The library created so spontaneously aboard the *Franklin* encouraged William Wood to attempt to place similar libraries aboard other naval vessels sailing from New York. Wood probably proposed his library plan to a number of ship captains between the years 1821 and 1826, for later, he claimed to have supplied subscription libraries to the *Franklin, United States, Erie,* and to two other warships.[1] In 1823, only sixteen vessels of war were in commission, and the number of men in the navy was the lowest it had ever been since the close of the War of 1812. Secretary of the Navy Samuel L. Southard in his annual report to the president for that year was able to sum up the activities of his department in just five octavo-sized pages of narrative text. The navy was mainly employed in protecting American interests in the Mediterranean Sea and in the Pacific Ocean, although it was pressing a kind of war against the pirates of the West Indies with some of its smaller craft. In his report, Southard remarked upon the success and prospects of the missions of the various men-of-war, and mentioned by name the commanders of vessels significantly employed. Many of these ships and officers were heroic veterans of earlier naval wars and were well known by all who took an interest in American naval affairs. The navy was constantly in the public eye. From the day it was anticipated to send a warship abroad, to the time that the order was executed, through to the day that the ship was paid off, news items concerning the ship and the names of her officers appeared regularly in the newspapers of the day. On occasion, the text of a commander's orders as communicated to him by the secretary of the navy was printed in the press. Dispatches from the commander en route and on station might also receive the same notice. Almost every day a letter from a captain or other crew member of a warship would be printed in some newspaper, relating to an incident or item of interest that occurred in connection with a ship's cruise. In the case of at least one naval commander, Captain James Biddle, his ship's company, at the completion of a voyage on the frigate *Congress,* even submitted a card of thanks to the *Norfolk Herald* on Christmas Eve, 1823, citing his humane and considerate treatment. This was a variation on another prevalent journalistic custom of the day whereby some merchant ship passengers publicly acknowledged the courtesy and expert seamanship displayed by a ship's captain at the end of an ocean passage.

Although a naval officer might enjoy being portrayed favorably in a newspaper one day, he might the next day find himself put on the spot in its crowded columns. A seemingly unfavorable comment, an open letter addressed to him, or the unsavory details of his court-martial, if that fate had befallen him, could and did appear in print. This, of course, called for a letter to the fourth estate by the maligned officer, in which he, as a public official, explained his actions or defended his honor. One such letter of explanation was sent to the New York *Evening Post* on August 21, 1821, by the captain of the sloop-of-war *Hornet.* Master Commandant George C. Read let it be known why he refused to accept a library for his crew proposed by the "Committee of the Seaman's Library." His reasons were understandable, for the *Hornet* had just returned from the Mediterranean and it was not known what the immediate plans were for the sloop or her crew. Read observed that "The men attached to the Franklin are going on a long cruize and require amusement for mind and fancy; but the Hornet is just returned from one to her native shores, where Jack, if he has any leisure time, would prefer spending it in the arms of his sweetheart." However, Read assured the committee that if the *Hornet* was fitted out for another cruise under his command he would very early accept its kind offer. Within two months the *Hornet* was back in action, having captured the pirate schooner *Moscow* off the coast of Santo Domingo on October 29, 1821. Read was not her captain at this time, but the *Hornet* might then have gone to sea with at least a donated seamen's library, if not a subscription library.

A few paragraphs in various New York newspapers of 1823 attest to the existence of libraries aboard the frigate *United States* and the sloop *Erie.* William Wood's connection with their formation is also confirmed, even though neither he nor his committee was mentioned directly. Using the pages of the *American* to publicize his plan, Wood chose a new pen name and composed a letter intended to enlighten, or perhaps soften up, the recently designated commander of the *United States,* the frigate ordered to relieve the *Franklin.* The letter written in Wood's unmistakable style appeared in the October 21, 1823, issue of the paper:

> To Captain Hull:
>
> SIR—when the *Franklin*, Commodore Stewart, was laying in our harbour, the crew subscribed *one dollar* each, for the purchase of a suitable LIBRARY; the amount was $720, and produced *fifteen hundred* volumes of Voyages, Travels, History, Geography, & religious works. Accounts from the Franklin state that the library has produced the best effect upon the seamen; and if Sir, you will allow your noble crew to perform a similar act, you will gratify them, and oblige.
>
> "NEPTUNE."

"Neptune" was at home amid the printed hyperbole of the journalists and other anonymous correspondents with their many axes to grind. In those days a warship or her crew was likely to be "noble" or "gallant" when mentioned in the popular press, and "Jack" or "tar" was invariably applied as a fanciful substitute for "sailor" or "seaman." It is also obvious from this and other letters that Wood's figures on the size and cost of the *Franklin's* library varied with each telling of his story. Perhaps in this instance, Wood wrote in haste, for Commodore Isaac Hull was already in Washington, on his way to join his ship at Norfolk, Virginia, when the letter appeared in print. The following day, the *Post,* commenting on the good effects of the *Franklin's* library, as learned from "Neptune's" letter, went on to hope that Hull and other captains in the navy would encourage the introduction of libraries aboard their ships: "Books impart useful knowledge, and occupy those leisure hours which might otherwise be employed in vicious pursuits."

On December 6, 1823, the *American* reported that Hull had acceded to the wishes of his "noble crew," who had subscribed for a library of about 1,000 volumes which was to be sent to Norfolk from New York. Noting this article, the president of the infant New York Bethel Union in a year-end address to his brethren observed that "every Christian heart must have beat high with joy, on reading even a newspaper account that Commodore Hull had ordered a library of one thousand volumes for the use of the crew," and that the natives of the Sandwich Islands would be impressed with the *United States* because she was "armed with fifty guns, for her seamen to fight, and with her thousand volumes for her Seamen to read." He did not bother to mention how the library came into being. If the bethel union had some direct connection with the library, doubtless he would have told of it. But the admonition of the prophet Hosea provided him with the hope that the bethel union would achieve future similar triumphs, by following "in the path of benevolent exertion."[2]

About the same time that Commodore Hull and his family arrived at Norfolk, Nathaniel Ames, a seaman, was being conveyed by the steamboat *Potomac* alongside the *United States*. Ames had shipped for a long cruise but he later admitted that the three and a half years spent by him aboard the frigate were the happiest in his life. He had already passed three other happy years at Harvard and some time at sea, so he was in a good position to record life as he saw it aboard an American man-of-war. Unlike Herman Melville, who sailed in the *United States* twenty years later, and who based *White-Jacket* upon his experiences aboard the "Neversink," Ames wrote a straight autobiographical account while on the frigate, devoting about one-fourth of his book, *A Mariner's Sketches*, to the voyage. Ames was less harsh in his opinions about the navy than Melville, who later read his book and appropriated some of Ames's thought into *White-Jacket*.

Life aboard the *United States* while anchored in a foreign port, as Ames described it, was almost idyllic. He seemed to relish the routine afloat, stating: "I was out of the reach of love, religion, and politics . . . . I had enough to eat and drink, my duty was light, and I understood it thoroughly, and I had but little to do, except to keep from being 'pressed' into a boat, and to walk straight enough to avoid treading on the toes of *Mrs. Discipline* oftener than I could help. . . ." Within the routine, adequate time could be found to read, and he observed, "Sailors universally are extremely fond of reading and are far better judges of books than they are allowed credit for."

Unfortunately, Ames's cogent observations were not directed toward the crew's subscription library, for he neglected to comment upon it in his book. Instead, he noted that the sailors "were generally well-supplied with books by the kindness of the officers, whose friends sent out Scott's novels, and other new and interesting works, as fast as published in America." Also available to the crew, according to Ames, were the Philadelphia and Baltimore newspapers, which ships from those ports brought out fairly regularly. Perhaps this supply of fresh and new literature was more memorable or accessible to Ames than the books subscribed for in Norfolk, but for whatever reason he omitted telling about the library, Ames at least indicated the importance of another source of reading matter for seamen on a foreign station. The old method of communication by letter or parcel via trading vessel was less uncertain for such ships as the *Franklin* and the *United States* because they maintained a more or less fixed location for long periods of time. Even at that, Ames complained that it once took nineteen months to receive a letter sent to him from Boston aboard a ship that wandered all over the Pacific before delivering it.

An officer who served on both the *United States* and her escort the *Dolphin* at this time, also wrote about life in the Pacific Squadron. In his *Journal of a Cruise of the United States Schooner Dolphin* (1831), Lieutenant Hiram Paulding told of his ship's adventurous pursuit of the mutineers from the whaler *Globe* in 1825-1826. On her way back to Callao from the Mulgrave Islands, where the mutineers were found, the *Dolphin* stopped at Honolulu, thus becoming the first naval vessel of the United States to visit Hawaii. Contrary to the hopes of the president of the New York Bethel Union of having a large American warship with her impressive library demonstrate Christian goodness to the inhabitants, the crew of the little *Dolphin* only demonstrated their great displeasure in the form of a riot upon finding out that the resident Yankee missionaries had influenced the island chieftains to place a taboo on prostitution. Although no mention of libraries aboard the *United States* or her two support vessels was made by Paulding, it is probable that the *Dolphin* and the sloop *Peacock* had small crews' libraries aboard. These vessels had outfitted for the same cruises as the *Franklin* and *United States*, respectively, and no doubt William Wood had contacted their commanders at the time about the subject of libraries.

A little more is known about the library aboard another small vessel of the navy, the sloop-of-war *Erie* of the Mediterranean Squadron. Her library was mentioned in William Wood's "glass of champagne" letter of October 6, 1824. Further details were reported in a religious magazine which emphasized Chaplain Jones's involvement in the formation of the library. The Reverend Cave Jones, of the Episcopal Church in New York City, had assumed the chaplaincy at the navy yard in Brooklyn in the summer of 1823. Later in the year, at his suggestion, and "through the instrumentality of a benevolent gentleman," who could only have been William Wood, the *Erie* was reported to have been provided with " a well chosen library." It consisted "of about five hundred volumes, of which one hundred were adapted to the use of the crew, containing among them a suitable number of moral and religious books.[3] The cost of the library was borne by the officers and men of the sloop,

which departed New York for the Mediterranean on November 6, 1823.
Chaplain Jones had also furnished the *Erie* with a supply of Bibles, to
be distributed through all the messes, the wardroom, and the cabin; and
the captain, Master Commandant David Deacon, had promised to have
divine service performed every Sunday during the cruise.

The brand new ship-of-the-line *North Carolina* also took a subscription
library to the Mediterranean in 1825. About a month before she sailed,
while lying at anchor in the Potomac River off Ragged Point, Maryland,
she was inspected by President James Monroe, Secretary of the Navy
Samuel Southard, and several congressmen, heading up a party of about
forty distinguished visitors. It being a Sunday (January 30, 1825), the
important guests were gratified to witness the entire crew listening with
solemn attention to the performance of divine service by the ship's chaplain. After inspection and worship and while awaiting the dinner hour,
"the visitors were led to notice a very handsome and well selected library." It consisted "of about eleven hundred volumes, purchased by
private individual contributions from the officers and men belonging to
the ship." The library had probably been shipped to the *North Carolina*
from New York while the warship prepared for sea at Norfolk. It is notable that William Wood did not later claim to have furnished this library, even though it was carried on the newest and most imposing vessel
in the navy at that time and had been seen by a president and other
government officials. However, as already noted, he did comment on his
connection with, and upon the intended fate of, the libraries furnished to
the *United States* and the *Erie*. The crews of these vessels, he maintained,
had agreed to release the libraries upon the return of their ships, in order
to form a library at the New York Navy Yard. The foundations for this
library, he also claimed to have laid with the help of Chaplain Cave Jones
at the time the *Erie* sailed to the Mediterranean in 1823. But a permanent
shore based library was not fully realized at the navy yard until the U.S.
Naval Lyceum was founded there some years later.

The frigate *Constitution*, and the sloops-of-war *Cyane* and *Ontario*
had also been likely prospects for William Wood's solicitations. They
had sailed from New York in 1824 and became units of Commodore
Rodgers's Mediterranean Squadron. On an earlier cruise the *Ontario* had
been the scene of a mutually enlightening experience between a group of
American naval officers and civilians, and Lord Byron at the port of
Leghorn. The poet, while being shown the junior officers' quarters aboard
the *Ontario,* was delighted to see a New York edition of his poems there.
An American, who was a visitor to the squadron with Byron, recorded
the incident of the book of Byron's poems: "He took it up with every
appearance of pleasure, and seemed to interpret it as an earnest of his
fame," for Byron at the time was in a mood rather to have received "a

nod from an American, than a snuff-box from an emperor." The youthful American observer of his nation's navy at its cultural best was George Bancroft. He would, one day, have quite a bit to say about the libraries carried aboard naval vessels and about the education of officers for the service, as secretary of the navy. On May 21, 1822, however, the books that he and Lord Byron saw aboard the *Ontario* at Leghorn were probably the personal property of the officers, for the sloop had sailed from New York several months before Wood's seamen's library committee was organized there in 1821.

William Wood's plan of initiating subscription libraries aboard ship continued to bear fruitful results without his fitful, guiding hand. Especially through the third decade, and into the fourth, the purchase of libraries by crews of U.S. naval vessels was a common practice. The idea appears to have been readily adopted and sustained by the officers and men themselves with little outside assistance. Those who had once sailed in ships with crews' subscription libraries grew to expect them aboard every man-of-war. But in order to place a library aboard ship, three conditions needed to be satisified. The crew had to be willing and able to purchase it, the responsible officers had to give their permission to do so, and someone had to initiate the action. A sailor's complaint about the lack of the accustomed seamen's library aboard the frigate *Potomac* in December of 1831 indicates how essential these requirements were and how well established the idea of subscription libraries had become by that date. In a letter written while at the Cape of Good Hope, the sailor observed:

> Our time would be very pleasant if we had a library on board
> for us sailors, but I am sorry to say that I have not found a book
> worth reading among the crew. The like I never saw on board
> of any ship but this. Libraries are common on board every
> sloop of war, supplied by subscription among the crew, and se-
> lected by the chaplain. It was proposed by our crew some weeks
> before our departure, but . . . and so we sailed without it,
> and now here we are, placed beyond the means of supplying our-
> selves. Conceive for yourself the evil of being confined for three
> years within the walls of a ship, without having a single book to
> read. I can neither beg, borrow, nor steal one from either of the
> men, for they are equally as poor as myself.[4]

This short letter told more about seamen's libraries aboard ship than did two book-length narratives which were published in 1835 as a result of the *Potomac's* 1831–1834 voyage of circumnavigation. Following the fashion of other contemporary naval personnel of a literary bent, both the schoolmaster, Francis Warriner, and Commodore John Downes's private secretary, Jeremiah Reynolds (who later figured prominently as a promoter of the first American exploring expedition), wrote books concerning the frigate's cruise. Although Reynolds commented upon the officers' library (which was then furnished by the navy), neither mentioned the presence or absence of a crews' subscription library or provided any clue which today might help fill in the elision that appeared in the sailor's letter from the Cape. Thus it was likely the crew was without its own books, at least in the beginning of the voyage.

This state of affairs was repeated on the next voyage of the *Potomac* in 1834, but was remedied somewhat by the purchase of $100 worth of schoolbooks—grammars, arithmetic texts, and geographies—when the frigate reached Gibraltar, her first port of call. The crew paid for these books, and their chaplain, Charles Rockwell, appears to have played a part in obtaining them. Apparently, a proposal to purchase a subscription library valued at $400 had been presented prior to sailing from home, but it was defeated by some of the officers of the ship who claimed that there were not enough funds for the use of the ship at the time, even though the crew had been willing to match an offer of $200 made by a "benevolent gentleman" in Boston. This incident is reminiscent of an earlier one related by Chaplain George Jones. In his travel book, *Sketches of Naval Life*, he mentioned that a chaplain had attempted to solicit contributions of books from his friends for the seamen aboard his ship, which was then about to depart on a cruise. But the officers attached to the ship soon stopped him, for they did not want it known that a naval officer had to beg for anything for his ship. Although this occurrence apparently took place before subscription libraries became popular in the navy, it illustrates yet another method tried in the attempt to supply books to seamen. Jones, who endorsed the attitude of the officers, advised his fellow chaplains to use caution when soliciting for books, lest both the ship's officers' and the national pride be insulted in carrying out the good deed.

Once a library was subscribed for and brought aboard ship, the limited amount of accessible space encountered there more or less determined the physical location of the library, while naval routine afloat regulated its use and administration. These factors, being somewhat uniform throughout the ships of the same class in the navy, also tended to prevent a wide variation in the location and handling of the libraries from ship to ship. As with many other shipboard matters, the commanding officers, acting within the customs and usage of the service, determined how the library was to be governed aboard his ship. In May of 1838, on a cruise to the East Indies, Commodore George C. Read spelled out specific instructions in his order book concerning the subscription library aboard the frigate *Columbia,* a sister ship of the *Potomac.* He charged a professor of mathematics, J. Henshaw Belcher, with the supervision of the library. The professor was to maintain a circulation record, allowing one book at a time to a man, and the transaction was to be entered in a ledger. Upon the return of a book, if it was found to have been carelessly abused, the borrower's privileges were to be terminated. Commodore Read was particular in this regard, because it had been proposed by the subscribers (*i.e.*, the officers and the crew), "to present the books uninjured to the Naval Hospital at Norfolk, on the return of the ship to the U. States.[5]" Perhaps the commodore had already heard complaints about the inaccessibility of the library, for he also elaborated on the location of the collection: "The books are at present, put up on shelves in the Ward-Room until a book case can be fitted up at the Cabin bulkhead for the greater Convenience of the Officers & crew; but their present location is the best in the ship, & cannot prevent any person obtaining what he may wish to read."

Despite the carefully written instructions which were to insure the proper use and easy availability of the books, the library seems to have had an uncertain existence aboard the *Columbia*. The very person who was to have it under control later criticized its handling and abuse in the inevitable book about the voyage, which he wrote. Actually, three books appeared in 1840 as a result of the *Columbia's* cruise (Chaplain Fitch W. Taylor's *The Flag Ship: or A Voyage Around the World in the U. S. Frigate Columbia,* William M. Murrell's *Cruise of the Frigate Columbia Around the World,* and *Around the World, a Narrative of a Voyage in the East India Squadron,* by Joshua S. Henshaw); but only professor Henshaw's (he had changed his name from J. Henshaw Belcher, by this date) mentioned the crew's library. Either Henshaw took his duties lightly, as he was actually accused of by Commodore Read in another instance, or else he was somehow disassociated from the library early in the voyage. The latter circumstance seems more plausible, for Henshaw became digusted with his position, as it related to rank or status aboard ship before the frigate ever set sail. To his dismay, Henshaw learned at the last moment that the professor of mathematics was not a member of the officers' wardroom and that he had to mess and sleep elsewhere. He never did gain the privilege of the wardroom and, according to his account, the library apparently was never moved from those quarters to the cabin bulkhead as promised. This situation, Henshaw noted, caused some grumbling among the crew for they objected to the fact that the officers used their library as an ornament for the wardroom, "where the sailors seldom could see it; and that in some instances, those officers monopolized the best books." At one time some officers who conducted a Sunday school for the apprentices managed the library a while with the result that no books were issued to the men for many days. One crew member, fearing the worst, was of the opinion that "these religionists intend to keep the men's library to themselves to barter it away for bibles," and that everyone would then be required to read a verse or two twice a day at quarters.

Henshaw had observed that the "General Library" of 360 volumes was frequently used by the crew when it was first introduced but the novelty wore off early in the voyage. When the *Columbia* rounded the Cape of Good Hope in a storm, many of the books, neglected on deck and in the mast tops, were blown away or washed into the scuppers. Others were torn or dropped overboard by the crew, so by September of 1838, just four months out, the size of the collection was somewhat reduced. A similar situation also took place on the ship-of-the-line *Delaware*. After less than a year aboard ship, the extensive subscription library had been dissipated, "owing to the carelessness of those in charge." Daniel Noble Johnson, the purser's clerk of the *Delaware*, lamented having difficulty in finding an "instructive book" to read as a consequence, and noted in his journal on Sunday, March 20, 1842, that there had been "no registry kept of the books or subscribers," so the books had soon become "so scattered about the ship, that it was found impossible to collect them, and they never were recovered."

In the case of the *Columbia*, some crew members continued to read the remaining books as a form of recreation but the jaded professor, after living more than two years among sailors, could only express his reservations about the benefit of the library when he got to writing about it in his book. Yet other naval authors of the period did not hesitate to mention the good effects of libraries aboard ship, or to offer suggestions toward their improvement. One of the scenes depicted in *Life in a Man-of-War* had to do with the joyous opening day of a purchased library of 300 or 400 volumes aboard "Old Ironsides" in 1839. The books in the library had already been numbered and their titles noted in a catalog "which was forcibly dragged" from one eager sailor to another in their efforts to make selections. Henry J. Mercier, the author, attributed to the crew the notion that they "felt pleased to think that they had now in their possession a stock of intellectual food to beguile the heavy tediousness of the cruise, or to refresh their thirst for mental acquirements."[6]

The Reverend Charles Rockwell, of the *Potomac* (1834–1837), observed that some of the larger naval vessels had subscription libraries consisting of several hundreds of volumes. He believed that great good had resulted from them and advocated that the government should supply a "well selected and appropriate library for the use of the crew" of every ship of war. Noting the practice of disposing of subscription libraries at the end of a voyage by means of auction or lot or abandonment, Rockwell recommended that instead, the libraries should be carefully preserved and reshipped aboard other naval vessels. The idea to reuse or keep intact subscription libraries appears to have entered into library proposals from the time of the *Franklin* to that of the *Columbia,* but the fulfillment of such promises after lengthy voyages was, understandably, not always achieved, with the result that the libraries were probably often disposed of in the manner mentioned by Rockwell.

Of more concern, at least to William McNally, a seafarer aware of the benefits of subscription libraries, and author of *Evils and Abuses in the Naval and Merchant Service Exposed* (1839), was how to get the navy to furnish books to seamen.[7] If the government would not purchase them outright, then, he claimed, the crew should be allowed to buy books from a source available aboard every man-of-war—the "slush fund." According to McNally's estimates, about $450 to $800 might be obtained from selling the slush, or grease, which each ship accumulated in the process of cooking the salt pork and beef that was served to the crew of a sloop or frigate during a three-year voyage. The slush was the rightful property of the crew, he argued, for each man was allotted a certain ration of meat, and from this meat the collective boiled-off slush was obtained. Rather than have the first lieutenant, who fell heir to the slush fund, spend it, as was then the alleged practice, on such luxuries for the ship as Turkish rugs for the cabin, or cushions for the boats, or for a carpet for the wardroom, McNally asserted that an advance could be made on the anticipated sale of the slush before the voyage, and from it books could be purchased for the crew. Or, as he naively believed, "any bookseller would furnish three or four hundred dollars worth of books on the credit of this fund which could be remitted to him as chance offered." If the money or credit were thus made available, the crew "could have a handsome library, as well as be furnished with the popular newspapers and periodicals, from different parts of the United States."

McNally's proposal (as well as an almost identical earlier argument which had appeared in the March, 1836, number of the *Army and Navy Chronicle*) went unheeded in subsequent naval regulations. The 1841 regulations, published two years after his book, specified that any proceeds derived from the sale of slush were to be expended by the captain of a vessel for only three purposes—as premiums for the most accurate gun captains at target practice, for musical instruments and sheet music (another of the uses McNally had objected to), and for furnishing dress clothing for side boys and messengers.

By way of comparison, and as a commentary on the parallel educational outlook of the services in regard to the lower ranks, it is of interest to note that the U.S. Army, in its regulations prior to 1849, allowed soldiers' libraries to be formed on military posts through a fund "accumu-

lated by savings in the bake houses on soldiers' bread, and taxes on the
sutlers of the posts." These libraries, consisting of newspapers, pamphlets, and bound books, ranged in size between 100 and 1,000 volumes
and were used by soldiers and children on military reservations. Troops
detached from a garrison were "entitled to take with them their propor-
tionate shares of the fortification's library."

SEAMEN'S LIBRARIES IN THE U.S. NAVY. Overlooked or ignored
by contemporary writers of the naval scene was the fact that the navy
did attempt, for a brief period, to provide books to its sailors both
afloat and ashore. The very first communications that Secretary of the
Navy Abel P. Upshur dispatched upon taking office in 1841 were to the
commandants of three navy yards and to the several navy agents in-
forming them of the books which were to be allowed the various units
of the navy. As will be discussed more fully in chapter VII, the navy
since 1828 had provided its ships with certain books for the use of the
officers in order to encourage their self-education; so Upshur's list
concerning officers' libraries was nothing new. From time to time previous secretaries had added to or revised the lists, but the letters sent to
the commandants and navy agents by Upshur on October 12–13, 1841,
included, in addition to the listing of books to be allowed for officers,
a list of books, "for the use of seamen on board vessels of the Navy."
    The inclusion of books for seamen among the lists of allowances sent
out by Upshur was not without more immediate precedent. In the Royal
Navy, an Admiralty order dated August, 1838, directed that libraries
were to be established on each ship for the use of the crews. The libraries
were to be furnished at the public expense, and were to be placed in the
charge of the ships' schoolmasters. The larger vessels received 270
volumes exclusive of Bibles, while the smaller craft were supplied with
100 volumes. The books were reported to have been "judiciously chosen
with the view of combining amusement and instruction," with the emphasis placed on the latter object. These libraries and the value of elementary
education were commented upon favorably by a naval physician in a
lengthy report on health in the Royal Navy, ordered printed by the
House of Commons in 1840.[8]
    Meanwhile, in the U.S. Navy, other positive decisions related to
library matters had recently been generated partly as a result of the
navy's program to recruit and train young native Americans as seamen.
In 1837, a naval apprentices act was passed by Congress in the hope of
overcoming the persistent problem of attracting and retaining suitable
seamen in the navy. One of the effects, administratively, of the new
apprentices program was to put the navy into the business of educating
seamen. Heretofore it had officially provided books for officers' libraries

aboard ship and had furnished instructors for the education of young midshipmen. Unofficially, there had been experiments of varying success over the years in the education of boys and seamen. Now, in order to back up its commitment to instruct apprentice boys of thirteen to eighteen years of age in reading, writing, and arithmetic, the navy had to provide books for their use. One way was to allow the apprentices access to the officers' libraries. Fifty-four "pupil apprentices" aboard the ship-of-the-line *Ohio,* who attended class every other day, and were taught the three "Rs" and navigation, were reported, in March of 1839, to have free use of the ship's library, and to be mostly "very devoted readers." The apprentices' school aboard the *Ohio* was also praised in almost identical passages in two different books which appeared twenty-one years apart and which were written as a result of the ship's Mediterranean cruise of 1839–1841.

In 1840, Secretary of the Navy James K. Paulding authorized the purchase of books and stationery for the use of apprentices aboard receiving ships. He also granted them the extraordinary privilege of taking their books with them when they were transferred to seagoing vessels. This disregard by Paulding of petty accountability and of governmental parsimony, which had always been the watchword in public expenditures, was a noble expression of his hope for the success of education in the navy.

But Secretary Upshur's subsequent order of 1841, which allowed books for seamen, seems to have gone unnoticed outside of the navy, and within the service itself, its impact was lessened by the presence of subscription or other informal shipboard libraries. The seamen's library was originally conceived of by the Board of Navy Commissioners, who drew up a small list of inexpensive books and submitted it to Secretary George E. Badger on May 13, 1841 (fig. 5 and appendix A). Only fourteen title entries comprised the list, yet two of the entries provided for the purchase of several volumes each of miscellaneous works (*i.e.,* "Various Narrations of Imprisonment, Shipwreck, Perils and Captivity," and "Selections from Family Library") which could bring the total number of volumes in a library up to perhaps 150 or more, or its cost up to $100 (a figure which the Board of Navy Commissioners originally estimated for the typical seamen's library).[9] A preponderance of seafaring works dominated the list, but some balance may have been introduced by a selection of books from the "Harper's Family Library" series, which itself consisted of 105 excellent nonfiction volumes in 1840 (171 volumes in 1844), priced at forty-five cents each.[10] The seamen's libraries must have varied in content and size from vessel to vessel, each acquisition probably having been determined by the availability of titles at the time of procurement, and on how liberally the order was interpreted.

List of Books to be allowed for the Libraries of seamen
on board vessels of the Navy.

Dana's two years before the mast
Oracle of the Arts –
Robinson Crusoe
Brannans official letters (late War)
Various narrations of imprisonment, shipwreck, perils and
         captivity –
Gardens Anecdotes of the Revolution –
Naval Monument
Sketches of Naval life in the Constitution & Brandywine
Pauldings Journal in the Dolphin
Picture of Australia
Sewards narrative of his Shipwrecks, and discovery of certain
         Islands –
Penny Magazine (bound)
Selections from Family Library
Cities and principal Towns of the Cabinet Cyclopedia –

5. Seamen's library list of the U.S. Navy, 1841–1843.
National Archives

Even though the navy provided these libraries to its vessels, their crews continued the custom of purchasing subscription libraries. The duality of the source of naval libraries was specifically noted in a personal journal kept by Joseph T. Downey, a seaman aboard the sloop-of-war *Portsmouth* in 1845–1847. He mentioned in connection with the observance of the Sabbath at sea that: "The libraries, of which we have two, the one furnished by the Government, the other bought by private subscription, are now opened, and the books consisting of Histories, Travels, Lives of Celebrated Men and other Sterling works distributed to all that call for them." Inasmuch as the *Portsmouth* had sailed from Norfolk on January 23, 1845, it can be assumed that the governmental library that Downey referred to was a fairly complete seamen's library, although, perhaps, he also meant the officers' library as well.

An exchange of correspondence between William Wood and Secretary Upshur helps to underscore the public's general unawareness of the status of naval libraries and finally fixes Wood's position in relation to subscription versus government libraries. From his home in Canandaigua on March 12, 1842, Wood wrote Upshur, ostensibly to congratulate him for some action which had resulted in "giving the Navy a 'God send' in Bibles." Wood apparently could not resist telling again his now twenty-year old story about the *Franklin's* library, for he repeated it once more, this time adhering somewhat closely to the version that Lieutenant Matthew F. Maury had written for the *Southern Literary Messenger* two years previously, which had probably refreshed his memory. Wood concluded his letter with the plea:

> I venture to trouble you Sir with these items in the hope that while your Excellency steers the Navy an order will be sent to the Commander of every Ship which leaves the U.S. to invite the crew to subscribe for their own benefit to a Library . . . .

Secretary Upshur was quick to send Wood a reply. He agreed that it would be gratifying if naval seamen would voluntarily and at their own expense procure libraries, but declined giving any order in that regard. Had the navy's libraries for seamen been adequate or even well-known at this time, there would not have been any need for him to advocate the continuance of voluntary subscription libraries, or for Wood to beat a dead horse. In fact, Wood's letter written a half-year after Upshur's notice of allowance of books for seamen reveals Wood's probable ignorance of the true situation, and further puts the lie to his, or his friends', later claims that he influenced an order from the Navy Department "for every ship bound abroad to take a suitable number of volumes for use of the sailors." No correspondence by William Wood regarding seamen's libraries other than that already quoted appears in the files of the secretary

of the navy for the period 1821-1857. Unless there was some earlier
personal contact between Wood and a secretary of the navy, or with
others who might have influenced a secretary, it appears that Wood was
only indirectly responsibile, by virtue of his past exertions, for the
eventual provision of libraries to officers (1828) and to seamen (1841)
by the navy.

While William Wood, in the manner of the Ancient Mariner, was
retelling his faded story of the *Franklin* to a secretary of the navy for
perhaps the last time, an American wanderer, Herman Melville, was
absorbing experiences which the world would one day remember as the
stuff of great literature. He was later to comment unfavorably on the
quality of the library he found aboard a U.S. man-of-war, and his
remarks would be taken as fact for many years by those in search of
information about life at sea in the 1840s. More recently, Melville
scholars, as indefatigable as Captain Ahab in pursuit of their own white
whale—the very genesis of Melville's writings—have to some extent
sorted out the fact from fiction in those of Melville's works having autobiographical bases. In the process, it has been amply shown that Melville was a masterful appropriator and borrower of other writers'
material. His *White-Jacket* (1850), in which chapter 41 is devoted to
"A Man-of-War Library," incorporated facts, phrases, and ideas from
other books about life at sea. What Melville wrote about the world of
the man-of-war, "Neversink," in *White-Jacket* was not necessarily what
he experienced when he served aboard the frigate *United States* in 1844.
Of importance here is to note that Melville's description of the frigate's
library is unreliable as historical fact. It has also been demonstrated in
a dissection of chapter 41 that much of its substance came from Henry
J. Mercier's book, *Life in a Man-of-War*.[11]

The research, which revealed the description of the "Neversink's"
library to be little more than the effective literary license of a great
writer, has also happily uncovered some positive information concerning
naval libraries of this period. When the *United States* was preparing to
depart the Pacific Station upon being relieved by the frigate *Savannah*,
she was reported to have been stripped of her charts and excess equipment, including part of her library. It was only natural for this to have
been done. The transfer and trading of charts from ship to ship was a
common occurrence in the navy. Certain charts, unique because of additions and corrections made on board one ship, became valuable to another about to sail the same waters, perhaps for the first time. One such
chart which was used on board the *United States* in her 1843 passage from
Callao to Honolulu, and supposedly given to the *Savannah*, was used by
the frigate *Congress* on the same route in June of 1846. Somehow this
chart, with the course and daily distances run by the *United States* still

recorded on it, was acquired from the *United States* by the *Congress*.[12]

No doubt at the time that the transfer was made, it was officially noted or remembered against a future day of reckoning. Government property of any kind was not simply given away in the naval service, and this stricture included books. The longstanding custom of recording or otherwise remembering the titles of books issued to various naval vessels was evident at all levels of the Navy Department, from the written personal recollections of a midshipman to the official records of the secretary. Books issued to ships for the use of their officers had to be accounted for, and the titles allowed each vessel were in accordance with an authorized listing.

At the time the *United States* sailed from Norfolk in January of 1842, the new October 12, 1841 lists of book allowances for officers' and seamen's libraries were in effect. It is probable that many of the titles allowed were in the officers' library of the *United States* when she transferred several books to the *Savannah* on July 6, 1844, before departing for home. Of the titles reported as given over to the *Savannah,* namely, "*Prescott's *Ferdinand and Isabella,* 3 volumes; *Bancroft's *History of the United States;* Darwin's *Voyages of H.B.M. 'Adventure' and 'Beagle,'* 4 volumes; Livingstone's *Atlas;* Hough's *Military Law Authorities* and *Courts Martial;* and *Harper's Family Library,*" three (identified with asterisks), and the atlas were probably from the ship's or officers' library. The Harper's Family Library, consisting of seventy-two volumes, was probably from the seamen's library; and the Darwin could have been from either collection.

Whether Melville read these or other books (especially those which might have been in the crew's library) while aboard the *United States* is a matter of conjecture. Many variables, such as loss and transfer of books, inaccurate listings or substitutions of titles in the allowances provided to either the officers' or seamen's libraries, need to be considered in any attempt to reconstruct the library or libraries Melville had possible access to while serving on the *United States*. His statement in *White-Jacket* that, "There was a public library on board [the "Neversink"] paid for by government, and entrusted to the custody of one of the marine corporals . . . ," while not challenged by Melville scholars, is also suspect. This "public library" in total might have been made up from a subscription or a religiously donated library, of which only a part was the official seamen's library paid for by the navy. In this case there would have been many other books available to the crew, and more than likely several of these would have been of the unappealing variety that Melville recalled as being "selected by our Chaplain."

Melville's comment on the librarian's "very cross and irritable" disposition seems to have been suggested by the character of the captain's

clerk aboard the *Lexington* to whom William McNally had to bow and
scrape whenever he received permission to borrow a book from the
officers' library. Lastly, the military rank of the "little, dried-up" librarian, a marine corporal, and the manner and place of stowage of the
"Neversink's" library—"a large cask on the berth deck"—are beyond
even the vague limits of the pattern of library custody and accommodation aboard naval vessels of the period. As a matter of fact, a logbook
entry for Saturday, February 24, 1844, noted the location of a library
on the *United States* in the "main deck cabin" area. On this date, it was
recorded that the cabin, pantry, library, and flag room bulkheads had
been taken down, "leaving the battery flush fore and aft." It is possible
that more than one library (*i.e.,* seamen's, officers', subscription, etc.) had
been shelved in this part of the frigate.[13]

Thus, while most of the elements of the then-existing shipboard
library situation are found in Melville's fanciful description of a man-
of-war's library, each had been altered slightly by him in order to convey
a somewhat negative total impression. The library's source, content,
users, custodian, and its effect all received the patronizing notice of
White-Jacket, Melville's seaman-critic of the navy and autobiographical
hero of the tale. To have ventured a positive opinion about the library
or the literary fare available to seamen aboard the "Neversink" would
not have been in keeping with Melville's intent to emphasize the flaws
and to ridicule the routines of naval life. Even the library, provided for
the good of his messmates, had scant redeeming qualities in the eyes
of the otherwise humane White-Jacket.

This fictional view of the naval shipboard library scene, then, was the
one more popularly read and believed until recently, although another
lesser known, terse, but factual, description existed alongside of it. If
anything, the latter has been thought to complement Melville's fuller
treatment. Its author, the Reverend Walter Colton, in October, 1845,
embarked with Commodore Robert F. Stockton on the historic voyage
of the frigate *Congress* to Hawaii and California. While awaiting the
day of sailing, Chaplain Colton recorded in his journal, which was later
published as a book, *Deck and Port,* the following entry:

> Wednesday, Oct. 29 [1845] . . . I have been occupied to-
> day in arranging in suitable cases the library of the crew—a
> library comprising between three and four hundred volumes.
> For many of the miscellaneous and religious books in this li-
> brary I am indebted to the Presbyterian Board of Publication,
> to the Sunday School Union, to the American Tract Society,
> and to the liberality of Commodore Stockton. My acknowl-
> edgments are also due to the American Bible Society for a

donation of Bibles adequate to the wants of the crew. No national ship ever left a port of the United States more amply provided with books suited to the habits and capacities of those on board. This desideratum has been supplied, so far as the crew is concerned, with comparatively little aid from the department. The government furnishes the sailor with grog to burn up his body, a Christian liberality with books to save his soul. The whisky ration is a curse to the service, and a damning blot on our national legislation.

Colton's reference to the small amount of assistance he received from the navy in his attempt to assemble the library reflects again on the limited nature of the official crews' libraries and hints at the short duration of their actual existence in the service, for at this time, books for all authorized naval libraries were no longer being purchased by the Navy Department. On February 9, 1845, the secretary of the navy had issued an order to the effect that ships fitting out for cruises were to be supplied only with books already on hand at the navy yards. This order would have limited the selection of books for the *Congress* to those titles in stock at the Norfolk Navy Yard. But even if Colton had been able to choose from the complete list of books allowed to crews' libraries, he was not content with wholly secular titles. He also wanted books of religious character, and in seeking for them elsewhere, he did not hesitate to criticize the navy for having to do so, as is evident from the passage quoted above. On September 17, 1845, the chaplain had written to his friend Dr. H. H. Boardman of the Presbyterian Board of Publication and asked that the *Congress* be supplied with "some of their excellent publications" for her library. He again observed, "We can have no appropriation from the Government for this purpose. The day for such appropriations has not yet come, though I think the star that harbingers it is above the horizon. . . . The Books will constitute a part of the Library of the Frigate Congress and remain permanently with her. . . ."[14]

The library situation aboard the *Congress* as Colton depicted it was probably representative at the time, and is almost as complete a picture of the scene as could be desired. His description not only serves to show up some of the factual defects already cited in connection with *White-Jacket,* but at the same time, it tends to reinforce at least the mood or feeling concerning the heavy religious content of a man-of-war's library which Melville sought to portray. Colton's comment on the liberality of Commodore Stockton indicates that the commodore either provided books or money or both in the formation of the crews' library. Just a few years earlier, Stockton had donated $4,000 to the American Whig So-

ciety of the College of New Jersey, a literary association of his boyhood
alma mater. Not only was he inclined to be generous in the support of
learning, but at sea, Stockton expressed his strong religious sentiments
to the crew of the *Congress* at divine worship, thereby sustaining his
chaplain in both word and deed.

The Reverend Walter Colton was further supported in his cause
through the distribution of religious tracts. After breaking out his supply
of tracts on the second Sunday at sea, he wrote: "It would have encouraged the hearts of those who supply these sources of salutary instruction, to have witnessed the eagerness with which our sailors took
them. In a few minutes there were three or four hundred men on the
decks of our ship reading tracts. . . ." Colton did not exaggerate the
number of takers, for a passenger on the *Congress,* witnessing the crew
at divine service that day, noted in her journal: "Nov. 9th, Sunday. . . .
After inspection, divine service was held. This is always impressive on
the ocean. For the first time we all attended. The band played a hymn,
the Chaplain read service, 'Old Hundred' was sung accompanied by
the band. A good discourse by the Chaplain followed. After service,
the name of each man was called and as he answered he passed the
officers with his hat off. Later we noticed several hundred of them about
the deck with tracts which the Chaplain had distributed. Mother reading
a 'History of Missionary Enterprises in the South Sea,' by Rev. John
Williams who was murdered and *eaten* at the New Hebrides."

Miss Elizabeth Douglas Turrill, the observant passenger, also commented on several other titles of books her family read throughout the
voyage to Hawaii. Her father, Joel, had been designated the U.S. Coun-
sul-General to the Sandwich Islands by President James K. Polk, and
the *Congress* was their means of transportation to his new post. While
she never mentioned a library being aboard the frigate, a few of the books
supplied to the Turrill family by Captain Samuel F. DuPont, commander
of the *Congress,* probably were from that source. The captain early in
the voyage loaned thirteen-year old Elizabeth a copy of *The Missionary's
Daughter* (a juvenile religious book often included in sailors' libraries),
and at the same time gave her father a pamphlet reprint of Lieutenant
Matthew F. Maury's treatise on the Gulf Stream to read. To Mrs. Turrill he loaned *The Diary of Lady Willoughby.* Their host on another
occasion sent the family an account of the *Bounty* mutineers, probably
Pitcairn's Island (number 31, of the Harper's Family Library series), a
likely title from the official crews' library.

Chaplain Colton's sanguine pre-voyage forecast of an impending
action by the government to provide books, or the funds to buy them,
for seamen was a sad miscalculation on his part. The star that he thought
he saw on the horizon was actually setting, not rising, and it signaled

the withdrawal of financial support to crew's libraries by the navy. No official concern over seamen's libraries or the provision of books to seamen was again expressed by the Navy Department for several years after the 1845 order of curtailment. In 1855, the chaplain of the sloop *Jamestown* wrote the secretary of the navy to inquire whether any allowance was available for the "purchase of bibles or other books for the men." He was told that there was no allowance, and that only books already furnished (for officers' libraries) were authorized.[15] By 1858, the navy again had recognized the seaman's need for books to the extent that the secretary of the navy was authorized, according to the naval regulations dated that year, to "make an allowance, at his discretion, for books for the use of the petty officers and persons of inferior ratings on board of vessels going on long or distant cruises," in addition to providing for the never quite discontinued officers' libraries.

SEAMEN'S LIBRARIES AND THE AMERICAN SEAMEN'S FRIEND SOCIETY. The brief episode of government support for seamen's libraries was all but lost in the floodtide of religious activity on behalf of naval and merchant seamen which prevailed at the time of their introduction. As noted in chapter II, during the first third of the nineteenth century, various means of supplying American seamen with religious books, Bibles, and tracts had been employed by religiously motivated groups. Chief among the many organizations scattered along the Atlantic and Gulf coasts and in every large port of the United States, and on its rivers, lakes, and canals, was the American Seamen's Friend Society, which attempted to represent the seaman at the national level.[16] The society had as affiliates many active seamen's aid societies, some of which predated its founding by several years. By 1834, there were forty-two autonomous seamen's organizations affiliated with the American Seamen's Friend Society. The national society gradually enlarged its influence over the years until it embraced practically all undenominational work for seamen in seaports and inland cities. Although the American Seamen's Friend Society had supported some overseas library activities since the date of its reorganization in 1828, it lagged behind its counterparts in Great Britain as well as behind some of the local societies, in the provision of books and libraries to seamen at home and at sea. In 1835, the British and Foreign Sailors' Society had reported that it had 100 "Loan Ship Libraries," comprising a total of about 3,000 volumes in circulation, and had available in its chapel a library of upwards to 1,500 volumes "daily open to sailors." A year earlier, the recently organized Seamen's Library and Tract Association in Philadelphia had begun a program of placing a library of "well selected and useful books" on board every vessel belonging to the port; and in Boston more than 400

volumes of books, "most of them quite valuable," had been collected
with the view to lending them to ships' officers on foreign voyages. The
Boston Seaman's Friend Society also reported that the American Tract
Society at Boston had donated fifty-three volumes of its standard publications to its library program in 1835, and that it contemplated furnishing each vessel of the port with similar libraries. This practice, which also
began in New York about the same time, finally projected the American
Seamen's Friend Society into a program of supplying libraries to ships.
The first libraries that it furnished were regarded as permanent shipboard collections. They were made up from sets of the publications of
the American Tract Society, to which other donated books procured
by the American Seamen's Friend Society were added. Each library,
packed in a case, consisted of sixty to eighty volumes. By 1839, the
society had supplied 159 vessels with such libraries.

The remarks made by Richard Henry Dana, Jr., on the value of books
aboard ship in his then-recently published *Two Years Before the Mast,*
might have influenced the executive committee of the American Seamen's Friend Society to enlarge its library program in 1843. That year,
the society decided to make available at cost a sixty-volume "Sailor's
Library" of selected books which shipowners and others could purchase
for any vessel. Quoting Dana in its initial announcement, the society
believed that the library would be "like a spring in a desert land" aboard
ship, just as Dana had found books to be on the culturally barren coast
of California. The "Sailor's Library" was composed of fifty titles, about
two-thirds of them religious in nature (one of the titles being Marks's
Retrospect) and the balance made up of miscellaneous titles (fig. 6, and
Appendix B). They had been chosen for inclusion in "Library No. 1"
for "variety and interest in matter, simplicity in style," and for economy
and instructional value, as well as to make a "good moral impression"
on seamen. Arrangements were made with the firm of Mark H. Newman
of New York City to act as publisher for the "Sailor's Library," and the
library was offered for sale in a "neat and substantial case" for $25. It
could be obtained in New York from either the society or from Newman's, and elsewhere from book firms located in Boston, New Bedford,
and New London. Tappan and Dennet, the Boston publisher who
handled the library, advertised it in one of its books, *Thirty Years From
Home,* by Samuel Leech, in 1843, as "Recently published: *The Sailor's
Library* consisting of sixty volumes selected by a committee of the
Seamen's Friend Society—in a book-case, with lock, key, &c. Price
$25.00."

The initial response to the "Sailor's Library" as reported by the society
was fairly strong. Several shipowners in New York, New London, Ston-
ington, and other ports had their vessels supplied with the library the

1843]   SAILOR'S MAGAZINE.   281

NEW-YORK, MAY, 1843.

ANNUAL MEETING.

THE fifteenth anniversary of the American Seamen's Friend Society, will be held on Monday evening, the 8th inst., at the Broadway Tabernacle, N. Y. An interesting meeting is anticipated.

ALL READY.

We are happy to communicate the information to shipowners, shipmasters, and others interested in seamen, that the Sailor's Library is now ready for orders.

To such as feel an interest in the mental and moral improvement of the mariner, the list below given will afford real satisfaction. They will find that in making the selection, the committee have studied variety and interest in matter, simplicity in style, economy, instruction, and good moral impression. To those making long voyages, this library will be what Dana found a book to be on the coast of California: "Like a spring in a desert land."

The real excellence of the volumes, and the small amount for which they are furnished, we doubt not will be a sufficient temptation to buy; and we shall not be disappointed if many of these libraries find their way to cabins in the mountains as well as cabins on the waves.

No. 1.
SAILOR'S LIBRARY.

SELECTED UNDER THE SUPERVISION OF THE AMERICAN SEAMEN'S FRIEND SOCIETY.

CATALOGUE.

Abbot's Young Christian
Alexander's Biblical Dictionary
Bunyan's Pilgrim's Progress
Baxter's Call with Chalmer's Preface
Buck's Religious Anecdotes
Brown's Concordance

VOL. XV.—No. 9.

Bancroft's Life of Washington, 2 vols.
Benevolent Merchant
Cowper's Poems, 3 vols.
Circumnavigation of the Globe
Charles Morton
Doddridge's Rise and Progress
D'Aubigne's History of the Reformation
Dairyman's Daughter, &c.
Early Navigators
Emma
Fool's Pence, &c.
Florence Arnott
Gray's Chemistry
Gurney on the Sabbath.
Great Secret
Hale's History of the United States
Hitchcocks Geology
Jay's Prayers
Life before the Mast
Life of Columbus
Memoir of Harlan Page
Memoir of Gordon Hall
Martyr Lamb
Meditations on Prayer
Michael Kemp
Missionary's Daughter
Nevin's Practical Thoughts
Nelson on Infidelity
Old Humphrey's Addresses
Old Humphrey's Observations
Old Humphrey's Thoughts for Thoughtful
Paley's Natural Theology
Polar Seas
Pitcairn's Island
Retrospect
Shepherd of Salisbury Plain, &c.
Sargent's Temperance Tales, 6 vols.
Seamen's Friend
Smith's Geography and Atlas
Tracts for Seamen
Uncas and Miantonomoh
Views of the Saviour
Widow's Son
Zebulon, or Claims of Seamen.

The undersigned, a committee of the American Seamen's Friend Society, appointed for the purpose of selecting a suitable library for seamen, have approved of the above-named books, and have made arrangements with Mr. Mark H. Newman to publish the same.

We therefore cordially recommend this Library No. 1, to the patronage of ship-
36

6. "Catalogue" of the "No. 1 Sailor's Library," 1843.

first year at the $25 price; or at $1.00 for each member of a vessel's crew, which might indicate that seamen were expected to subscribe for a library as well. The next year (1844), the price of the library was reduced to $20, and its name changed to the "Miscellaneous Library" for ships. Included in the library at no extra cost were three Bibles and a dozen New Testaments as an added inducement for purchasers. At this time, the society also began to make available through the liberality of the American Tract Society, two of its libraries, the "Christian Library" and the "Youth's Christian Library" at half price. The former was described as "45 neatly and well bound volumes" in a case for $10 (normally $20); and the latter as "containing 40 neatly bound volumes, for $5, or with case $6. The usual price [being] $10 and $11." The two American Tract Society libraries were typical of the standard collections of books that various publishers made available to the many Sunday school libraries which flourished in the United States from about 1825 to the 1880s.[17]

All three libraries were especially recommended by the American Seamen's Friend Society for whalers and other vessels engaged on long voyages. The frigate *Constitution* had a set of the Christian Library aboard, supplied by the Episcopal Floating Chapel of New York, when she left on a three years' cruise in 1844; and a portion of the books provided to the Reverend Walter Colton on the *Congress* in 1845 by the American Tract Society, probably consisted of titles from its standard libraries. The same year, the sloop *Portsmouth* was reported to have been supplied with books and tracts originating from the American Seamen's Friend Society, the American Bible Society, and the American Tract Society, which materials were probably either a part of, or separate from, the subscription library Joseph T. Downey mentioned as being aboard her at the time. Also, in 1850, some of the books sent for by Chaplain Charles S. Stewart for the crew of the *Congress*, then on another voyage at Montevideo, might have been from these sources.[18]

The American Seamen's Friend Society continued to advertise its libraries, and also furnished other libraries made up in part from donated books, which in 1853, averaged about 50 to 117 volumes each. At this time the society was hoping to win a contested legacy which would give it funds to expand its library program. In 1858, a more systematic program of loan libraries was inaugurated, which nevertheless, still depended upon the purchase of libraries for ships by parties interested in the welfare of seamen. The purchased libraries, at first called "Sea Missions," were loaned by the society to one or more religiously converted crew members who were expected to hold religious services or to institute Bible classes aboard their ships, as well as to act as librarians or keepers for the collections. The society noted that this work of evangelization by lay labor was more apt to be successful, for it took the ship's library out of the officers' cabin and placed it with "the colporteur, or sailor missionary, in the forecastle." Support for the plan was specifically solicited from Sunday school children, who subscribed or contributed their pennies in order to buy the $10 libraries which were then assigned to various ships by the American Seamen's Friend Society. The society knew that money and support could be obtained from the popular Sunday school movement, which then was enjoying its peak years, and it set out to tap the financial resources of this "growing power" in the land. Once the "hearts of the children" had been "turned to the sailor," the society reported that they took hold of the good work with much interest and spirit, and as a consequence, the larger part of the libraries in circulation were soon owned by children's groups.

The libraries were first sent to sea from Boston and New Bedford, and then from New York. Within four years' time there were 325 libraries afloat "in the care of as many religious officers and sailors." At this time (1862) it was estimated that 16,000 volumes were available. Each library purchased was given an identification number and its history was henceforth noted among the records of the society. In this connection, the *Life Boat,* "a little sheet published monthly by the society, designed chiefly for children and Sabbath Schools," was begun in 1858 in order to publicize the program.[19] Its pages were for the most part filled with letters of testimony by seamen regarding the good effects of the libraries, along with anecdotes of an inspirational nature about the seamen's cause. Most of the letters printed in the *Life Boat* were variations on a standard theme which told how the presence of the sea missions helped convert sailors to the Christian faith or suppress swearing and drinking, or how the religious books supplanted the reading of novels and light literature aboard ship, and took the place of card playing or other pastimes. Occasionally, between the lines of these stereotypic reports of evangelical realization, a hint of actual shipboard conditions concerning literacy, or the desire to achieve it, was brought to notice. The sailor missionary in charge of Library No. 28, for example, wrote that only two men in his black crew could read, but the library, likened to a medicine chest by him, seemed to have been a cure "for all the diseases of sin" on the ship, for those who could read, read to those who were unable to. The master of another vessel, containing Library No. 61, noted that inasmuch as his crew was composed chiefly of foreigners, the library would have been more useful if it had contained "books of different languages," although the crew members who were able to read English had read the volumes in the library with great interest.

Not only were merchant and naval seamen and shipboard passengers reported to have derived benefit from the libraries, but other persons,

directly or indirectly, might be subjected to the solicitude of zealous sea
missionaries. Libraries were left at hospitals; foreign pilots regardless
of their own religious beliefs were handed testaments, Bibles, and tracts
upon boarding a Christian vessel; and books from the libraries were
even loaned to landsmen. Uusally the recipients were described as being
grateful for the attention given them, but the Civil War introduced a few
exceptions to these rote-formula reports. One incident, recounted in the
patriotic *Life Boat,* told how the crew of the appropriately named Confederate privateer *Jefferson Davis* did not want Library No. 136, which
was aboard the Yankee bark *Alvarado* when captured at sea in 1861.
The rejected library was next acquired by the ship *Carolina,* where it
was, of course, properly appreciated by the crew, and it eventually found
its way back to Boston. In a more heroic vein, the seaman in charge of
Library No. 322 was moved to imitate Captain James Lawrence's "Don't
give up the ship" exhortation when his vessel was faced with the danger
of sinking in a storm. He was heard to shout to a pious shipmate as he
left on a errand on mercy in the ship's boat, "If anything happens to the
ship, *be sure you save the library.*"

The libraries, which were usually loaned to ships for the duration of a
voyage, were packed in strong cases with locks and hinges made of brass
(so the hardware would not rust), and the books that made up their
contents were "selected with great care," being "generally furnished by
publishers at the lowest cost price." A few letters in the *Life Boat* mentioned the titles of the more popular religious items contained in the
libraries, such as, *The Sinner's Friend, Pilgrim's Progress,* and Doddridge's *Rise and Progress.* One contributor to the *Life Boat* noted that it
was easy to tell which books had been read the most, for they were more
soiled than the others, and some smelled "pretty much of tar." A large
warship, like the steam frigate *Minnesota,* was furnished with several
libraries simultaneously. In 1862, this vessel had three libraries aboard
which were fastened to the main mast on the berth deck. Both the ship's
crew of 586 men and the prisoners she had aboard were able to avail
themselves of the books. Library No. 220, on board the frigate *Sabine,*
was located in the sick bay but was intended for the use of the entire
ship's company. The sea missionaries who were in charge of the libraries
were responsible for the return or renewal of the libraries at the completion of a voyage; and the presence of these volunteer librarians and
their libraries seems to have been readily accepted by officers in both
the naval and merchant services. On the larger naval vessels which already carried chaplains as members of the crew, the sea missionaries
were especially welcomed. Chaplain Charles S. Stewart praised the
work of a seaman "coleporteur" aboard the steam frigate *Niagara* in
1861, and remarked, "I have made him Librarian of all my books for

the men," which would indicate that the frigate was supplied with more
books than just those of the American Seamen's Friend Society. Other
naval officers who were attuned to the religious, philanthropic, and
temperance causes involving seamen at the time also lent their support
to the society's library program. Captain Andrew H. Foote, for example,
when in command of the navy yard at Brooklyn, helped distribute the
society's libraries. In 1861, he sent out Libraries Nos. 324–326 to the
naval vessels, *Vandalia, Cuyler,* and *Daylight,* where they were reported
to have been gratefully received by their commanding officers. Sympathetic masters and mates of merchant ships were also desirous of obtaining libraries for their vessels and helped the society by frequently
acting in the capacity of sea missionaries for their crews.

The loan library program initiated by the American Seamen's Friend
Society became one of its permanent operations, and it grew over the
years until some 13,543 new libraries had gone to sea by 1932. Yet, as
successful as it was, libraries were carried aboard only a small fraction of
the number of ships in actual service in the earlier years. In 1862, the
ratio by the society's own estimate, was about one library to every one
hundred American vessels.[20] If this was indeed the case, then some fraction of the other ninety-nine percent of vessels were furnished with libraries from other sources, such as local seamen's friends groups, shipowners, private donors, and the crews themselves. It is not always clear
from contemporary accounts what the origin of a library aboard a
merchant vessel, when mentioned, might have been. For instance, the
whaler *North America* in 1839 was reported to have had a library of
200 volumes, and other sperm whalers were said to have carried similar
collections, but how the library came to be placed aboard the *North
America,* or what its true contents were, was not commented upon.[21] The
relatively smaller library that may have been aboard the *Acushnet* (the
whaler that served as the model for Melville's "Pequod" in *Moby Dick*)
on one or more of her voyages appears to have been made up of mostly
secular titles of general and popular interest; but another library purchased for a Nantucket whaler by her owners for $16.24 in 1840 con-
sisted of thirty-five titles, many of which were either religious or juvenile
in character.

Although libraries or collections of books intended for the use of
ships' crews were quite common onward from the second decade of the
century, it is obvious that throughout the period of sail, many merchant
vessels and some warships went to sea without any of the kinds or com-
binations of seamen's libraries available. John Ross Browne, who
shipped in haste in the capacity of landsman aboard a New Bedford
whaler in 1842, regretted in leisure that he had not brought any books
with him, for he found only a few books and newspapers that he could

borrow among the officers and crew. These he was compelled to read and re-read throughout the voyage. And as late as 1860, the surgeon's mate aboard the steam frigate *Mississippi* had to reiterate the familiar plea: "It would be a most worthy undertaking for our benevolent people to see that [our ships-of-war] are fitted out with suitable libraries before they leave the United States, of the proper kinds of books, for the sole use of the men." The idea of having shipboard libraries had become firmly established by mid-century, even if the means for providing them were still not always assured.

Notwithstanding the prominence which was given to the sea missions in the affairs of the American Seamen's Friend Society after 1858, other important activities were engaged in by the society and its affiliates in regard to the furnishing of libraries ashore and afloat before and during the sea mission period. These activities involved one or more of the four library services to seamen which were described in chapter II. Of particular note is the effort put forth to provide safe and Christian boarding-houses for seamen, which invariably included libraries or reading rooms as part of their facilities. The "Sailor's Home" opened by the society at New York in 1841 was perhaps the best known at the time. The six-story building located on Cherry Street contained reading, recreation, and dining rooms, and 130 sleeping rooms capable of accommodating 300 seamen. A "Marine Museum" begun in the office of the society prior to 1838 was also part of the home. It had as its nucleus some geologic specimens which Josiah Holbrook, the founder of the American Lyceum movement, had contributed. In 1843, the museum was composed of "several cabinets of natural curiosities" donated to the collection by seamen patrons. The library consisted of about a thousand volumes at this time "of interesting and instructive books, with an abundance of newspapers, magazines, maps, charts, &c." It had been started by a hundred-dollar gift, and was added to by donations of books from interested persons. One of the larger gifts to the library, 680 volumes, had been received shortly after its formation from a man living as far away as Newburyport, Massachusetts. The reading room and musuem were described as "spacious apartments." It was expected that "much good" would be gained by the seamen who could peruse daily "the well selected" books in the library. Seamen could also take advantage of the school which was taught in one of the rooms. For a small fee they could apply to learn the elements of mathematics and navigation, or reading and writing. Every Wednesday there were free "musical and temperance concerts, and astronomical and other lectures" offered for innocent enjoyment and instruction. The home in these respects offered some of the benefits of the landsmen's mechanic institutes, and also anticipated by a few years the goals and facilities of the Young Men's Christian Association.[22]

Before the home was built on Cherry Street, the society sponsored three boardinghouses, one of them exclusively for black seamen. The "Colored Sailor's Home," begun in 1839, was maintained on a separate basis. In 1850, it was reported to have had 600 boarders that year, out of an estimated black seaman population of 2,000 men who sailed from the port. At this time a new library was proposed for the home by a prospective donor who offered to give one hundred volumes if a suitable bookcase was provided. The *Sailor's Magazine* noted that, "To meet this expense, the keeper of this house, who had made large expenditures in fitting up a new house, is obliged to appeal to the friends of the colored sailor, to enable him to comply" with the condition. Donations in money or books were to be sent to the society, or to the home, located on Pearl Street.

SEAMEN'S LIBRARIES IN HOSPITALS. Books and libraries were provided to sick and disabled American seamen ashore in hospitals at an early date. The first volume of the *Sailor's Magazine* in 1828 contained a short article supporting the cause of libraries and reading rooms for sailors. In it a physician in New York was reported to have commented on the reading habits of sailors. The doctor observed that the seamen patients at the "hospital of the city," who had access to a library, "read more than all the other occupants of the house," and also noted that, separate from the library, the sailors themselves took "several daily papers." Almost thirty years later, the chaplain of the Seaman's Retreat, a hospital on Staten Island for mariners, pointed out the use of such libraries for the reinforcement of religion among seamen, who, as patients confined to bed, were often deprived of the benefits of chapel and other services. The chaplain maintained that books in foreign languages were needed for seamen in hospitals, and that books "would be a medicine to help" cure disease and "would be a fountain of healing waters" that would tend to cleanse and elevate "the character of a most useful class of men."

The U.S. Navy, which early went its own way in regard to medical treatment for its seamen (merchant seamen since 1798 supposedly were to have been provided for by marine hospitals to which they contributed a small portion of their wages), also at times supported libraries in its hospitals for the use of seaman patients. On April 8, 1834, the Board of Navy Commissioners was of the opinion "that a small number of cheap

Books would probably be useful, for the perusal of the convalescent" at
the hospital near Norfolk.[23] Two years later the members of the board
changed their minds and advised the secretary of the navy that "under
the present imperfect and incomplete organization of the Hospitals"
it would not be expedient to allow them libraries. However, on September 30, 1843, the same seamen's libraries that were allowed to warships
and to navy yards were also authorized for naval hospitals.

The apparent lack of knowledge in the navy about this order (or the
short span of existence of the navy's libraries for seamen) is again evident
in the fact that on November 18, 1844, the secretary of the navy approved
the creation of a combination chapel and library in a spare room at the
naval hospital at New York. The chaplain of the hospital was to purchase the furnishings, and the navy's literary surgeon, Dr. William S. W.
Ruschenberger, at the hospital, was to select the books. By the time the
chaplain had made his arrangements, only $30, out of an original allow-
ance of $150, was left for books; so the secretary was asked for more
money. He authorized an additional $70, again specifying that the sur-
geon should select the books.

The example of the hospital library at Pensacola, Florida, indicates
that the dual method of subscription and official authorization of seamen's libraries also carried over to naval hospitals. This library, founded
in 1847, was "raised by voluntary subscriptions of the inmates of the
hospital, and of benevolent individuals, officers of the navy, &c." The
secretary of the navy also had directed that $150 be given "from the Naval
Hospital fund." In 1850, the library was reported to contain 1,337 volumes, and to be open from morning to evening every day. Each patient
was allowed to borrow one book at a time. The library was considered
the property of the hospital, under the direction of the surgeon in charge,
and the steward of the hospital was named as the acting librarian.

* * * * *

Libraries for American seamen in the nineteenth century were thus
derived from several main sources: secular donation, subscription, the
government, and religious donation or purchase. Aboard ship, a library
might consist of one type exclusively, or a blend of two or more kinds.
Subscription libraries purchased by ships' crews, or libraries donated
by secular groups or private individuals, were more likely to mirror
the reading fare of contemporary society ashore. The early subscription
library was also relatively the largest type of shipboard library, often ex-
ceeding in size the libraries of wealthy persons and certain cultural
institutions on the American frontiers.[24] The religiously provided libraries as exemplified by those of the American Seamen's Friend Society

afloat and ashore endured, whereas shipboard subscription libraries flourished only a quarter-century or so, and the authorized seamen's libraries in the navy withered away within a few years of their introduction.

The sustained continuity of effort and modest funding by organizations motivated to further the cause of religion among seamen helped assure the success of their libraries. The early plans of these societies which included libraries as one of the means to accomplish their goals were never abandoned. With some effect, the benefits to be derived from libraries for seamen were enunciated regularly by those both within and without the movement. No less a champion of seamen's rights than Richard Henry Dana, Jr., bore witness to the effectiveness of shipboard religious reading and instruction. In the concluding chapter of *Two Years Before the Mast* (often left out of editions of this work), Dana remarked generally on the good which was achieved by societies devoted to the welfare of seamen, such as the American Seamen's Friend Society. In particular he noted the value of religious instruction as the first step for some seamen to acquire the skill of reading, or to begin to think and act as Christians. Earlier, the Reverend John Harris (1838), in a prize essay sponsored by the British and Foreign Sailors' Society, had brought his "Moral Claims of Seamen" to the attention of the Christian world.[25] This essay, and a later article by Timothy Dwight Hunt on the "Wants of Seamen" emphasized the good of seamen's libraries and the need for their universal provision. At the same time they mentioned the status of contemporary education and library facilities available to landsmen, and maintained the right of seamen to be provided with equal religious, educational, and cultural opportunities. Yet while many of the seaman's problems in these areas were unique due to the very nature of his calling, to a large extent, the attempts made to solve them had been in keeping with the times. By mid-century, as far as books and libraries were concerned, most of the means for providing them to seamen had been tried or established afloat and ashore. The tasks of the future would be to improve upon the accepted methods, to enlarge the scale of operations, and to broaden the educational philosophy of the agencies primarily concerned with seamen as a group.

Chapter VI

Books in the Navy, 1798–1827

The government of the United States has no theoretical school for her marine officers, but each national vessel, when going on service, receives on board a certain number of midshipmen, and thus forms a practical school at little expense as to money, and attended with the happiest results.

—Auguste Levasseur

During the period of the rise and progress of books and libraries within the general American maritime community, the U.S. Navy, which contributed to the overall success of the movement, and yet was somewhat independent of it, was engaged in working out its own book and library arrangements in order to fulfill its several needs. These needs were mostly centered around three basic responsibilities of the navy as a unit of government. Very early in its history, the navy had to provide for the proper administration of its vessels and facilities, to superintend the professional development of its officers, and to promote the advancement of learning in general. In carrying out these responsibilities, as far as the broad subject of books in the service was concerned, the Navy Department sooner or later became involved in the distribution of materials which pertained to the government and navigation of vessels, and the authorization or procurement of books and texts for use in various school and teaching situations, as well as the acquisition of books for the use of the department itself, or for its various offices and shore establishments, in the provision of books for use in scientific endeavors and on exploring expeditions.

Books often received special and individual consideration at a high level within the Navy Department because of their unique and obvious qualities for transmitting knowledge and authority. Unlike the hundreds of other items the navy had to allot and control in its daily affairs, books were not apt to be lightly regarded as just one more commodity, especially during the early days of the service. However, from purchase to disposal, books were made to fit the pattern of the navy's way of existence and became themselves part of this existence. Thus to tell of the role of books in the old sailing navy is to tell something of the administrative history and operations of the early Navy Department, but more importantly it is to tell of another significant development in the social history of the navy, for books and libraries contributed much to the betterment of life in the service.

The history of books in the early navy is set against a background of fundamental changes that took place in naval construction, education, and administration, notably between the War of 1812 and the Civil War. In this period the navy was to begin to experience the transition from sail to steam. It was finally to establish a permanent naval school; and the Navy Department was to be reorganized for the second time in its history. Several overdue problems concerning retirement and seniority of officers were dealt with, and various social reforms were accomplished. Flogging was abolished in 1850, duelling was outlawed seven years later, and the grog ration was done away with in 1862. It was a period of relative peace. Besides the showing of the flag abroad by the navy during this time, other important matters that occupied its attention were the suppression of piracy and the slave trade, the mounting of exploring expeditions, the *Somers* mutiny, and participation in the Mexican War.

Much of the history of books in the navy was, of course, influenced by the larger occurrences and decisions which brought about change and improvement in the service. As a small confluent current within the mainstream of naval history, the handling of books and the development of libraries can be delineated by a chronology of events which contributed to its own history. A few dates in this separate history serve to mark the milestones in its progressive course. The year 1828 stands out as the most significant of these dates, for it was at this time that libraries were officially established aboard ship for the use of naval officers. Thus, for purposes of the present study, the broad subject of books in the navy can be divided into two appropriate periods of time, 1798–1827, and 1828–1860—before and after the introduction of libraries.

In the discussion of the early period, presented in this chapter, the beginning usage of books in the navy will be treated in three parallel accounts, which represent the attitudes of the Navy Department toward books in fulfilling its three responsibilities, to provide for (1) the government and navigation of its vessels, (2) the advancement of learning, and (3) the education of its officers. The first topic will be pursued only to 1828, for about this time, navigational materials and books in general more or less ceased to have a common history in the navy, and it would be beyond the scope of this book to follow the history of navigational and regulatory materials further. The second topic, the advancement of learning, is represented by the account of the beginnings of the library of the Navy Department, and is also terminated at this date; however, the broad subject of the advancement of learning is again continued in chapter VIII in connection with the navy's participation in the cause of science and geographic exploration. Finally, the third and largest topic, the account of books and libraries in relation to the methods and means of education in the early navy is begun in the present chapter and concluded, with emphasis on the evolution, ripening, and decline of the ship's library, in the following chapter.

BOOKS FOR THE GOVERNMENT AND NAVIGATION OF SHIPS.

The earliest mention of books in the official correspondence of the Navy Department appears to deal with the distribution of the rules and regulations of 1798 within the service. For several years, and as a matter of routine, the secretary of the navy personally sent out copies of the regulations then in force whenever a new officer was commissioned or a ship was in need of them. During the tenure of Robert Smith (the second man to hold the office of secretary), an instructive little book, *The Mariner's Dictionary,* was also usually sent to new midshipmen. It, like the navy's regulations, was inspired, and, in part, copied from English sources. Moreover, its publisher, William Duane, one of the pioneer printers of Washington, made no attempt to hide the fact that his 1805 *Dictionary* was "improved from an English work," (*The British Mariner's Vocabulary,* attributed to J. J. Moore, and published in 1801). He also took the liberty of dedicating the book to "Robert Smith, Esq." Nevertheless, the secretary discontinued its distribution, perhaps due to the depletion of copies, in April, 1808, although he remained in office for another year. No other similar instructional book was provided gratis to young officers for years to come. A worthwhile practice had died aborning, and furthermore, it was soon forgotten.

Other materials of a prescribed nature, in addition to the departmental rules and regulations, were also sent to individual officers and ships alike. Copies of the statutes which pertained to the service and copies of special laws to be enforced by the navy, such as the ineffectual Embargo Laws of 1808, were widely distributed. In 1814, a listing of naval officers by rank and seniority, the "Navy Register," was authorized for yearly publication.[1] Together with the annual report of the secretary of the navy it served to present the status of the service. Only to this extent did the early government attempt to inform or instruct those in its employ by means of printed matter, for these materials, produced at the public expense, fulfilled the responsibility of the government to make known its laws and actions. Commanders of ships, however, might receive along with their sailing orders other pertinent items which had a direct bearing on their cruises. For example, Lieutenant Otho Norris, commanding the schooner *Shark,* bound for the coast of Liberia on November 3, 1826, was sent a copy of the laws of the United States in relation to the suppression of piracy and the slave trade. And "a volume on the subject of the Fisheries published in 1822" and extracts of the treaties between the United States and Great Britain of 1783 and 1818 were furnished to Lieutenant Isaac M. McKeever on a subsequent voyage of the *Shark* on July 9, 1827.

Another vital concern to the Navy Department from its beginning was the distribution of signal books or codes of signals devoted to the various purposes or forms of this means of communication. Copies of private or other signals were frequently requested by, or were routinely sent to, commanding officers afloat. Newspapers were also often sent to ships' commanders while on station. Captain Thomas Tingey received some newspapers along with the "Laws for the Government of the Navy" and a letter discussing his future employment, in an early 1799 dispatch.[2] On May 24, 1825, files of the *National Intelligencer* and *National Journal* were sent to Commodore Isaac Hull in the Pacific. They were to afford him and those under his command, according to the secretary of the navy, "full information of all occurrences of a general nature worthy of being communicated."

Other books which assisted in carrying out the internal regulation of a vessel or the external governing aspects of the navy on the high seas might be provided to ships, not so much as a matter of course, but by purchase and then apparently only at the request of a squadron or ship's commander. These books usually pertained to courts-martial or international law, and had a definite reference value aboard ship. Jacobsen's *Laws of the Sea,* Alexander Macomb's, Stephen Ayde's, and John MacArthur's treatises on courts-martial, and Vattel's *Law of Nations* were among the titles often requested. Ship commanders also desired to have with them, on distant voyages, appropriate published works by or about celebrated navigators and their voyages. As previously noted in the case of the *Franklin* fitting out for sea in 1821, Commodore Stewart obtained from the *Columbus* eighteen volumes of the voyages of Vancouver, Cook, and La Perouse. In requesting these valuable sets, Stewart was following the example of the many prudent mariners before him, who when they set sail, first took with them copies of

Hakluyt, and later, the succeeding accounts of famous voyagers, in order that they might be guided or counselled by these books while in the remote regions of the world.

The geographic and general descriptive information contained in sets of this nature, along with the serviceable charts and plates which usually accompanied them in the form of pictorial atlases, were indispensable to the seafarer. Then too, apart from the practical value of these works, they might have served to teach and inspire, for from some of the accounts and journals of the great navigators, the perceptive seaborne reader could also glean lessons of humane and enlightened leadership. Books such as these were in constant demand by early American naval officers, and were supplied to them throughout the period of sail. Collectively, the purchased books of voyages and the few legal titles furnished by the government served as incipient libraries. The practice of providing such books for reference, if not for self-education, probably influenced and made easier the introduction of the broader concept of the official ship's library which was to follow in 1828.

The handling of purchased books in the early navy is illustrated in matchless perspective by an incident in 1817, which prompted the secretary of the navy's office to expend considerable time and effort in order to trace the whereabouts of one set of Vancouver's voyages. It began with what could be considered a kind of historic interlibrary loan negotiated by Captain James Biddle with the New York Society Library. Just before leaving on his voyage to claim the Oregon country for the United States, Captain Biddle resourcefully obtained from John Forbes, the long-time librarian of the New York Society Library, one set each of Cook's and Vancouver's voyages. Biddle had promised Forbes that the navy would replace the copies borrowed from the library with identical sets, and after he secured in writing the word of Navy Agent John Bullus of New York that this would indeed be done, Biddle sailed away with the books on the sloop-of-war *Ontario*.[3]

When Bullus reported the transaction to Washington, it was recalled in the Navy Department office that a set of Vancouver's voyages had already been procured for Captain Charles Morris on the *Congress* the previous year. In 1816 this frigate had prepared in Boston to sail on the same mission as the then-current voyage of the *Ontario,* but was diverted from it at the last minute. To further complicate matters, Captain Biddle, apparently on leave in Philadelphia at that time, had obtained the set of voyages for the *Congress.* The Navy Department now wondered what had become of it after the *Congress's* orders were changed. Inasmuch as the *Congress* had just conveniently returned from the Carribean Sea while Bullus's report was fresh in everyone's mind, it was probably thought that if the set was still aboard, it could be removed and sent to the New York Society Library. A letter was written to Captain Morris aboard the *Congress* at Norfolk about the matter. He replied on October 17, 1817, saying: ". . . A set of Vancouvers charts were procured for the Congress through Captain Biddle & were to have been taken from Philadelphia [to Boston] by an officer of the ship then in Virginia. This officer however having taken passage by water [and thus having by-passed Philadelphia] the charts were left in Philadelphia, I believe in possession of Captain Biddle or his Brother. I procured a damaged set of Vancouvers voyages without charts in French at Boston & they are now in this ship." So the set of books was apparently still in Philadelphia! The Navy Department was nearing the end of its quest. It followed up its new lead with an inquiry to Charles Biddle of Philadelphia on October 23, 1817. Although Biddle's reply appears to be lost today, Secretary B. W. Crowninshield had learned by November 7 that the books had left Philadelphia on October 14, with the *Franklin* prior to her departure for the Mediterranean Sea. He wrote to her commander, Charles Stewart, then at Annapolis: "A set of Vancouver's voyages & charts was taken on board the Ship Franklin by the Sailing Master, or other officer, from the Navy Yard Philadelphia; and as the purchase was made expressly for the use of the Captain of the U.S. Frigate Congress upon her intended cruise, you will therefore, please to send the Voyages and charts aforesaid to the Navy Agent at Annapolis, to be delivered to Captain Arthur Sinclair of the Ship Congress."[4] A week before, Navy Agent Bullus had been instructed to purchase replacement sets for the New York Society Library and the case was now closed.

The relating of this episode in the daily affairs of the Navy Department, 156 years ago, also tells something about the availability of certain nautical books in American seaports. The status of the local book market determined which editions or titles could be purchased, especially on short notice. While Captains Biddle and Morris had to improvise or settle for substitute choices of books of voyages in New York and Boston, respectively, Captain Sinclair, aboard the *Congress* in 1817, was unable to obtain the latest nautical almanacs in Baltimore, and had to request, on November 26, that the Navy Department purchase them in New York for delivery to him.

The secretary of the navy often became personally involved in transactions regarding books, even though the Board of Navy Commissioners might have been more likely to be concerned. The board, which consisted of three senior naval officers, was established in 1815 to assist the secretary of the navy in the administration of the department. It had as its general authority the procurement of stores and provisions, and the construction, arming, and equipping of naval vessels. Included in its scope of activity was the important duty of supervising the purchase and allocation of charts, nautical instruments, and some navigational books. The provision of these items to ships had always been an important concern of the department. During the American Revolution, and for a time thereafter, if a navigator was in need of professional books, he was supposed to provide them himself. A precedent for this practice appears in the British *Regulations and Instructions Relating to His Majesty's Service at Sea* (1734), addressed to the master of a vessel, which stated: "It is expected that he do provide himself with the proper Instruments, Maps, and Books of Navigation, and keep an exact and perfect Journal . . . ." With the deletion of the word "maps" and other slight changes, the entire article was copied for the U.S. *Naval Regulations* of 1802, although no specific mention of this requirement appeared in the two earlier codes of naval regulations (the Colonial rules of 1775, and the *Marine Rules and Regulations* of 1798) which preceded it.[5] That the practice of, or tendencies toward, requiring the master to furnish his own books was in vogue at the time is further indicated in an essay on the general duties of officers of ships of war which Thomas Truxtun appended to his book on latitude and longitude in 1794. Commodore Truxtun was probably then the most informed officer in the navy, for his knowledge bridged both traditional seamanship and modern navigational technique, so his statements probably reflected current thought. In commenting on the duties of the master in his short treatise, Truxtun retained the sentence of the British rules which required the master to "provide himself with proper instruments, maps, and books of navigation."

A shift in this requirement from the master to the government itself occurred before or with the promulgation of the next major revision of the U.S. naval regulations distributed in 1818. Books, at least navigational books, then gained the same status that barrels of salt pork and whiskey had always enjoyed, inasmuch as they were officially recognized as allowable items. The charts, nautical books, and instruments belonging to the ship were to be delivered to the master and charged to his account when he assumed his duties. This was in keeping with the navy's custom of assigning responsibility to officers or petty officers for certain allotted stores used in connection with the "departments" which they respectively superintended (*e.g.,* Sailmaker's Department, Boatswain's Department, etc.). The master, under command of the captain, was in charge of navigating the ship, so whatever nautical books allowed were to be procured for his department. In 1825, for example, two copies each of Bowditch's *Navigator* and Blunt's *Coast Pilot* were among the items claimed for the frigate *Brandywine* as deficient against "the stores allotted by regulation to a ship of this class."[6] The following year, the only book items officially specified for the master's department in a table of stores approved by the secretary of the navy at that time, were three nautical almanacs for ships-of-the-line, and two copies each for frigates, sloops, brigs, and schooners. Navigational charts were to be supplied by an order from the Board of Navy Commissioners' office on requisition by the commandant of a navy yard when a vessel fitted out. Navy agents or ships' pursers then made the necessary purchases.

Despite what the early regulations and tables of allowances prescribed, there is evidence to the effect that in actual practice other conditions prevailed in regard to the purchase of navigational books. Longstanding custom, as well as immediate circumstances and changing routines, probably decided which precepts then "on the books" of the Navy Department were literally followed. It was one thing to prepare instructions to apply ideally to men and ships. It was another for them to remain relevant under all conditions or for any length of time. Some light is shed on the actual status of nautical books in the early navy by the correspondence of Edmund M. Blunt, a New York dealer in nautical publications and instruments. Over the years, and with varying degrees of success, he attempted to interest the navy in buying his nautical almanac, which was an abridged edition of the British *Nautical Almanac and Astronomical Ephemeris* that he published under royal license. Blunt started out as a printer of sermons, and at one time operated a bookstore and circulating library in Newburyport, Mass. After moving to New York in 1811, he shortly became America's foremost publisher and seller of nautical books and charts, at the "Sign of the Quadrant." His publishing success was due, in part, to the combination of plagiarizing and improving upon certain British nautical publications. Since no international copyright agreements were in effect at the time, the enterprising Blunt was able to bring out his improved versions of successful foreign nautical works and keep the profits for himself. He also tried to eliminate or diminish the competition between his own and other publications. To this end, from the first year that Blunt began to publish his nautical almanac, he had entertained hopes of selling it in quantity to the navy. In 1811 he wrote to Navy Secretary Paul Hamilton and to former President Thomas Jefferson about the superiority of his edition over that of a competitor, John Garnett of New Brunswick, New Jersey, who he claimed had just supplied 150 copies to the navy. He also quoted a price per hundred copies of his almanac to the navy. That same year, Blunt wrote Hamilton again, this time asking that "some" be bought and enclosed a sample copy.[7] He also attempted to persuade the navy to purchase in quantity other items published by his firm. In early November of 1826, Edmund and George Blunt offered to sell at a twenty-five percent discount the following works of theirs, if bought at the quantities listed:

500	Bowditch Navigators	@ $4.00 [less 25%]
200	Blunt's Coast Pilot	4.00

400	Seamanship & Naval Tactics	4.00
200	Ward's Lunar Tables	1.50
200	N. Almanacs Blunts Ed. 1828	1.50
100	N. Almanacs Blunts Ed. 1827	1.50[8]

According to the Blunts, the publications (which included several charts not listed here) were required by all of the navy's ships for the next year's service. They went on to say that, "We make this proposition in consequence of the constant evasion of the orders heretofore given by the Navy Department for the purchase of Nautical publications at the Store of E. M. Blunt." But the Board of Navy Commissioners was still not about to buy an apparent excess of books in order to receive reduced prices or to eliminate retail dealers, who had to purchase these publications from Blunt and then supply them to the navy. Secretary Southard was advised that the proposal was not in the public interest, and the navy commissioners reiterated an earlier instruction of June 28, 1822, that the New York navy agent should make individual purchases on the most favorable terms, from time to time, as needs required. Two years earlier, the commissioners had turned down another proposal to subscribe to Blunt's spurious "*Seamanship and Naval Tactics,*" on the grounds that its author was not identified. As fighters of pirates on the high seas, the commissioners were apparently also wary of encouraging literary pirates on land.

On June 28, 1827, Secretary Southard had evidently reconsidered the need for buying several copies of the Blunts' publications, for he sent a copy of their catalog or list of books and charts to Commodore Isaac Chauncey at the New York Navy Yard with instructions for him to examine a few of the items that he had marked on the list. If Chauncey thought that the publications were accurate "and such as we ought to possess," he was to purchase twenty-five copies of each and distribute them to the navy yards at Boston, New York, and Norfolk. It was likely that the list sent to Commodore Chauncey was not much different from the 1826 list reproduced above, in which case the commodore would have been quite familiar with the merits of the books and charts, for the navy had made many individual purchases of Blunt's publications over the years. In fact, there probably were copies of some of Blunt's works, which had been taken from ships in ordinary (such as the copy still extant of the Bowditch which had been on the bibliothecally historic voyage of the *Franklin*), available for Chauncey's inspection at the navy yard. At that time, all reusable and valuable materials, including books, removed from ships were placed under the custody of naval storekeepers and were piled in storehouses at the navy yards with the idea that these materials could be requisitioned from the public store when again needed for another vessel.

The Blunt items that Commodore Chauncey was to examine may have been intended by the secretary of the navy for use at the naval schools then in existence at the New York, Boston, and Norfolk navy yards, for just a month before, the navy commissioners had authorized the commandants of all seven of the service's navy yards to procure twenty-four other book titles for the use of officers at these stations. The titles listed in their order of May 3, 1827, were mostly technical or legal in content, and appear to have been selected to form a library reference collection rather than one for study or teaching purposes. Four additional titles, supplied directly from the commissioners' office, rounded out the list. The commandants were instructed to have the volumes lettered on their backs and sides with the wording "U.S. Navy Yard [and location]" in gold. The books were to be protected by whatever regulations the commandant of each yard established, but were not to be removed from the station without his written permission. Any loss or injury to the books due to neglect was to be made good by the party responsible for it. Although this action by the navy commissioners seems to be unrelated to the efforts which were soon to be made by the secretary of the navy to provide libraries to officers for study, the precedent for navy yard libraries probably served as the opening wedge for the provision and handling of other libraries within the service. At any rate, the navy yard book collections appear to be the first libraries ever allowed to U.S. naval units through administrative initiative.

THE NAVY DEPARTMENT LIBRARY. The purchase of books by the early navy was not confined solely to the purpose of supplying wants of individual ships and yards. A need for a collection of books within the Navy Department devoted to naval and allied subjects was perceived the same year that the Congress of the United States decided to provide for a library to serve its own needs. While destiny was to transform this parochial legislative collection into the prestigious Library of Congress, the book collection of the Navy Department remained just that for a considerable number of years. Notwithstanding this deficiency in achieving an exalted status, the library of the Navy Department more or less fulfilled its intended purpose. Certain incidents related to its history supply additional information about the provision and use of books during the formative years of the navy. This history will be the subject of the next few paragraphs since it serves to complement both the discussion which has gone before on the initial provision of requisite professional books for use on ships, and the discussion which is to follow on the initial provision of books for educational use.

From the very outset, the men in government who were responsible for the organization of the navy regarded books as essential to its administration, and their outlook encouraged the acquisition and retention of books within the service. The Department of the Navy came into being on April 30, 1798, when President John Adams signed the congressional act creating it. Hitherto, naval affairs had been conducted, not too efficiently, under the War Department. President Adams was interested in the success of the U.S. Navy as an institution of the government and to this end wanted to employ every means to insure its proher development. In a letter to Benjamin Stoddert, the first secretary of the navy, Adams set the course for the department in regard to books which would assist in attaining its goals. On March 31, 1800 he wrote:

> The President of the United States requests the Secretary of the Navy to employ some of his clerks in preparing a catalogue of books for the use of his office. It ought to consist of all the best writings in Dutch, Spanish, French, and especially in English, upon the theory and practice of naval architecture, navigation, gunnery, hydraulics, hydrostatics, and all branches of mathematics subservient to the profession of the sea. The lives of all the admirals, English, French, Dutch, or any other nation, who have distinguished themselves by the boldness and success of their navigation, or their gallantry and skill in naval combats. If there are no funds which can be legally applied by the Secretary to the purchase of such a library, application ought to be made to Congress for assistance.[9]

Two subsequent events might have prevented the immediate implementation of the president's request. The first involved the removal of the seat of government from Philadelphia to the city of Washington in mid-year 1800. Secretary Stoddert announced the official order to move the Navy Department to his clerks on May 30, and in early June, its various records were sent overland, while the printed books already in its possession and pieces of office furniture were sent by water. It appears that the department operated in an unsettled state in Washington until May, 1801, when it finally moved into more permanent quarters. By this time the second limiting event had occurred in the form of the defeat of Adams for reelection, with the resultant naming of a new naval secretary. The moves from Philadelphia and within Washington, in addition to having a disruptive effect on the business of the department, must have resulted in some loss of books. Upon inquiring after a copy of a signal book which he had furnished the office, Commodore Truxtun was informed on December 28, 1801, that "in consequence of the travelling state in which the Department has been in for sometime," all copies of it had been lost. Truxtun was advised to request from Captain John

Barry a copy of another signal book that the navy had adopted for use. Thus it appears that a book collection of sorts existed prior to the Navy Department's moving and that it was used in some reference or loan capacity.

History repeated itself just thirteen years later. Another move was made—this one quite in haste—and another signal book was not to be located afterwards. During the War of 1812, the Navy Department vacated its offices just before the British invaded Washington. The valuable effects of the department, including the library, were moved out of town in boxes and trunks to a place of safety on August 22, 1814. Everything remained secure except for certain official papers relative to navy accounts settled and transmitted to the Treasury Department. Secretary of the Navy B. W. Crowninshield was later unable to use the war as an excuse for not being able to find the only copy his office had of Commodore John Rodgers's signal book, which Commodore William Bainbridge inquired after on November 14, 1816. It had been in the department since 1812, so Crowninshield stated, "and all the books were saved when the British destroyed the public buildings in 1814."

In 1805, the seemingly uneconomical operations of the Navy Department prompted the second secretary of the navy, Robert Smith, to think of sending Commodore Edward Preble abroad in order to obtain first-hand information on how the major naval powers maintained comparatively less costly navies. The department's book collection at this time could not have been much, for in corresponding about the project, Preble echoed President Adams's proposal that a naval library be collected in the department. Although Preble was not sent to Europe, other attempts were soon made to acquire appropriate books overseas. On February 20, 1808, Lieutenant William Lewis was advanced $300 to buy in France two sets each of certain military books, from a list furnished him by Robert Smith. Lewis got as far as New York, but was still there on gunboat duty in late March, 1809. Whether the mission was finally accomplished by him or someone else is unclear.

A more notable opportunity to purchase books abroad was presented in 1825, when Commodore Charles Morris was given the special assignment to accompany General Lafayette on his return to France aboard the specially built, manned, and named frigate, *Brandywine*. The old Revolutionary War hero had just completed a long, triumphal tour of America, where incidentally, during one of the many ceremonies he took part in, he had physically and spiritually touched an adoring lad, Walt Whitman, at the cornerstone laying of the Brooklyn apprentices' library.[10] After arriving overseas with the marquis, Morris toured naval facilities in France and England, and visited many of the cultural attractions of the two countries. He was also to carry out a request of his peers on the Board of Navy Commissioners to select according to his judgment "valuable professional books and improved charts" in Europe; for the navy commissioners had $150 to $200 with which to support their project to purchase "the most approved and authentic works" then available.

During the infant years of the navy, books and charts were also acquired as gifts from authors and compilers, who sent them as gestures of their good will, or with expectations of deriving some hoped-for benefit from the government. Some of the gift items were addressed to the president of the United States, who if he did not keep them himself, probably handed them on occasion to his secretary of war or navy. George Washington received some charts of North America, dedicated to him by a London chart maker, who also sent others to Thomas Jefferson while he was president.[11] A comment by Jefferson in acknowledging the receipt of a book of tables on navigation and nautical astronomy by Joseph Mendoza y Rios, F.R.S., again points up the fact that the government did consider purchasing navigational books for ships at an early date. On May 4, 1806, Jefferson wrote the author, ". . . I have recommended to the Secretary of the Navy of the US to avail our public vessels of this publication by procuring such number of copies as he shall think their wants and our duties will justify." Both Edmund Blunt and John Garnett wrote to former President Thomas Jefferson, as a man of science and influence, in hopes that he would convince the navy that their respective almanacs be adopted. They enclosed copies of their publications as favors, but they did not receive more than letters of advice in return. Paul Hamilton, the third man to become secretary of the navy, in a letter of thanks to Dr. Edward Cutbush, Surgeon, USN, alluded to the possibility of the Navy Department's patronage being extended to his book, *Observations on the Means of Preserving the Health of Soldiers and Sailors,* if Cutbush still retained the copyright. The doctor had sent a gift copy of his treatise, published in 1808, to the secretary on July 5, 1809.

Depending upon their merits, some books brought to the attention of the Navy Department might receive support through direct subscription. For example, twenty sets of Louis de Tousard's *American Artillerist's Companion,* published 1809–1813 in Baltimore and Norfolk, were subscribed to by the navy, possibly with the view of distributing them to ships and yards; but it appears that a prospectus to subscribe to *A Treatise on the Science of War and Fortification* was never returned to its solicitor and author, John M. O'Connor, of the army. He had in his request of August 13, 1817, attempted to pit army against navy by stating that he hoped the navy would not lag behind the liberality of the War Department in support of his work. His obvious campaign to provoke rivalry between the services on his own behalf was modern in approach, and if he did not succeed in selling his book to the navy at this time, he did at a later date, for it was supplied to the navy yard libraries in 1827.

In 1810, Robert Fulton's motive in corresponding with Secretary Paul Hamilton and other government officials was not to sell books, but to get the United States government to test further his idea of underwater explosions in naval warfare. To do this, he used a book to explain his inventions and was successful in convincing Congress to appropriate $5,000 for experimental tests.[12] Several copies of his little *Torpedo War and Submarine Explosions* were sent to six senior naval officers by the secretary on May 4, 1810, with a request that they read it with the object of informing the inventor, through Commodore John Rodgers at New York, of the possible ways his system could be circumvented. Apparently they studied the book well, for Commodore Rodgers created a formidable defense for the 16-gun brig *Argus* and defeated the main experiment in New York that October. A copy of the House Committee report on the practical use of the torpedo made after the experiments were conducted was sent to Rodgers without comment by the secretary when it appeared some months later.

The Navy Department also subscribed to several newspapers from different parts of the country in order to obtain information helpful in the conduct of its daily business. Two London newspapers as well as such periodicals as the *Edinburgh Review, North American Review, Niles' Weekly Register,* and about six others were being received in 1823. Thanks to a House resolution of that year which required the executive departments of the government to transmit lists of the periodicals and books which were purchased over a period of five or six preceding years, there are enumerated in a House document all of the titles purchased by the Navy Department for the years 1817–1821. A total of some $1,326 was spent during this period for approximately 110 listed book and continuation items, which ranged in price from a half-dollar to $142 per listing. This is in contrast to $9,267 expended by the State Department, $8,674 by the War Department, and $4,032 by the Treasury Department for similar materials for their offices.[13] The purchases made by the Navy Department were for titles in the categories of periodicals, history, travel, biography, mathematics and science, law, commerce, reference, and miscellany, with the first three named categories accounting for well over one-half of the total. The Board of Navy Commissioners had to submit a list, too. Their purchases for 1817–1822 amounted to $980.98 for sixty-six items, mostly devoted to voyages and travels, which were probably imported from England. The total Navy Department expenditure was about $2,307 for books and periodicals, which was the smallest amount of money spent by the four departments.

By the year 1824, only slightly over one-half of the 110 titles reported purchased for the five-year period were still in the office of the Navy Department. A surviving manuscript catalog of the library of that date contains a total of about 128 titles. The categories of naval and military history, travel, biography, government, and periodicals account for about ninety of the titles, which were mostly in English. Another manuscript catalog, prepared in March 1829, incorporated several additions to the 1824 catalog and had a total of about 196 titles. But while it increased by some sixty-eight titles, another thirty-five that were listed in the 1824 catalog were now missing, making the net gain only thirty-three titles in five years. Books were being purchased, but their retention was precarious. Apparently some books were loaned or given to individuals and ships, or transferred within the Navy Department (*e.g.,* to the library in the Board of Navy Commissioners' office), or they simply disappeared. President Adams's dream of a comprehensive naval library had fallen short of its goal after twenty-five years of a sieve-like existence. It appears that by 1829, the library was not much more than a small collection of books under the care of one of the clerks in the office, and that its growth and quality were now more dependent on accident than design.

BOOKS AND NAVAL EDUCATION. The history of education during the early years of the navy is one of sporadic teaching efforts on sea and land. From the very inception of the service, the necessity to train young men to become officers was deemed essential by the Navy Department. The philosophy of naval education was then well enough defined: professional knowledge was to be gained through practical experience coupled with proper study. Yet the methods and means to implement the educational goals of the department were left in the hands of the individual commanding officers and a few chaplains. As a result, no uniform plan for universal instruction emerged for many years, although the benefits of such an arrangement, preferably in the form of one naval school ashore, were officially advocated very early. The many teaching situations employed on land and sea in the service led to some false starts and a few successes. These successes and failures alike, viewed in isolation by writers of naval biography and popular naval history, have provided them with material enough to claim that one or another naval hero was the first to set up classes for midshipmen, or that a particular school was the direct or spiritual precursor of the present-day Naval Academy. Thus, much that has already been recorded on the subject has been written *in vacuo,* or as part of romanticized and vainglorious accounts, the total falling short of presenting a true or complete picture. Notwithstanding the need for a full and modern history of education in the navy, the key part that books played in the educational process is evident from the various original accounts and from other sources. The remainder of this chapter will be devoted to depicting the usage of books in the navy under the prevailing educational conditions of the times.

Informal Instruction and Private Libraries. One of the earliest recorded educational situations in the navy occurred under unusual circumstances during the Barbary Wars. While enforcing the blockade against Tripoli in 1803, the frigate *Philadelphia* had the misfortune to run aground. Her crew was then captured by the enemy and jailed in the Pasha's castle, where they remained for nineteen months. During this time, the American sailors were befriended by the Danish consul, Nicholas C. Nissen, who attempted to alleviate their trying condition. Among the favors he performed for Captain William Bainbridge and his imprisoned officers was to supply them with certain books in French and English. Some of the books Nissen obtained for the prisoners might well have been aboard the *Philadelphia* at the time of her capture. The details concerning the books that he supplied them with were early obscured in legendary stories of the crew's incarceration. There is general agreement, though, that the books obtained from Nissen were put to good use in a school of instruction. During certain hours of the day the subjects of mathematics, navigation, and naval tactics were apparently taught to the midshipmen by the older officers; and the senior officers used their enforced leisure to improve themselves through varied and intensive reading.

Although impromptu instruction was later conducted among American naval prisoners in Dartmoor prison in 1815, the organized classroom exercises of the *Philadelphia's* officers were probably patterned after similar arrangements which may have been in effect aboard some of the larger ships at that time.[14] If classes were more successful in the Pasha's castle than aboard ship, it was no doubt due to the greater amount of time and supervision that was devoted to serious study by the imprisoned officers. Success of another kind also resulted from their use of books, for not only did the books afford an opportunity for self-improvement, but their continued exchange, arranged by Nissen, served as a covert means of communication between Captain Bainbridge and Commodore Edward Preble, the commanding officer of the Mediterranean Squadron at Syracuse. By writing in invisible ink (citrus juice) on the paper wrappings of the books, the two officers sent each other secret messages via the cooperative Danish consul. Through these messages it was agreed that the *Philadelphia,* having since been refloated by the enemy, should be destroyed, which was subsequently done by the American ketch *Intrepid.*

Charles Morris, who also served in the Tripolitan campaign as a mid-shipman (in fact he was the first man from the *Intrepid* to board the *Philadelphia*), described the limited educational outlook afloat in relation to his own development, which was perhaps typical of the time. In October, 1804, a few months after the burning of the *Philadelphia*, Morris was ordered to the frigate *President*. He later remarked in an autobiographical sketch:

> Hitherto my opportunities in the squadron for reading or study had been very limited. There were no books among the officers after I joined the Scourge [a brig of 16 guns to which Morris was previously attached], and few in the squadron devoted any part of their time to their use. It was my good fortune to find an exception in Lieutenant Daniel Murray of the President, and to obtain his friendship. He was a good classical scholar, well read on many subjects, conversant with the French language, and at this time studying the Italian. My fondness for reading had not been lost and it was now not only encouraged but usefully directed by Mr. Murray, whose library was placed at my disposal. My subsequent improvement may, in a great degree, be fairly attributed to his influence. . . .[15]

David Glasgow Farragut was similarly encouraged in his formative years during and after the War of 1812, and other references are to be found from this period to the tutelage extended to the younger generation of officers by their seniors, and to the private libraries owned and shared by generous naval officers. Prominent among such libraries were those of Commodores Edward Preble and Oliver Hazard Perry. Preble's library on the frigate *Constitution,* in excess of 110 volumes in 1803, consisted mostly of professional works of interest to mariners of his day (and for some years after), but included also several titles in history and travel, and a very few in law and belles lettres. On the frigate *Java* in 1816, Perry's "well selected library" on the history and antiquities of the Mediterranean region "was freely placed at the disposal of the curious." Perry encouraged everyone to read, and classes for midshipmen were reported to have been conducted under his watchful eye on this cruise.

Books and charts were prized aboard ship. But an officer having them in his possession ran the risk of losing them through the ordinary hazards of life at sea, or by theft while in port. Like other valuables, books were also subject to plunder and booty on the high seas, or to the spoils of war. Despite the niceties which were supposed to prevail among gentlemen officers in regard to personal property on occasions of naval capture, books might be taken by members of boarding parties while their commanders conveniently looked the other way. Commodore David Porter complained of receiving such treatment from the captain of HMS *Phoebe,* who captured the frigate *Essex* in March of 1814. Porter wrote, "besides being deprived of books, charts, &c. &c. both myself and officers lost many articles of our clothing, some to a considerable amount."[16] Two and one-half months later, upon the recapture by the British of one of Porter's prizes, the *Sir Andrew Hammond,* a similar occurrence caused him to note that the two American officers aboard her "had the mortification to find themselves robbed of a number of valuable articles, including a sextant, two tea-spoons, several books," and a pair of pistols.

The temptation to appropriate a few books as souvenirs of battle was by no means limited to the British. Lieutenant Isaac Mayo, USN, while helping to scuttle the vanquished HMS *Penguin,* probably acquired the several volumes of the *Bulletins of the Campaign* which are now in the library of the U.S. Naval Academy. They were presented in 1876 by his widow, and each bears a bookplate which explains: "Captured in H.B.M.S. 'Penguin' by the U.S.S. 'Hornet', off Tristan d'Acunha, March 23, 1815." A carved figure of a penguin was also removed from the brig at this time by order of the *Hornet's* commanding officer, the daring James Biddle, who later sent it to his father as a memento. On an earlier occasion, Mayo, who appears to have collected many kinds of trophies, acquired a small volume of Milton's poetical works from the British sloop-of-war *Peacock.* The fore-edge of this book (also in the U.S. Naval Academy Library) is marked with a brownish-colored stain, which according to a hand-written note on its front endpaper is blood from the death wound of Captain William Peake, R.N., who fell in the action between the sloop-of-war *Hornet* and the *Peacock* on February 24, 1813. Although the *Peacock* sank before the *Hornet* could take off survivors, there was apparently enough time, if the note in the rescued Milton is to be believed, to search the captain's cabin for valuables.

Navigational books and charts belonging to a captured ship were often more valuable than any of its other possessions. When Commodore Porter rounded the Horn in the *Essex* in early 1813, he had a desperate need to acquire appropriate charts. He then had only one chart of the whole western South American coast with him, and it was of such small scale that it could only be relied on for direction and the determination of gross features of topography. Porter hoped to find better charts aboard the first ship he could capture. As he expressed it, he had more desire to gain possession of them "than can well be conceived; for, at this time, good charts of the coast would be the greatest treasure we could meet with."

The flourishing existence of private libraries at sea around the period of the War of 1812 is further substantiated by a unique proposal that was made to form a library in common aboard HMS *Leander*. In 1816, two officers attached to this ship, who were surprised and astonished that "so useful an establishment as a public library on board his Majesty's ships of war" had been neglected up to then, offered to combine their separate book collections of "some hundreds of volumes" with those of their fellow officers. The originators of the proposal submitted a list of twenty-three well thought-out regulations for the government of the intended library. The plan called for a library committee to be appointed from the membership, as well as a librarian, who was to have sole direction of the library. Along with the books to be jointly held (each man still reserved title to his own books), other books and periodicals were to be purchased from a monthly subscription charge, which each subscriber was to be assessed. Although members could suggest titles for purchase, it seems that the main purpose of the library was to provide for scientific or professional reading. It was of course pointed out that the advantages of a "well arranged and properly conducted library" would "be productive of the most lasting and incalculable benefits" to the junior officers. In order to receive as much support as possible, there was even a provision for "friends of the library" who could donate books or money to help sustain it.

The *Leander* proposal appears to be the second publicized instance of adapting the idea of the subscription or proprietary library to the needs of various readers aboard ship. It was made the same year that the Reverend William Marks's book, *The Retrospect,* was published. As already noted, Marks had organized a religious subscription library for sailors aboard HMS *Conqueror* before the year 1810. Perhaps the proponents of the *Leander* library were aware of Marks's experiment or had read his book, as William Wood might have done several years later; but it is possible that these events were not directly influenced by one another. The idea of having crew members participate in the formation of a library appears to have been spontaneously reintroduced in one form or another from time to time, even into the twentieth century. Although the proposal for the *Leander's* library appeared in the widely read *Naval Chronicle,* no further notice was made to it or similar libraries in later issues of the magazine. Whatever the success of the plan in the Royal Navy, it apparently was never formally tried at sea by officers of the U.S. Navy.

Instruction Ashore: Navy Yards, Receiving Ships, and Other Facilities. Several schools were begun ashore, mostly aboard receiving ships at certain navy yards, during the beginning years of the service. It appears that these schools had a common conception and each followed the same course of development, inasmuch as they were fostered and encouraged by the Navy Department. Individually their fragmentary histories contribute to the knowledge of the status of education as a whole in the navy at that time.

The Washington Navy Yard was perhaps the first site at which formal instruction was held. During the years 1804–1810, classes in navigation and mathematics were taught by Chaplain Robert Thompson on board the frigate *Congress,* which was then in ordinary at the yard. On March 26, 1807, the chaplain sent Secretary of the Navy Robert Smith a list of fifteen books and several instruments which he considered absolutely necessary "for the use of the naval mathematical school and the navy-yard, Washington." He had already purchased seven of the books for $31, and suggested that the other items be bought from the firm of W. and S. Jones in London. The total list of books was confined to commonly available mathematical, nautical, and astronomy titles, except for two items on the orrery and globes published by the Jones firm; and it is probably indicative of the scope of the curriculum offered at this and other naval schools of the period. Chaplain Thompson died in 1810, but his school was continued by Chaplain Andrew Hunter, who also died in the post thirteen years later.

Another early school was started by Commodore Isaac Chauncey for the squadron on Lake Ontario at Sackett's Harbor, New York. He reported the fact to the secretary of the navy on November 30, 1814, stating that about sixty lieutenants and midshipmen were in daily attendance, and that they were being taught by his chaplain, the Reverend Cheever Felch. The commodore ended his letter with a question which was to be asked with increasing frequency by commanders ashore and afloat: "May I be permitted to purchase a few books for the use of the School?" At another lake station (on the Detroit frontier), a resourceful midshipman took matters into his own hands and borrowed, in the fall of 1813, several books to read over the winter from a sympathetic resident who had saved them from "the depredations of the enemy." Eight years later the lender was still waiting for his books to be returned, though by this time the enterprising officer had left the navy.[17]

In the instance of the school at Sackett's Harbor, no lasting benefit was derived from it, for the naval establishment on the lake was ordered to be shut down within a half-year of Chauncey's request. Chaplain Felch then went with Commodore William Bainbridge to the Mediterranean Sea aboard the *Independence* in 1815, but may have briefly conducted a school for the squadron aboard the flagship at the Boston Navy Yard prior to her departure. When he returned in 1817, according to his account, he began a school at the Boston yard on June 5, 1817; and in 1819 he started work on his "System of Studies for Midshipmen." The Navy Department was interested in the publication of this work, possibly as a course to be instituted throughout the service. Felch received an extra allowance to prepare it, but in 1831 the department had no record that it was ever completed, although he had reported that he was almost ready to finish it eleven years earlier. The fact that Felch had been asked to resign from the navy, for conduct unbecoming an officer and gentleman in 1825, probably terminated his interest in the project, if indeed he was still working on it then.

Concern for the proper teaching of midshipmen was evidenced by creation of the special rank or position of schoolmaster in the navy in 1813. In an act of Congress of that date, which provided for the construction of four 74-gun ships-of-the-line, schoolmasters were authorized for the service. For a time thereafter, chaplains (who by the naval regulations of 1802 had the additional duties of schoolmaster) continued to teach in their usual situations, and also helped out on the 74s. As Chaplain George Jones explained his duties aboard the frigates *Brandywine* and *Constitution* in 1825–1826: "It is the Chaplain's business to instruct [midshipmen] in Navigation. It is true, in large ships, a distinct officer is usually employed as instructor; but the laws impose it also on the Chaplain, and he is sometimes required to 'lend a hand.' "[18] Although Jones referred to the instructor as an officer, the seagoing schoolmaster of this period did not hold a warrant or commission, but was simply hired by the ship's captain.

Early in the second decade, schools were also begun aboard ships berthed at the navy yards in New York and Norfolk. A letter of Captain John B. Nicholson at New York, dated July 18, 1821, to the Board of Navy Commissioners, mentioned that many midshipmen who were attending the naval academy (as these early shore schools were sometimes called) aboard his ship, the *Washington,* 74, seldom applied themselves to their studies. This was another plaintive remark of the times often repeated by those responsible for providing education in the navy. Midshipmen attached to the sloops *Hornet* and *Cyane,* and the 74s *Franklin* and *Ohio,* which were at the yard, also studied mathematics and navigation with the *Washington's* schoolmaster, Edward C. Ward. The arrangement indicates that an effort had been made to have the available midshipmen in the yard report to one chaplain or schoolmaster for instruction as had been done at Sackett's Harbor and Boston. In December, 1823, Chaplain Cave Jones was reported to be instructing midshipmen in mathematics and other subjects aboard the *Washington,*

at the New York yard. It was at this time and place that he and William
Wood were successful in getting the crew of the *Erie* to subscribe to a
library of 500 volumes.

In Norfolk, the same pattern was more or less followed in setting up a
school at the navy yard. Captain Arthur Sinclair was responsible for
its inception aboard the frigate *Guerriere,* in ordinary, in 1821. He, however, anticipated a more ambitious teaching program inasmuch as he
mentioned to his schoolmaster that instruction in mathematics, navigation, history, geography, English grammar, hydraulics, and other subjects would be useful to the young officers attached to the yard. French
and fencing were included among the other subjects. Instruction in them
was to be given by a French teacher and a fencing master, respectively,
who were "to be procured at the expense of the young men."

The practice of engaging teachers for privately supported instruction,
especially in foreign languages, was resorted to for many years in the
navy. In 1816, the *Java* apparently had a teacher of Spanish and French,
and had a fencing instructor so employed for the midshipmen. The opportunity of serving as a hired tutor (or as a musician) aboard an American
warship at times also afforded a foreigner the means of gaining passage
to the United States. One such teacher of Spanish advertised his availability to the general public as a "professor" of this language in the July
11, 1821, issue of the *National Intelligencer.* Sr. Mariano Cubi, a native
of Castile, was proud to give as a reference his several months of experience in that capacity aboard the sloop *Peacock,* then just returned from
a cruise; and four obliging "officers" of the vessel signed their names to
the advertisement attesting to the claim and to their satisfaction with
Cubi's abilities as a teacher.

While arrangements were made for special instructors to teach a group
of officers *in situ* at their own expense, some midshipmen and officers,
as individuals, took advantage of other educational opportunities ashore.
A few, over the years, attended courses at various colleges and even
West Point. Others, including merchant seamen, took advantage of
private lessons or short classes in navigation, astronomy, mathematics,
and languages, which were given in "schools" conducted by instructors in
their homes or in waterfront locations. Edward C. Ward, who also
taught midshipmen for the navy, in 1821 advertised that he would teach
"gentlemen designed for, or belonging to the sea" in his own "Naval
Academy" at the corner of Fulton and Water Streets in New York.

During the 1820s a school popular for military education was the
American Literary, Scientific and Military Academy conducted by
former Captain Alden Partridge, USA, at Norwich, Vermont.[19] Several
young naval officers enrolled in the complete course in navigation and
seamanship which was offered at Captain Partridge's academy for a few

years. The captain had long been aware of the necessity for an institution for the education of young officers in the navy, and had attempted to accommodate his facilities accordingly. He even moved the academy to Middletown, Connecticut, for a time, apparently to be near the sea and shore, and so be more accessible to potential seafaring students. The library at his academy in 1827 consisted of 1,100 volumes in many fields, while that of West Point was about the same size, and Yale was under 8,000 volumes. John Pintard had much to say about Partridge's academy and the activities of its founder. One item of appropriate interest in this regard pertained to several lectures that Captain Partridge was to give in New York in 1826. Pintard hoped to distribute the proceeds obtained from these lectures to the infant mechanic apprentices', and mercantile libraries, and to found a "Military Library" for the use of militia officers of the city.

Instruction at Sea: The Beginnings of Navy Libraries for Education. Although the navy provided limited instruction ashore, it did not require midshipmen to attend the classes, and did not provide traveling expenses to those away from a navy yard who might desire to take advantage of the opportunity offered at one. An estimate of the number of midshipmen who at one time were taking instruction at the navy yard schools was put at about one-seventh of the total in the navy. Most of the others, it is presumed, were taught at sea where the same teaching goals influenced the kind and amount of instruction that was offered. If learning was impaired on land by midshipmen having too much leisure and too many outside temptations to distract them, at sea conditions appear to have been just as bad, although to impressionable landsmen like Auguste Levasseur and Henry Marie Brackenridge, taking passage on U.S. warships, it might have seemed otherwise.[20] The learning process afloat was further limited by shipboard routine and other restraints, including the nonavailability of materials. As noted earlier, in the case of the *Franklin* prior to her departure in 1821, her schoolmaster had requested certain books for his department, only to be told that the young officers requiring the books should provide them themselves.

This situation still prevailed aboard the smaller vessels of the navy in 1827. When Master Commandant Lawrence Kearney, on January 30, submitted to the secretary of the navy a list of a dozen or so books which a teacher aboard his sloop, the *Warren,* had suggested as "serviceable . . . in teaching the young gentlemen," he was told that no library was allowed by the regulations to vessels of the *Warren's* class. Secretary Samuel Southard further explained, "I cannot approve the purchase of them at the public expense without sanctioning a similar allowance for all the Sloops of War, however serviceable it might be to give the junior officers every opportunity of instruction; heretofore they have furnished their own books." He did, however, authorize the navy agent at New York to send the *Warren* six copies of Darcy Lever's *Young Sea Officer's Sheet Anchor.* The sloop's purser was to sell five of the copies to those officers who wished to own one; but the sixth copy was to be retained for the use of the ship.[21]

A supply of the *Sheet Anchor,* purchased by the department from Carey and Lea in 1825, made this and similar acts of seeming generosity possible. Upon the recommendation of the navy commissioners, who had received what they considered an attractive proposal from the publishers, at least 100 copies of the book were obtained at $5.00 each, with the view of making them available at cost. The young officers were then to have "the opportunity . . . to provide themselves with that useful work, for a far less price" than they would have had to pay separately at the booksellers. Secretary Southard on at least two earlier occasions distributed several copies of the book to naval vessels with instructions for their sale according to the plan. In these instances, he also made what might have been the first unsolicited gestures toward supplying free books for educational purposes. When he dispatched thirty copies of the *Sheet Anchor* to Commodore Isaac Hull on June 2, 1825, to be apportioned among the vessels on the Pacific Station, he wrote that free use of them was to be granted "to all the young officers during their leisure hours." To Commodore Charles Morris, on his mission to accompany General Lafayette back to France on the navy's showpiece, the *Brandywine* frigate, Southard that September 1, sent twenty-five copies "for the use of the Officers of that vessel."

As was implied in Secretary Southard's letter to Master Commandant Kearney on the *Warren,* the conditions concerning books for teaching had improved somewhat for ships-of-the-line since the *Franklin's* cruise of 1821–1824. On January 5, 1828, Commodore John Downes was allowed a total of seventeen copies of seven different books for the use of the school aboard the *Delaware,* 74, before her departure to the Mediterranean Sea. The books that the commodore was permitted to procure, as listed by the navy commissioners, consisted of two copies each of three mathematical texts, and two books on navigation, three nautical almanacs, and four copies of Bowditch's *New American Practical Navigator.* Two sextants, a pair of eighteen-inch globes, and "two cases of small mathematical instruments" were also allowed.

One other bit of evidence helps complete the survey of the status of books and instruction during this period. It involves the preparations which Andrew H. Foote and Charles H. Davis made in order to ready themselves to take the examination for the rank of passed midshipman. While aboard the *United States* (at the time when Commodore Hull received copies of the *Sheet Anchor*) the two midshipmen studied together, using the resources at hand to develop their own study-aid which took the form of a manuscript text-book.[22] Although Davis later recalled the so-called book and his studies, he did not mention being taught aboard the frigate, or the presence of any kind of library. When he arrived in New York in 1827, he applied for leave, in order that he might go home to Boston and study further for the examination.

* * * * *

The methods and means employed by the government in order to provide a naval education to young officers were more or less in keeping with the times. An ambivalent attitude toward higher education prevailed in antebellum America. Practical educational experience gained through an apprenticeship or by hard work was considered of more value than a college education, which was mostly regarded as a luxury of the rich. Yet many colleges were founded during the period. Most, however, were provided with little financial support, and thus exhibited the stultifying effects of a penurious existence. Conservative in outlook, the early colleges clung to a classical curriculum which was taught mostly by ministerially oriented teachers. An emphasis was placed on order and discipline, and the textbook-inspired lessons were often learned by rote. The colleges offered little in the way of relevance to the needs of ordinary society, and their libraries contained little to promote scholarship.[23] The U.S. Military Academy, founded at West Point in 1802, was the only college to have a formal program in engineering in the 1820s. And the government was not convinced that it needed another such institution to train naval officers. It was thought that mathematics, navigational theory, and foreign languages could be taught and learned anywhere, but the ship at sea was the best place to learn to become a naval officer.

Thus, the navy was left to bridge the gap between practical instruction and professional education as best it could with limited resources. By not having a formalized college of its own, it was perhaps more receptive to current civilian pedagogic practices and more susceptible to popular educational movements than it might otherwise have been. In the second decade, as evidenced by the activities of William Wood, religious and benevolent groups, and others, the encouragement of education for Everyman through the use of libraries was in the wind; and the navy, ever mindful of its dilemma, accordingly trimmed its sails in order to take advantage of this fresh concept.

Chapter VII

Libraries in the Navy, 1828-1860

To the fortunate, there is no life
like that of a sailor—we roam
the world at no expense; our libraries
travel with us . . .

—Frederick Chamier

THE SHIP'S LIBRARY: *Origin and History.* The schools provided
for midshipmen at the navy yards and at sea were more or less regarded
by successive secretaries of the navy as a temporary expedient against
the day when Congress would establish one permanent academy ashore.
Several proposals were entertained in the legislative chambers to this
effect over the years, but no positive action was ever taken. Following
on the heels of another defeat of a bill in Congress in 1827 to create a
naval academy, Secretary Samuel Southard, who had endured a relatively long tenure and hence gained an appreciation of the problems that
beset the navy in regard to education, began to assert the initiative. He
encouraged the employment of schoolmasters aboard sloops-of-war,
provided for better classroom facilities ashore, and made available
more materials—books and ancillary supplies and equipment—needed
for teaching and study. The means for providing books had always
been at hand, but the idea or desire to supply them uniformly in quantity,
that is, as libraries, had never been broached.
　Coincidentally with the rekindling of interest in the spiritual and educational goals of the American Seamen's Friend Society in New York,
and in keeping with the popular movement toward the establishment of

libraries for various occupational groups ashore, Secretary Southard
launched his own library-oriented educational program. On January 21,
1828, he wrote to Commodore John Rodgers, president of the Board of
Navy Commissioners:

> I should be very glad to make such an arrangement as will
> provide books for the use of our vessels in commission, es-
> pecially such as are necessary for the studies of the Midshipmen,
> and should be gratified by an answer to the following ques-
> tions—
> 1. Out of what funds can they be best provided?
> 2. What books ought they to be?
> 3. Under what regulations placed on board the vessels?
> 4. What disposition made of them on the return of the vessels
>   to port?[1]

Rodgers and his two fellow board-members, Commodores Lewis
Warrington and Daniel T. Patterson, were not long in replying. They
answered the secretary's questions on January 24, and attached a list
of thirty-seven book titles which were grouped in four categories: "Mathematics, History, Philosophical, and Miscellaneous." The books were
entirely different from the ones they had previously authorized for the
navy yards in May of 1827, and for teaching purposes aboard the *Delaware* a few days earlier. Their recommendations must have been dictated from memory, for a few of the titles included on the list did not
exist as such, and several spelling errors and omissions of words further
confused the listing. Nevertheless, Southard, after correcting the more
obvious mistakes, on January 28, sent the list of books to the commandants of five navy yards in the form of a department circular, or directive.
His historic order incorporated almost word for word the suggestions
which the navy commissioners had furnished him concerning the administrative handling of the libraries, but the first paragraph contained his
own sentiments on the subject. He wrote:

> I enclose a list of books which it is thought would be useful
> and lend to the promotion of study and diffusion of knowledge
> among the junior Officers of the Navy while at sea.
> Whenever a vessel is about to sail on a cruise from the sta-
> tion under your command you will order the Navy Agent or
> Purser to purchase the books mentioned in the list which are to
> be paid for from the appropriations for contingent expenses
> and placed on board in charge of her commander.
> You will instruct the commander to direct the School Master,

or some other suitable person to see that proper care is taken of the books, and when he returns to the United States to have them packed up in a box, labelled and delivered to the commandant of the yard where he may arrive.

The sloop-of-war *Falmouth* was the first vessel promised a library. Her captain, Master Commandant Charles W. Morgan, had written to Southard from Charlestown, Massachusetts, on January 15, to inquire about books and instruments for a school aboard his ship, and to report that a schoolmaster had been "provided from Harvard University with the best recommendations from the professors" of that institution. This letter may have triggered the secretary's action, for Southard had put off answering the *Falmouth's* captain until after he issued his library order. He then informed Morgan that Commodore James Barron at the Gosport Navy Yard would furnish the *Falmouth* with the necessary books upon her arrival at that port.

Unlike the order to provide libraries to the navy yards issued a half-year earlier by the navy commissioners, the order to provide libraries to ships for the use of officers caused some inquiries and comment from various parties concerned with carrying it out. This was due in part to the errors contained in the listed book titles and to the inclusion on the list of some items which, as it turned out, were not readily available on the American book market. The navy agent in New York, James K. Paulding (who at this time was gaining a literary reputation, and who would himself later become secretary of the navy), after attempting to purchase all of the titles, concluded that eight of them could not be had. He had made inquiries among the booksellers in Philadelphia and Boston as well as New York without success. Because the sloop-of-war *Hornet* would soon require a library, he wrote to Secretary Southard, on May 5, 1828, to suggest that certain substitutions be made. At this time Paulding recommended one addition to the list which he believed had no equal as a book, and which would serve to inspire naval officers with "a noble ambition."[2] The book was his old friend Washington Irving's *History of the Life and Voyages of Christopher Columbus,* which had just been published. Southard added it to the list and readily adopted Paulding's other practical and worthwhile suggestions and at the same time authorized all the navy yards to make the modifications on May 16, 1828.

Another change to the list came about when Master Commandant John D. Sloat in December, 1828, suggested a pair of globes as a substitution for Charnock's *Naval Architecture* and the *Analectic Magazine,* two items which Paulding had previously reported unavailable. Sloat's command, the sloop-of-war *St. Louis,* at the Washington Navy Yard, was furnished a library for $398 from Pishey Thompson's bookstore of that city. A few of the titles purchased for the library were not on the official list, and a few others, in addition to the two already mentioned, were not supplied. Notice of this transaction was sent to Navy Agent Paulding in New York on December 17, 1828. Southard still had some copies of Lever's *Sheet Anchor* on hand which the department had purchased back in 1825. On December 19, he sent the *St. Louis* twelve (one for the library and the balance for sale), and a copy of a work on treaties of the government, which he told Master Commandant Sloat to handle as a library book.

From the Philadelphia Navy Yard, Commodore William Bainbridge, long accustomed to the apportionment of stores to naval vessels according to their respective classes, inquired of the secretary, on October 17, 1828, whether it was intended that the sloop-of-war *Vandalia* should be furnished with the same library as larger vessels. The answer was affirmative. Southard meant to furnish all of his officers with the same quality and quantity of books regardless of the kind of ship they served on. In 1831–1832, the library list was reissued, and made to apply to navy yards as well. This new list of titles included all the modifications to the original 1828 list, and appeared in the *Rules of the Navy Department Regulating the Civil Administration of the Navy,* published in 1832 (fig. 7, and Appendix C). It served, with further changes, until revised in 1839.

During the years between the appearance of the 1832 regulations and the compilation of the revised list of books in 1839, the ship's library (also referred to as "officers' library," and "cabin library") became a standard feature aboard naval vessels. Secretary Southard left office in 1829, but fortunately his project was nurtured rather than abandoned in its infancy by his two immediate successors, John Branch and Levi Woodbury. Secretary Woodbury felt strongly enough about books to mention in his 1831 annual report to the president that it was believed "greater benefits of education to the youthful midshipman, while at sea, could be obtained by a more liberal compensation to schoolmasters, and sedulous attention to the purchase and preservation of nautical books and instruments." There was a final question in 1834 from Commodore Barron concerning whether some books imported to complete the libraries at the Philadelphia Navy Yard should be approved; otherwise, the program appeared to have been accepted as one of some permanence within the service. Secretary Woodbury authorized their purchase on April 5, thus indicating his administration's full support of the library plan.

Some notice of the new libraries was also taken by a few contemporary naval writers. Enoch C. Wines, a schoolmaster aboard the *Constellation*

CHAPTER XXI.

BOOKS.

§ 1. The following list of books will be furnished for the use of vessels of war when on a cruise, and for the use of the Yards:

Elements of Trigonometry
Euclid's Elements
Bowditch's Navigation
Douglas on Marine Artillery
Marshall's Hand Book on the equipment of guns.
Ramsay's Universal History
History of Rome
Milford's Greece
Rollin's Ancient History
Gibbon's Decline and Fall of the Roman Empire.
History of England
Marshall's Life of Washington
Botta's American Revolution
Modern Europe
Vattels Law of Nations
American Atlas, compiled on the plan of Le Sage
La Voisne's Atlas

Pair of Globes
Jacobson's Sea Laws
Charnock, and others, on Naval Architecture
State Papers
Federalist
Walsh's Appeal
Ledyard's Travels
Vanconver's Voyages
Ross's Voyages
Parry's Voyages
Franklin's Voyages
Life and Voyages of Columbus
Encyclopedia Britannica with its supplement
North American Sylva
Work on conversion and preservation of timber
Hutton's Tracts
Arnot's Natural Philosophy
Nicholson's ditto
Bible and Prayer Book

§ 2. Books furnished at the public expense, for the libraries of ships or yards, will be confined to the above catalogue.

§ 3. All books furnished, must be receipted for by the commander of a vessel or station, and accounted for when he quits the vessel or station. *Sept.* 1831.

(*Note.* An original list of books was furnished 28th January, 1828, which was modified on the 16th May following. On the 11th December, same year, other works were authorized to be added ; and on the 23d February, 1831, the above list, embracing all previous modifications, was ordered.)

7. Library list for U.S. naval vessels and navy yards, 1832.

(1829–1831) mentioned in his book, *Two Years and a Half in the Navy* (1832), that "of late years" it had become customary for a "public library" to be supplied to vessels in active service. Because he probably had access to the new 1832 naval regulations, he erroneously assumed that Levi Woodbury, then secretary of the navy, was responsible for the inception and content of the library. Wines's opinion of the catalog of books printed in the regulations was that it did not contain a title that should not have been there, "and in the quality and quantity of solid aliment," it left "perhaps little to be desired." Yet he did think that more books, written in any literary form, which contained descriptions of countries and places visited by naval officers should have been included, for he had observed that these were the kinds of books most sought after aboard ship. He also mentioned the location of the library as being in the captain's cabin, which aboard a frigate was located in the space abaft the mizzenmast on the main or gun-deck. The captain's cabin was divided into four compartments: the forward cabin, the after cabin, and two staterooms. "One of the state-rooms was appropriated to the library, and the other was the captain's sleeping-room." A pair of the frigate's main guns was also housed in the captain's cabin; so in effect, he shared his accommodations with two other symbols of authority on shipboard— the guns representing might, and the books, wisdom. When the frigate was cleared for action, the bulkhead that separated the forward cabin from the rest of the deck was removed so that the guns could be worked.[3] It was in this area, also, that a library aboard the frigate *United States* was located in 1844, according to her log. Aboard the frigate *Potomac* in 1831–1834, the library specified in her sailing orders, and in charge of her schoolmaster, was said to have been shelved in the "hurricane house," which in this case was probably a "round house," or an extra stern cabin such as Commodore Stewart had constructed on the *Franklin* in 1821 as a "light half poop" directly above the captain's cabin.

William McNally, a gunner, described the library furnished by the government for the *Lexington* in 1831–1833 as being made up of large, handsomely-bound volumes, chiefly professional in content. He also mentioned that books from the library were loaned to him through the kindness of Master Commandant Isaac McKeever, but that he "had to bow and scringe to his clerk" in order to get them. Two other accounts fail to mention specifically the library for officers aboard the *Guerriere* in 1829, or the *Brandywine* in 1830, although a "public" subscription library is noted for the former, and a library comprising several hundred volumes, which was probably also a subscription library, is referred to in the latter. If there was either an official or a subscription library aboard the sloop-of-war *Concord* in 1830–1832, it was not mentioned in a recent extensive biography of Matthew C. Perry, the sloop's commander at the time. Rather, the library referred to is more reminiscent of the one Alexander Slidell Mackenzie described as being aboard Oliver Hazard Perry's frigate *Java* in 1816.

Chaplain Charles Rockwell commented upon the library aboard the *Potomac* in 1834–1837 in general terms. He observed that it consisted "of an Encyclopaedia, a few standard works of national and natural history, a collection of voyages and travels, works on gunnery and naval tactics, and navigation, the state papers of the United States, &c." But he criticized the library for being deficient in works on science and geography, even though he thought their presence would not have done the officers much good. In his estimation their early literary and scientific education had been neglected for want of a naval academy. His consideration of the library was obviously directed toward its value as a reference rather than a teaching resource. The disgruntled mathematics professor, Joshua Henshaw, on the *Columbia* in 1838, also brought up the subject of science, only to note the lack of accommodation for "philosophical instruments and for cabinet specimens," and the absence of a billet for a naturalist. He said nothing of the ship's library, which he was supposed to have been in charge of, in addition to the crew's subscription library. William M. Murrell, aboard the *Columbia* on the same voyage, was silent about both libraries. Perhaps these two writers took the ship's library for granted or did not think it important enough to mention in their accounts.

The existence of the ship's library provided at least a plausible reason to deny some of the requests for the purchase of special books for teaching which were still directed to the secretary of the navy and the Board of Navy Commissioners by schoolmasters and ship commanders. Certain books requested for the *Concord* and the *North Carolina* in 1836, and for the *John Adams* in 1838, were denied on the grounds that the books and instruments already aboard these vessels were deemed sufficient. The requesters were further advised, as others had been in the past, that any additional books that were thought necessary were to be procured by the "young gentlemen" at their own expense. Consciously or unconsciously, the first steps toward an officially promulgated and uniform reading list had been taken and enforced.

Several recommendations for additions or substitutions to the libraries were sent to the secretary of the navy over the years by officers who were interested in improving the contents of the libraries. Although some positive action was usually taken on these individual requests, only a few items so approved were ever added to the official list for all libraries. Several other requests were either flatly denied or were put off and then apparently forgotten. When Navy Agent James K. Paulding wrote to Secretary Woodbury in 1832 to recommend that Commodore

David Porter's voyages, and another work be substituted for Parry's and Ross's voyages, he received a terse reply to the effect that his communication had been referred to the navy commissioners, who were revising the list of books.[4] This was just a few months after the 1832 regulations were published. Yet five years later, the navy commissioners were reluctant to consider any changes in the list. They advised Secretary Mahlon Dickerson on June 17, 1837, that due to the differences in reading taste and outlook among officers, it would not be expedient to alter the content of the libraries without consulting the opinions of several of them; and they half-heartedly mentioned that a board of officers to decide the changes might be advisable. Commodore Lewis Warrington, who displayed a continued interest in the libraries, had written to the secretary at this time to suggest a few substitutions of titles for the libraries which he thought would be more beneficial and less costly.

When the list was finally revised in June, 1839, the deliberate proceedings outlined by the navy commissioners two years previously apparently were not followed. The revision, itself, appears to have been brought about by the publication of James Fenimore Cooper's *History of the Navy of the United States,* which James K. Paulding, now the secretary of the navy, had just read and admired. On May 20, Paulding wrote to his friend Cooper "as a fellow scribe" to tell him of the pleasure that the book had afforded him. Paulding thought so much of it that he declared, "I shall direct this [book], with your *nautical* Novels, to be added to the Libraries of the Public Ships, for I know not where our young officers can find better practical illustrations of Seamanship than they contain." The *History* was added to the list on the same day;[5] and Cooper's novels, *The Pilot, The Red Rover, The Water-Witch,* and *Homeward Bound* were prominent as the only items of fiction on the newly revised list, which appeared on June 10, 1839 (fig. 8, and Appendix D). Washington Irving's saga of the fur trade, *Astoria,* commissioned by John Jacob Astor also made the new list, not that Paulding had any use for the old "grub worm" as he later called Astor, but because the Irving book had appeared in 1836, and he probably did not wish to slight his brother-in-law. Perhaps Paulding justified the book to himself, at least, as being of interest to naval officers, should they ever venture to the Columbia River region. He was, in effect, following the advice of schoolmaster Enoch Wines, who had earlier recommended descriptive travel books for ships' libraries. Several similar books, a few written by navy men, were also included in the revised list, one of them being the Porter's voyages that Paulding had suggested in 1832, but which Secretary Woodbury had then chosen to ignore, and two others requested by Commodore Charles Read (apparently for his private use) on the *Columbia* in 1838.

1839, June

The following books will be furnished for the use of Vessels of War when on a cruise and for the use of Navy Yards, until otherwise ordered.

Navy Department, June 10th 1839.

Nicholsons Mathematics.	Porters Voyage 2d Edition published by Wiley N Y
Euclids Elements.	Ross, Parry's & Franklins Voyages
Bowditchs Navigation.	Life & Voyages of Columbus
Maurys do	Bancrofts History of the U States
Ramsays Universal History.	Prescotts Ferdinand & Isabella
Gibbons History – Decline & Fall of Rome.	Coopers Naval History of the U.S.
Fergusons History of Roman Republic.	do Pilot
Gillies History of Greece.	do Red Rover
Rollins ancient History.	do Water Witch.
Lingards History of England.	do Homeward Bound
Constitution of the U.S. & the different States.	Encyclopedia Britannica
Marshalls Life of Washington.	Huttons Tracts
Bottas American Revolution (until Bancrofts is completed)	Arnotts Natural Philosophy
Hallams constitutional History	Wood & Baches Dispensary
Vattels Law of Nations.	Walsh's Appeal.
Bradfords Atlas.	Kents Commentaries
Jacobsons Sea Laws.	Incidents of Travel in Egypt, Arabia & the Holy Land.
Gordons Digest, or Ingersolls abridgement of US Laws	A year in Spain
Treaties with foreign Powers.	Lives & Voyages of Drake Cavendish & Dampier.
Federalist.	Historical account of the Circumnavigation of the Globe,
Ledyards Travels.	from the Voyage of Magellan to the death of Cook
Astoria.	Plutarchs Lives.
Voyage of the Potomac.	Bibles & Prayer book
	Elem. Naval Tactics
	Translation of Kir de Horks naval tactics

Note:— In the foregoing lists are comprised, with a few exceptions, the works authorised for Vessels on a cruise & for Navy Yards, by the order of 23d Feby 1831. and such as have been since added.—

8. Library list for U.S. naval vessels and navy yards, 1839.
National Archives

Three technical items which had been officially added to the original list were still retained. They were a pharmacopoeia, recommended by Warrington in 1834, Lieutenant Maury's *Treatise on Navigation,* and Kent's *Commentaries*—both of which had been approved in 1836. However, other items such as the continuation of the *Military and Naval Magazine,* and the American "State Papers," which had been previously allowed for the service as a whole, did not appear on the new list. Neither did many of the items that had been authorized in individual situations. Of particular note is the absence of any books on the subject of steam engineering, even though Captain Matthew C. Perry had been given permission in 1837 to acquire Lardner's *Steam Engine* and other similar titles for use of the navy's first steam vessel, the *Fulton.* The newly revised list exhibited the interests and prejudices of a literary secretary of the navy who appeared to be more enamored with the romance of the sea than mindful of the realities of the day.

Paulding's list was relatively short-lived. As in the case of its predecessors of 1828 and 1832, there were almost immediate requests to add or substitute titles. About a half-dozen new books were allowed as additions within the next three years. The question of granting books on steam engineering appeared again from several quarters. Pressure was slowly being generated by naval officers interested in the application of steam in the navy. On April 8, 1840, Paulding changed slightly the words to the old navy refrain of refusal when he stated the reason for denying the purchase of Tredgold's *Steam Engine* to Navy Agent John R. Livingston. He observed, "the Department does not conceive that the government is under any obligation to furnish Engineers with books to enable them properly to discharge their duty for which they receive a liberal compensation." In justice to Paulding, it might be added that this policy was in keeping with the practice in the merchant marine, and it was also observed by other employers at the time. The employee was to become proficient in his chosen trade or profession at his own expense— an obligation still prevalent today in many fields, but no longer so in the armed services.

Steam presented yet another problem as far as books and libraries were concerned. Was the same list of books as established for vessels in general to be allowed to the new classes called "steamers"? This question, posed by Commodore Stewart from the Philadelphia Navy Yard, was relayed to Secretary Paulding on his last day in office, March 3, 1841, by the navy commissioners. He replied verbally to the effect that they should present their views on the matter. They did, but not to him. Being politically astute, the navy commissioners seized the opportunity to revise the entire list to their own satisfaction. They then brought up the subject again on May 13, 1841, and presented their results to the new secretary of the navy, George E. Badger, as a *fait accompli.*

In submitting the new list, the navy commissioners recommended that the number of books allowed a vessel should be dependent on its class, and enclosed a table of allowances which apportioned each title on this basis. Steamers were not left out, and navy yards were to receive the same titles as the largest vessels of war. The proposed list of allowances was made up of titles which had been on the previous lists, but most of the literary and travel additions made during Paulding's term in office were now deleted. In their stead were added books on gunnery, tactics, steam, mechanics, and others of substance, including a few titles in history, the classics, and literature. The list prepared by the navy commissioners reveals that they were not out of touch with the times or the requirements of their fellow officers in these regards. Significantly, they also recognized the educational needs of the men before the mast, for they stated in their letter to the secretary, "a cheap selection of books for the use of the Seamen is also recommended." At a time when naval chaplains, acting out of a feeling of frustration and righteous duty, were supplying ships with the only free materials available to them—religious books and tracts—the navy commissioners proposed that the government provide seamen with substantial secular literature; at a time when more books of professional interest and diversity were needed by officers, they selected wisely.

Secretary Badger endorsed the board's proposal on May 19, 1841, and at the same time inquired what the costs of the libraries would be and asked what the titles of the books intended for the seamen were. The commissioners replied a month later that the libraries allowed to ships-of-the-line, frigates, large steamers, sloops-of-war, and small vessels carrying over six guns would amount to $313.70 each. The contents of the seamen's libraries was listed on a separate enclosure and was estimated at about $100. The total cost of libraries was put at $413.70 for each seagoing vessel, or $421.70 for each navy yard, which was to receive certain additional works on courts-martial for $8.00. In a postscript, it was suggested that the libraries of sloops and small vessels might be reduced by half, as they did not "afford the room for the preservation of extensive libraries."

The new ship's library list must have met with Secretary Badger's early approval, for in mid-July he authorized Commodore Morris to purchase all of the proposed professional titles for his new command, the *Delaware*. Morris had been president of the Board of Navy Commissioners at the time the new list was prepared, and he was succeeded as president by Commodore Warrington, another board member. The presence of these two book-minded officers on the board at this time probably accounted for the quality of the lists which were produced. The 1841 officers' and seamen's library lists were the last prepared by the board, which was abolished the following year. But the lists also stand as historic milestones in the progress of education in the navy, for they mark the peak years in the program to provide libraries. No future library lists would ever be as essential to the navy. In a few years the sailor in the lower ranks would again be forgotten officially as far as libraries were concerned, and the founding of the naval school at Annapolis would alter the educational aspect of the officers' library and tend to lessen its total effect. The remaining history of the ship's library is in a sense anticlimatic.

On October 13, 1841, the two lists as prepared by the navy commissioners, with slight modifications, were made official by Abel P. Upshur, a day after he assumed the office of secretary of the navy (fig. 9, and Appendix E). Two years later they were again reissued under his signature through the Bureau of Construction, Equipment and Repair.[6] This administrative office, which was given the responsibility for libraries as part of its duties, was one of five bureaus (*i.e.,* Navy Yards and Docks; Construction, Equipment and Repair; Provisions and Clothing; Ordnance and Hydrography; Medicine and Surgery) created in place of the Board of Navy Commissioners when the Navy Department was reorganized by an act of Congress in 1842. In the new library lists of March 3, 1843, the content of the seamen's library remained virtually unchanged, but the ship's library catalog was altered to include brigs in the same column of the tables as sloops-of-war, and four book titles were deleted, while one was added to the list.

For the next two years libraries were supplied to vessels and navy yards in accordance with the new listings. The books acquired during this period, as it turned out, were made to serve the navy's needs until 1852, even though another catalog was prepared in 1844. About the time that the 1843 ship's library list appeared, work was begun on the revision of the tables of allowances for all kinds of stores and equipment in the navy, including libraries. Captain Thomas W. Wyman was named as the senior officer of a board of review to accomplish this purpose. He was aided by two commanders and several experienced officers and petty officers whose specialties were gunnery, carpentry, sailmaking, and seamanship. The chiefs of the bureaus (Charles Morris and Lewis Warrington among them) also took part in the review, which culminated in the publication by the department of a comprehensive, quarto-sized book of fourteen tables of allowances in late 1844.[7]

Among the tables was a four-page listing of 140 book titles headed, "Table No. XIII—Library Equipment." It specified the book allowances

9. First page of the library list for U.S. naval vessels and navy yards, 1841–1843. The companion seamen's library listing is reproduced in fig. 5 and Appendix A.

National Archives

for fourteen different classes of vessels, but did not list navy yards nor include any books for seamen's libraries. This was the largest and most detailed list ever prepared and is of interest in itself because it was a classified book catalog, possibly the first ever printed by the navy. The titles listed in it had been chosen for their professional value, and were arranged by subject in the following order: religion, law, science, technology, naval science, geography, voyages, history, and biography. Although these broad topic headings were not printed as such in the list, a close look at it reveals that a definite subject arrangement was used and that it was a slight adaptation of Jacques Brunet's scheme of book classification. The Brunet arrangement, developed in editions of this French bookseller's *Manuel du libraire et de l'amateur de livres,* was widely known and used in Europe, and had been introduced in the United States by the elder Benjamin Peirce at Harvard University Library in 1830. The compilers of Table XIII had either used it or another work based upon it, such as the five-volume *Catalogue général des livres composant les bibliothèques du Département de la marine et des colonies* (1838–1843), as a model for their own list.

A prefatory note in the newly prepared 1844 *Tables of Allowances of Equipment, Outfits, Stores, &c, &c, &c.* indicated that the tables were for "prospective use" and were not to affect vessels already in commission, except when they were in need of repair or refitting. Although the note was dated January, 1844, it appears that it was not until early 1845 that printed copies of the tables were distributed. Almost as soon as they were sent out, however, Table XIII was revoked on April 9, 1845, by George Bancroft, who had become secretary of the navy a month before. Bancroft ordered that until further notice, libraries were to be completed from the books already available in the public store, "agreeably to the list as it existed before the Tables of Allowances were issued," and that no new book purchases were to be made. Table XIII was to be considered as no longer in force. The Norfolk Navy Yard nevertheless contracted to buy all the books on the list, in addition to all the books on the 1843 ship's library and seamen's library lists. The report of this transaction is valuable today, for it indicates the probable prices paid for most of the individual titles the navy had authorized over the years.

Bancroft's order not to purchase any new books was probably prompted by a desire to economize. In 1842 Secretary Upshur had begun using the status of the appropriated funds as an excuse for denying special book requests, in addition to refusing requests because they were not listed as allowable books. Secretary Bancroft and his immediate successors, however, appear to have reverted to the pre-Southard approach of frugality and non-uniformity in the provision of books. The only differences at this time were that a book stock existed within the naval establishment, as well as the precedent for libraries.

As early as July, 1845, the pinch was being felt. The commander of the sloop-of-war *John Adams* at this time complained about the inadequacy of the ship's library (it was twelve titles short by the old allowance list), and requested to no apparent avail that it be furnished with "such additional works as should be allowed."[8] Purchases again were being questioned, and makeshift arrangements were suggested or ordered, such as having the *Ohio,* in 1846, forego the expense of acquiring certain sets of books because they were already aboard the *Independence,* in the same squadron. By 1849, even the 1843 list of book allowances had been abandoned. When Commodore Foxhall A. Parker inquired about the availability of certain books for the frigate *Raritan,* he was told that the Bureau of Construction, Equipment and Repair had in November, 1848, called for the book inventories of all the naval stations, and then divided them into "libraries of about equal estimation as to service and literature." The library with which his ship had been furnished was one of five that had been ordered to be put up in boxes at the Norfolk Navy Yard, and it was supposed to have contained the books he needed. If it did not, Commodore Parker was further told by Secretary William B. Preston that he was authorized to purchase them. On the same day (April 24, 1849), the secretary also wrote to the chief of the Bureau of Construction, Equipment and Repair and restated Bancroft's original order to furnish each vessel when ready for sea "out of the books now on hand and of a character suitable for the use of the ship." In 1850, the brig *Porpoise* was furnished by the Norfolk Navy Yard with a ship's library which was more suggestive of the first library than one of later vintage. It consisted of twenty-nine titles in fifty volumes, and the purchased portions of it were set at an assumed price of $50.

Not only did the practice of making up libraries from a static book stock provide ships with libraries of varying content and size, but the stock itself was not inexhaustable. It was also in danger of becoming a substandard, as well as a nonstandard commodity. If the navy did not realize this, Franck Taylor, a Washington bookseller did—at least as far as his sales were concerned. He wrote to the president of the United States, Millard Fillmore, about the situation on May 7, 1852, and he referred the letter to the Navy Department. Secretary William A. Graham, in turn, on May 10, asked Commodore Morris, as chief of the Bureau of Ordnance and Hydrography (the responsibility for libraries had been transferred to this bureau about 1850), to report on Taylor's principal object, which according to Graham was "to establish a regular system of arrangement and classification of Books for Libraries, and accountability while in use." Morris, who was assisted by the chiefs of the Bureau of Construction, Equipment and Repair, and the Bureau of Navy Yards and Docks, was also to submit "a Table showing the Books which you will recommend for the Libraries of the different classes of vessels in the navy; and also regulations for their preservation and care."

Commodore Morris was again involved in the book selection process. In a month's time his committee prepared the new list, which consisted of sixty book titles to be allowed to five classes of vessels and two classes of navy yards. It followed the 1844 printed *Tables of Allowances* in arrangement, but many of the titles had been deleted, some were substituted, and about twenty-five new titles were added. A few of the substitutions and new titles were from the older 1843 list that had more or less been in effect since that date, but fourteen or so titles were first-time listings, added at the end of the classified arrangement. These titles were concerned mostly with steam and naval science. On June 13, 1852, Commodore Morris submitted to Secretary Graham the new list along with the committee's recommendations for the procedures to be followed for the purchase, distribution, and accountability of books, which were essentially the same as those that had already been in force.[9] Although Graham left office in July without approving the list, his successor, John P. Kennedy, issued a general order putting it into effect, almost verbatim as recommended, on October 20, 1852. The navy was back on its course to provide vessels with books according to a current and uniform plan; but whether the newly revived program was fully implemented is doubtful. In 1854, Secretary Kennedy's successor, James C. Dobbin, in answer to a complaint by the captain of the steamer *Michigan* that his library was not standard for that class of vessel, informed him "that in the present reduced state of the appropriations to which the purchase of Books in chargeable, it is not deemed expedient to authorize an expenditure to complete the Library of the vessel under your command." Earlier, two other complaints about ship libraries based on the 1852 list were received by Secretary Dobbin. The commanding officer of the sloop-of-war *St. Mary's,* after finding that the third and fourth volumes of Kent's *Commentaries* and Gordon's *Digest* were the only law books in his ship's library, requested on September 27, 1853, fourteen other works on law, and several books on ordnance and gunnery "suited to the practice of Sailors and Marines when acting on ship and shore." He was not authorized any in addition to those allowed. Neither was the commander of the sloop-of-war *Germantown,* who obviously did not appreciate the exclusively professional nature of the library aboard his ship. He declared that six-sevenths of its contents was composed of "strictly mechanical, scientific or legal works—and of the remaining seventh, but one work is not naval."

Another list, authorized by Secretary Isaac Toucey, became effective on October 27, 1860. It comprised fifty-two titles and was very similar to that of 1852, with the exception of a few new titles. The ship's library had become, as the *Germantown's* captain observed, almost solely technical in content. The imperative need to educate officers aboard ship by any means available had passed with the founding of the Naval Academy fifteen years earlier. On the threshold of the Civil War, the ship's library had already assumed the lessened educative role that it would play in the modern navy. Nevertheless, it was still essential to officers aboard ship as a reference aid, and would survive on its own merit another 113 years of varying fortune, to this day.[10]

Procurement and Regulation. Some word needs to be said about the legal authority for, and the method of, purchase of books in the early navy. During most of the period covered by this study, books were usually bought out of a fund category of the Navy Department's budget called "contingent expenses." Each year, when Congress appropriated money to the navy, the wording of the appropriation act spelled out the allowable expenses of the service and limited the amount of money that could be spent for the purposes specified. At first only a few categories were mentioned in the statutes, but over the years, they were increased in number. The basic allowances had always been for pay and subsistence of officers and seamen, for provisions, for medicines and hospital stores, for repairs to vessels, for ordnance, for docks, for the support of the U.S. Marine Corps, and for contingencies. The contingent allowance was to take care of the miscellaneous, sundry, and unforeseen expenses not otherwise specifically mentioned in the appropriations acts. Over the years, with occasional downward fluctuations, the amounts appropriated for contingent expenses grew from $10,000 in 1802, to $220,000 in 1823, to $896,000 in 1860.

Prior to the year 1824, that portion of the annual appropriation acts which allowed money for contingent expenses was simply worded: "For contingent expenses . . . thousand dollars"; but beginning in 1824, the purposes for which the contingent money was to be used were set forth in the act. Some thirty to forty allowable contingent expenses were usually enumerated each year. These covered such objects as the expenses of naval agents, expenses of recruitment, traveling expenses of officers and transportation of seamen, cabin furniture for vessels in commission, pilotage, printing, coals for blacksmiths, lighterage and scow hire, postage, burial expenses, taxes, accidents to public vessels, etc. In the first enumerated listing, and for several years afterward, between the statement, for "chamber money to officers, in lieu of quarters . . . ," and "expense of pursuing deserters," the significant allowance for "purchase of books, charts, nautical and mathematical instruments, chronometers, machinery, models, drawings, and all stationery of every description, used throughout the naval service" was provided.[11] Beginning with the appropriation act for 1846, maps, charts and instruments, as well as books, were specifically allowed for the navy's "Hydrographical Office," but books, models, and drawings were still listed in the enumeration of allowable contingent expenses for the service as a whole.

Congress, early in its career, took a continuing interest in the expenditures made by the navy from the monies appropriated to it for contingencies, and required the secretary of the navy to provide an annual statement or report of all claims discharged against the contingent appropriation. These annual accountings, together with similarly required statements of all contracts for purchases of supplies and services, exist today as valuable sources of information on book purchases made by the navy, inasmuch as the reports were published in the official documents of the government. Usually the only data presented in these summaries of expenditures were the names of the payees and the amounts of the purchases, but occasionally specific titles of books, periodicals and newspapers, and the names of vessels or stations were also listed, such as, "Nov. 6, 1837 to E. G. Mygatt—For vols. 11 and 12 Sparks's Washington—$7.50," or ". . . 1829 P. Thompson, Contr[actor]. For books, stationery &c. for the St. Louis, sloop of war $546.50." Another form of statement listed the name of the person who made a purchase against the contingent fund along with an account number, such as (in 1836–1837), ". . . James K. Paulding, navy agent at N.Y. For books shipped to Pensacola—[paid to] Wiley and Long . . . $65.00"; or ". . . Nash Legrand, navy agent at Norfolk. For the 'Falmouth'—[paid to] G. Marshall, for two copies of M. Gunnery, $3.50; C. Hall, for library $480.00 . . . ," etc. While many purchases were made individually or locally on the open market because "public exigencies required the immediate delivery of the articles," books were also contracted for on bid or proposal like most of the navy's other stores and equipment, and individual book titles can be found listed in the reports of some of these contracts.

By precedent in 1828, and by custom and regulation thereafter, the secretary of the navy retained the authority for designating the books which were to be allowed as libraries for vessels and navy yards. During the period of the Board of Navy Commissioners, it was normally the responsibility of the commandant of the navy yard where a ship was fitted out either to authorize standard purchases (including books) or to order his storekeeper to provide the available items from the public store if available there. When the bureau system was instituted in 1842, commandants of navy yards were to send a requisition for needed items to the appropriate bureau, although they were still allowed to sanction purchases if there was not enough time to process them through channels.

Book purchases were most commonly made through navy agents who maintained offices in certain American seaports. Navy agents were appointed by the president for four-year periods (until 1866, when the position was abolished), and they received as compensation a percentage of the funds which they disbursed. The navy also made use of commercial firms as temporary agents of supply in certain foreign countries; and pursers aboard ship performed the purchasing and disbursing function for vessels in commission. All book purchases had to conform to the lists of allowable titles, or be specifically approved by the Navy Department before payment was officially completed and the account settled. The office of Fourth Auditor of the Treasury Department, established in 1816, audited the navy's accounts. Any additions or changes to the library lists which were approved by the Navy Department had to be reported to a number of persons concerned with procurement, both for informational and control purposes. For example, when Acting Secretary John Y. Mason, on March 25, 1845, ordered that the *London Encyclopaedia* was henceforth to be purchased in lieu of either the *Encyclopaedia Britannica* or the *Encyclopaedia Americana* because it could be bought more cheaply from one particular source, he notified by circular the commandants of the navy yards, the port captains, the navy bureaus, the shore stations, all navy agents, and the Second Comptroller and Fourth Auditor of the Treasury. And when changes were made to the list of books for navy yards and vessels of war on March 7, 1843, the commanding officer of every vessel in the service was to be notified as well. The actual shipment of a new title from the Navy Department office might also serve the purpose of notification when no purchase was necessary by the recipient vessel or yard. A printed or engraved letter simply informed the commanding officer that the item was to be used and accounted for like other books furnished to his vessel or yard.

Although six of the seven library lists of allowable books that were in force between the years 1828–1860 specified certain standard titles for each class of vessel, it is doubtful whether libraries of similar ships were exactly the same at any one time. The diversity of situations, and the uncertainties involved in updating and interpreting the lists and in the ordering process, made it difficult to achieve an ideal uniformity. A ship having been outfitted prior to a major change of lists, of course, carried a library made up from the older list. For example, the sloop-of-war *Decatur*, at Rio de Janeiro on June 1, 1842, had on board a library that matched, with a few exceptions, the 1839 list of allowances, although at this time the new 1841 lists of ships' and seamen's libraries were being applied to vessels then being fitted out at home. The accountability procedure for libraries is also illustrated in this example. When Commander David G. Farragut assumed command of the *Decatur* at this time, he furnished the relieved captain, Commander Henry W. Ogden, with a receipt for the ship's library, itemized by book titles. A duplicate of the receipt, along with receipts for the signals and cabin furniture of the sloop was also furnished to Commodore Morris, then in command of the Brazil Station.

A captain missing a book from his ship's library might be called upon to explain the circumstances of its loss. Such an instance and its consequences are recorded in a letter to the commander of the sloop-of-war *Boston* from the secretary of the navy's office, dated July 31, 1839. The fact that a volume of the *Encyclopaedia Americana* was lost from the library because there was no lock on the bookcase was not considered a good excuse. Commander Edward B. Babbitt was reminded that "under the regulation of September, 1831," all books were to be receipted for by the commander of a vessel or station, and that he was to be held accountable for the loss of the volume in question.

Despite the efforts to control both the purchase and return of books, nonauthorized books were acquired and retained. The schooner *Enterprise,* in August, 1839, while at the Philadelphia Navy Yard, was discovered to have many books that were not allowed by the regulations; and at the same time, she was also found to lack a great portion of those which were allowed. Similarly, in January, 1843, it was reported that "quite a number of books at the Naval Store at Norfolk" were not on the current list of books to be furnished to naval vessels. The surplus books were subsequently ordered to be shipped to Washington.[12]

The books purchased for ships and navy yards as libraries were usually uniformly bound in leather or in leather and boards, and each volume was stamped with gilt lettering. The precedent for this was established along with the first navy yard libraries authorized on May 3, 1827, and was reiterated through the years in subsequent orders or specified in bid proposals. Several examples of these bindings exist today in the libraries of the Navy Department and the Naval Academy. Those from warships usually bear the name of the vessel lettered at the foot of the spine. Volumes from the *Lexington, Plymouth, Cumberland, Ohio, Experiment, Preble,* and *Dale* are among those preserved. Also, a few specimens of books lettered with appropriate property designations from the Navy Department, the navy commissioners' office, the navy yards, and the bureaus still remain.

Evaluation. The libraries initiated by Secretary Samuel Southard for "the promotion of study and diffusion of knowledge among junior officers of the Navy while at sea" came to be used by officers of every rank, and for all purposes, on land as well as on sea. Thus for a time, the leaders and future leaders of the service had the same standard of reading fare available to them from which to inform themselves, broaden their outlook, or become influenced, if they chose to read. The ship's library became as much a feature of an American warship as her guns. In later published accounts of life at sea, it needed no introductory explanation when presented to the reader for the first time. Henry A. Wise, sailing master of the razee *Independence* during her cruise of 1846–1849, remarked in his book, *Los Gringos* (1850), "our chief resource was reading, and after absorbing heaps of ephemeral trash drifting about the decks, we sought the library and poured over ponderous tomes of physics, history or travels."[13] Wise further implied use of the library by his messmates, who consulted encyclopedias, gazeteers, and dictionaries for sportive or mischievous purposes (as was also done on the steam frigate *Powhattan* in 1854 in a book-oriented amusement, which in this instance, was called "twaddle"). He also observed that "books find their true value" aboard ship, and that the crew derived the full benefit of reading, but in doing so, "many a stupid author is thoroughly digested, and many labored narrations of voyages are carefully studied." In this regard, Wise believed that the authors of the dull books should have been grateful to the government for the purchase of their works. To a limited extent, it could be said that certain authors, publishers, and booksellers were indirectly aided or subsidized in the sale of their materials for the use of the navy, especially during the halcyon years of the libraries.

The content and cost of the libraries was also remarked upon somewhat inaccurately and slightly disparagingly by another naval officer, Dr. William P. C. Barton, chief of the Bureau of Medicine in 1842. In an attempt to emphasize the need for a "small compact medical and surgical library" aboard ships and at hospitals and shipyard sick bays, Barton wrote in his first annual report. "Extensive and costly libraries are furnished by Government to the commanders of all ships in the Navy often embracing a large portion of mere general literature." Apparently Dr. Barton was not too successful in his attempt to receive authorization of shipboard medical libraries, for on July 1, 1854, an assistant surgeon, who had inquired about the same subject, was informed by the secretary of the navy, "A few books are allowed to ships of war in the Medical Department. . . . But no Library."

To another observer, the ship's library could never have enough in the way of literary, historical, travel, and philosophical works. This writer, John Stuart Skinner (a successful publisher of agricultural literature and a former navy purser during the War of 1812), in a published letter (1841) advised a "young gentleman of Maryland, on his entrance into the Navy of the United States" how to court success in his new career. Much of his Chesterfieldian advice had to do with the importance of reading. Skinner recommended many books by title which the young midshipman might well "pack into one good sea chest" and benefit from reading. In concluding his long epistle, Skinner stated, "I well know that not many even of the books that I have enumerated, with many more that are equally worthy of perusal and study, are to be found in our ships of war at present; but there are none of them that ought not to be there." He further entertained the hope that soon an enlightened administration would more amply provide "for the moral and intellectual culture" of young officers.[14]

As for the quality of the books in the ship's library, a few of the titles available there at one time or another were the same standard works that Nathaniel Ames mentioned having read when he was a student at Harvard College. Between the years 1828-1843, thirteen out of the many titles which were chosen for the ships' libraries appeared on each of the library lists promulgated during this period. These titles are listed in Appendix E as items 1, 2, 6, 8, 11, 12, 13, 15, 18, 19 (three titles), and 26, although an encyclopedia and the Bible occurred on the 1832-1843 lists, and several other titles were included on more than one list. The fact that some of the same titles appeared on all or some of the individual lists, and that a few titles were out of print, perhaps indicates more that the Board of Navy Commissioners regarded these books as essential than that the board members were reluctant to choose currently available books. Further, the few works concerned with timber and wood identification on the early lists were later dropped, and books on steam, hydraulics, and mechanics appeared in their stead. It is possible that the library lists of the navy commissioners were prepared with much the same spirit and intent that present-day college professors provide supplementary reading lists for students in their courses.

As the Board of Navy Commissioners had recognized in 1837, the matter of book selection for the ship's library was in a large degree one of taste, if not budget, and it was difficult to satisfy everyone. Critics might question the choice of books and the costs of the libraries, but they did not advocate their abandonment. Indeed, the navy's own critic, Lieutenant Matthew F. Maury, who found much to condemn in the administration of the service, had only words of praise for the concept. Even though he shot wide of the mark in attributing the direct establishment of shipboard libraries solely to William Wood, Maury, as a contemporary observer of the effects of the ship's library, did not have to rely upon hearsay evidence in order to form an opinion regarding its worth. Perhaps his evaluation of the ship's library (and here he was referring to it only, for he wrote in 1840, one year before the government provided the seamen's library) comes close to recording the true value of this educational instrument during the period of its ascendency. Maury wrote in his third *Southern Literary Messenger* article, "The experience of every officer will sustain me in the assertion, that in the last fifteen or twenty years, the moral and intellectual condition of the Navy has been steadily advancing. And I think, upon a due examination into cause and effect, it would appear that this movement is in a great measure owing to the establishment of libraries on board of our public vessels. Furnishing libraries to our men-of-war, is the only effectual step that has ever been taken towards education in the Navy." To be sure, there had been more direct measures taken to provide education, and Maury himself was advocating another one, more "palpable and obvious" than libraries— the schoolship as a naval academy. But this was high praise from Maury, coming as it did when he was having a field day exposing the real and imagined ills of the navy in the name of reform; and it might have been sincerity more than rhetoric that moved him to extol the ship's library at this time.

SCHOOL LIBRARIES. The advent of the ship's library did not necessarily eliminate the need for the purchase of special books to be used in instruction by individual chaplains and schoolmasters, nor did it significantly change the program of instruction, such as it was, at the chief navy yards or aboard ship. Requests for such books for instruction were still received by the Navy Department, and although some were refused for the reason that libraries were then being provided, other requests were granted. Three years after the first ship's library list went into effect, Commodore Jesse D. Elliott, on October 21, 1831, was told by the secretary of the navy that the expenses of books and stationery for the use of the schools to be established aboard ships of his squadron in the West Indies would be borne by the Navy Department. Ashore, a year earlier Commodore Isaac Chauncey at the New York Navy Yard requested on behalf of the chaplain at the school there eight books which he believed were "much required." The list of books that was submitted by him on January 28, 1830, consisted of popular titles concerned with "moral and political philosophy," grammar, and rhetoric. Both this request and another of Chauncey's that pertained to the payment of money in lieu of the spirit ration to forty-one seamen, marines, and boys who had joined the temperance movement aboard the receiving ship at the yard were approved by the secretary on February 2, 1830.

Other schoolbook requests and recommendations, directed to the Navy Department over the seventeen-year period prior to the founding of the permanent naval school at Annapolis, appear to have been for books of a technical nature and more directly related to the professional subjects then being taught. Those that were selected for one classroom situation appeared also to have been made to apply to the other shore schools that were active at the time. Current practical and scholarly works were suggested for the schools by officers, schoolmasters, scholars, and others who were interested in improving the quality of the teaching program. In April, 1828, a book on trigonometry was suggested by

Ferdinand R. Hassler, sometime superintendent of the coast survey, and it was readily endorsed. The Board of Navy Commissioners had written to the secretary of the navy that Hassler "would not recommend it for the Naval Schools if it was not good"; therefore, they in turn recommended twenty-five copies for purchase, which were to be sent to the different navy yards where schools were established. Several recommendations by the highly regarded and scholarly Peter J. Rodriguez, emigré schoolmaster at the Norfolk school, received similar treatment. When he proposed Bagay's *Nouvelles tables astronomiques et hydrographiques* for purchase in 1831, the navy commissioners recommended that a set be bought for both the Norfolk and New York schools, and further noted "there is perhaps no man in this country more capable of deciding upon the value of the tables than Mr. Rodrgues [sic]." Three other works by foreign authors suggested by Rodriguez in 1834 were also recommended for purchase at the three navy yards by the commissioners.[15] Books by navy authors, written specifically to fill the educational void, also received recognition and were furnished to the schools or libraries. Fifteen copies of Maury's *Treatise on Navigation* were initially provided in 1836, and again in 1838, for the use of the schools and the department, and twelve copies of Brady's *Naval Apprentice's Kedge Anchor* (later titled, simply, *The Kedge Anchor*) were authorized for purchase in 1841 for each of the three receiving ships at the navy yards with schools. Lieutenant Benjamin J. Totten's *Naval Text-Book* (1841), which was available in the ship's library of 1841–1843, and was probably used in the schools also, was of unique origin. In compiling his book, Totten used as source material the manuscript copies of questions and answers which midshipmen had prepared (such as Midshipmen Foote and Davis had done in 1827) in order to pass their examinations. This information, Totten observed, had always been "greedily sought for by the candidates." He was surprised that the great fund of information so assembled "should not have been long since embodied and published for the use of this class of officers."

The books obtained for the shore schools were presumably kept apart from the navy yard libraries, and were made available in "libraries" at the schools aboard receiving ships or in other locations ashore in the yards. These school libraries were probably small, and contained whatever books the schoolmaster was able to provide. A midshipman who replaced a missing copy of Simpson's *Euclid* through the secretary of the navy on December 14, 1838, explained that the original copy had belonged to the "Naval School Library" at Gosport, Virginia, which indicates the existence of this kind of library at the time.

Although books were supplied for use at the schools, midshipmen still had to provide other required texts. In the naval regulations of

1833, it was required that they "shall keep themselves provided with a sextant or quadrant, Bowditch's Treatise upon Navigation, and blank journals." The 1841 and 1843 regulations allowed midshipmen to substitute an approved treatise for Bowditch. This was not too much in the way of a requirement when compared with that of the French government. The 1828 edition of *Ordonnance du roi sur le service des officiers, des élèves et des maîtres . . . de la Marine royale* listed several books, charts, and instruments which were uniformly required to be in the possession of the *élèves de la marine* before embarking on a cruise.

Whether the "young gentlemen" of the U.S. Navy supplied themselves with the necessary books was another matter. In an 1834 weekly report on the attendance and progress of midshipmen at a "school" at sea conducted by schoolmaster Laurent Girard aboard the *Delaware*, 74, one midshipman was reported to have been absent each day classes were in session and to have been studying "nothing" because of his "having no books." The twenty-three other students, some of whom had been absent because of sickness or "being on duty" were reported to have been studying either Spanish, Italian, or French.[16] Classes aboard ship tended to be somewhat chaotic. This atmosphere has been captured in many accounts, from that of the school situation aboard the *Java* in 1817, where a man who had fallen overboard passed within a few feet of the class, to the amusing student *versus* professor scenes described aboard the *Delaware* in 1842 by Daniel Noble Johnson, who believed that the subject itself was worthy of a painting by Hogarth. Other contemporary sources touched upon the diverse study and reading habits of individual midshipmen, which might well have involved reading a book on solitude while on the solitary duty of lookout at the fore-topmast-head aboard the *Vandalia* in 1839, or the asking for a year's leave in order to study French and Spanish in Europe, contingent upon obtaining free passage to the Continent aboard the *Delaware* in 1833.

The teaching of seamen apprentices, American boys between thirteen and eighteen years of age (previously mentioned in chapter V), which began in 1837 and lasted a short while, tends to cloud further the already unclear picture of naval education. It appears that at times certain chaplains and schoolmasters might have simultaneously taught apprentices and midshipmen. The books furnished to apprentices were for their elementary schooling and moral guidance. On May 30, 1839, Commodore Ridgely forwarded a list of eleven books which were adopted as suitable by the Navy Department for distribution to the apprentices aboard the receiving ships at Boston, New York, and Norfolk. The content of the list differed from the one prepared by the chaplain of the New York Navy Yard in 1830, for it contained a Bible and prayer book as well as arithmetic books, a geography text, a reader, and a speller. Inasmuch as the cost of the books for the entire list totalled only $4.36 per apprentice, it was proposed "to have the names of the boys written in their books, & each boy to take his books &c on board their respective vessels." Remaining inventories of books in the public store at Norfolk in 1843 and at New York in 1846 list several copies of "School Books" which were purchased for the apprentices, although the Norfolk list also had a few algebra and trigonometry texts included, which probably had been intended for midshipmen's use.

The decade between the years 1835–1845 might well be referred to as the period of the rise and fall of the teaching professor of mathematics in the navy. During this time the qualifications to become a teacher in the service were tightened by examination. Legislation was passed in March, 1835, which permitted only the secretary of the navy to appoint instructors, who were henceforth to be called by the dignified title of professors of mathematics. Regardless of his new title, the professor's lot in the navy was still an ambiguous one. He continued to have the problem of winning the respect of his charges and achieving status, especially as it concerned living and messing privileges among his supposed peers. During this ten-year period the number of professors was increased. A total of thirty-four professors at one time or another had teaching or other assignments on more than thirty vessels of war, at four naval schools, or with the Depot of Charts and Instruments, and the coast survey. Despite the efforts to provide more and better teachers, there was a desperate awareness of the inadequacies of the system as a whole by interested parties both within and without the service. Professors, officers, and others made known their negative views on the efficaciousness of the teaching process, and the Navy Department in turn tried to make the best of a situation which it felt powerless to change except through an act of Congress.

One last extension of the provisional educational program was tried in the form of another shore school, this time at the Naval Asylum at Philadelphia in 1839.[17] Through a combination of fortuitous circumstances, this school soon eclipsed the others in importance and in so doing, prepared the way for the establishment of the long-awaited single permanent naval academy, six years later. In August, 1838, Commodore James Biddle was put in charge of the Naval Asylum, which was a hospital and retirement home built in 1833 for naval personnel. A few months after his appointment a library was started there when the commodore received thirty-nine volumes of legal and miscellaneous books that Acting Secretary John Boyle sent on October 31, 1838, with a promise that "others from time to time as opportunities" presented would be transmitted to him. In November, 1839, several midshipmen were detailed from New York to attend the school to be conducted there by Professor David McClure. The school was to provide a place for mid-shipmen to prepare for their examinations, exclusively, over a period of eight months, rather than provide beginning or finishing courses, as were offered at the navy yard schools. The physical facilities of the Naval Asylum, though barren and far from ideal, were more like those of a college, especially when compared with the arrangements available aboard the receiving ships and ashore at the navy yards. At an examination held at the Naval Asylum in 1841, the midshipmen present had to display their knowledge of certain texts, *i.e.,* "Bowditch's *Navigator,*" "Playfair's *Euclid* (Books 1, 2, 3, 4, and 6)," and "Bourdon's *Algebra,*" in addition to their facility in Spanish or French, and in "mental and moral philosophy."

With the death of Professor McClure in April, 1842, William Chauvenet, a young professor of mathematics, took over the school and "commenced the work of reform so far as was possible within the limits of the system then existing." Chauvenet sought to improve the school by providing the proper books, instruments, and models for classroom use. One of his first requests, dated September, 1842, to Secretary Abel P. Upshur, for certain books and instruments was forwarded to the newly established Bureau of Ordnance and Hydrography, which was responsible for the supply of navigational books and equipment. In another letter to Secretary David Henshaw dated November 8, 1843, requesting several kinds of nautical instruments for the school, Chauvenet also mentioned his desire to give the midshipmen some elementary notion about steam engines. He had found a model engine "at Mr. Baldwin's" which was well suited to his needs for it was easily taken apart and put together, and was "finely finished" of "about one man power" and cost $60. It is of interest to note that at this school the subject of steam was not neglected and that an attempt was made to teach the theory or rudiments of the subject in the navy ashore at this time. In fact, another faculty member, James H. Ward, published a book on gunnery for use at the school, which also included "a concise treatise on steam."

The same month Chauvenet mentioned the steam engine to Secretary Henshaw, he evaluated Lieutenant Maury's text on navigation for the secretary, and reported it to be mostly suitable for those "whose abilities or previous attainments do not qualify them for a more extended mathematical course." He preferred Harvard professor Benjamin Peirce's treatise on spherical trigonometry, though he did allow that there was a place for both texts in the navy under the prevailing conditions. Chauvenet himself had also published a little book on the binominal theorem for use of midshipmen at the Asylum, and in its preface acknowledged his debt to Peirce's and Louis Bourdon's treatises on algebra. In September, 1844, Secretary John Y. Mason ordered that Maury's *Navigation* was to be adopted as the text book of the navy, and at the same time revoked a previous order which would have allowed the school to offer a two-year course of instruction. A year later the school, by then consisting of five faculty members who taught courses or lectured in gunnery, navigation, mathematics, and maritime law, was transferred from Philadelphia to Annapolis, Maryland.

As the many accounts of the history of the U.S. Naval Academy record, in 1845 Secretary of the Navy George Bancroft succeeded in founding a permanent naval school ashore, while his predecessors, who recognized its need and value to the country as much as he, had failed. Bancroft did not ask Congress to create a school; rather he did it on his own with the funds at hand, and by bold action. The blueprint for the action Bancroft followed had, in effect, been sketched nine years before at a meeting of fifty-five naval officers aboard the frigate *Constitution*.[18] Protesting the poor status of education in the navy, the officers drew up a list of resolutions which were forwarded to the secretary of the navy. They advocated that the position of schoolmaster be abolished, and "believing the expense incurred by Government in providing ships' schoolmasters and professors of mathematics for the benefit of the junior officers of the Navy . . . would liberally sustain a scientific institution," they requested that the funds used for schoolmasters' salaries be directed to the establishment and support of a naval school. Secretary Bancroft early realized that he could effect this change administratively without petitioning Congress for permission, and he did it quickly and quietly. At the same time, he secured by transfer from the War Department the site of old Fort Severn, at Annapolis. Once the school was started, Bancroft took great interest in all aspects of its progress, conferring occasionally, and corresponding frequently with the capable Commander Franklin Buchanan, whom he had appointed as the first superintendent.

As early as one month before the official opening of the Naval School, Commander Buchanan on September 11, 1845, forwarded to the secretary a request for certain books, perhaps destined for the library, which Lieutenant James H. Ward, one of the school's original staff members, believed would "add much to the value of his course of instruction in gunnery." Ward also wrote directly to Bancroft with Buchanan's permission two days later and again enclosed the original list, and added a supplemental one. Bancroft soon replied and authorized him to purchase up to $100 worth of books from the lists. As a consequence, some twenty-one titles, mostly of a technical nature, were purchased from the Franck Taylor bookstore in Washington, and the bill, which exceeded the authorization by twenty-five cents, was paid the following February.[19]

But with an eye toward economy, Secretary Bancroft was intent on using the book resources within the navy to furnish the school's library, and he set about tapping all likely book collections for materials. Books were now to be gathered and sent to Annapolis for the use of midshipmen, just as Thomas Bray had earlier exported his "Annopolitan Library" to colonial Maryland in the cause of religion. On September 28, 1845, a fortnight after receiving Lieutenant Ward's request, Bancroft wrote to Passed Midshipman William B. Fitzgerald, stationed in Washington, and requested him to return the Navy Department's set of *American Eloquence,* so that it could be sent to Annapolis. He later communicated with the commandants of the navy yards at Boston, New York, and Norfolk requesting a list of all the books which were the property of the government at the respective yards, and on May 19, 1846, again wrote to each and directed that certain books which were "required" by the school be sent to it. The letter dispatched to the Boston Navy Yard with its enclosed list of requested books still survives.[20] The enclosure was in the hand of James B. Howison, Commander Buchanan's secretary, which indicates that a desiderata list probably had been prepared at some point, and that the selection of the books from the yards was made by the Naval School, and not by Secretary Bancroft.

By September 3, 1846, about 364 volumes had thus been assembled, for on this date Buchanan forwarded, in compliance with Bancroft's "verbal instructions," a catalog of the books comprising the library of the school. Today, many of the books listed in this manuscript catalog still remain. A few of them are in their original bindings or else contain clues to their past history. On some, marks of prior ownership, such as the names of vessels, navy yards, or the Navy Department, are stamped with gilt lettering on the leather covers or spines; while others are inscribed in ink or pencil in various places. Several books bear the original Naval School bookplate, and some, including a book on ordnance formerly owned by the commanding officer of Fort Severn, have an added association value inasmuch as they had been the property of personages connected with the navy or the early history of the Naval Academy. The content of the original library, though small in quantity, was, nevertheless, diverse in coverage and of substantial quality. Many of the titles, of course, were those that the navy had for years supplied by regulation to ships' libraries for the all-around education of junior officers, and for use by self-reliant ships' officers conducting the affairs of their government far from its shores. These particular copies were now intended by Bancroft to serve all the midshipmen of the navy for years to come at the one naval school in Annapolis.

In response to the September 3, 1846, manuscript catalog which Buchanan had sent to Bancroft, a new secretary of the navy, John Y. Mason, on September 14, requested that Commander Buchanan prepare a list of "such additional books as are necessary to complete the library, having regard to the purposes of the School and the limited means at the disposal of the Department." Apparently only sixty-five additional titles were thought necessary to accomplish this goal and they were authorized for purchase. This time the firm of Wiley and Putnam in New York furnished many of the books. Other purchases had been made of science books from the John Penington bookstore in Philadelphia, which was probably well known by Professor Chauvenet, who had signed the bill for them. He might also have arranged for the binding of thirty-two other volumes by another Philadelphia firm, Cunningham and David about the same time. For several years Chauvenet acted in the added capacity of librarian at the school, as did also for a time, Chaplain George Jones.

The library slowly grew from about 850 volumes during its first two years of existence to 2,766 volumes in 1852. In December of 1850, it was enriched by a gift of several books and pamphlets from the French ministeries of public instruction and of marine. This donation had been arranged by Alexandre Vattemare, the famous French ventriloquist, who since 1839 had been responsible for operating an international exchange of books, whereby European libraries could send their duplicate materials to libraries in the United States. The Naval Academy (its name had been changed from the Naval School in July, 1850) appears to have received the French books and pamphlets as a result of a personal visit by M. Vattemare to various Maryland and other institutions in 1850. Somehow the Naval Academy was also presented with a bill for $10 in transportation charges for the gift of materials, and this did not sit too well with the still economy-minded administration. The following year $2,596.75 was authorized for the purchase of books for the library which had been recommended by the six teaching departments and approved by the academic board. At this time, the board also recommended that the training ship (a new feature in the academic program) which was assigned to the Academy, should be provided with a library "equal in amount to that heretofore furnished to Ships of War."[21] The ship's library had not been forgotten as an educational resource for midshipmen afloat, but wisely it was not, in this case, to be supplied from the Academy's own library.

Prior to 1860, work was begun on the only catalog of the library ever to be printed. It was prepared by Thomas G. Ford, the assistant librarian at this time, who first examined other printed catalogs, and visited "some of the Boston and New York libraries to obtain information." Professor Chauvenet initially supervised the project, but left the Academy in 1859 before it was completed in order to join the faculty of Washington University at St. Louis. Apparently Chauvenet and Ford were influenced in their work by the New York Society Library's printed catalogs of 1838 and 1850, for the Naval Academy *Catalogue,* published in 1860, is similar to the New York catalogs in format, wording, and almost in numbers of major and subordinate categories. However, the specialties of the library, *i.e.,* mathematics, science, and military and naval arts, were expanded, and the order of arrangement of the major categories, or the "general scheme," still followed that of the original manuscript catalog that Commander Buchanan had sent to Secretary Bancroft on September 3, 1846. Apparently at this early date there had been some decision to follow a modified Brunet classification of knowledge, rather than devise an artificial or specialized library scheme (as was then employed at the West Point Library), and the order of the 1846 listing was continued in the 1860 *Catalogue.*

While the nucleus of the library's collection was composed in part of books that had gone to sea in ships, the entire library of about 9,000 volumes was to become seaborne soon after the publication date of the new catalog. In April, 1861, it made the hasty coastwise voyage from Annapolis to Newport, Rhode Island, when the Naval Academy was moved there for the duration of the Civil War. Thomas G. Ford, in an unpublished autobiographical sketch, colorfully but perhaps not too accurately, recalled how he, as assistant librarian, packed the books for the voyage and how he had slept in the library with a horse pistol under his pillow to protect his charge, when it was thought that Annapolis might be taken by the Confederates. Ford also claimed that the books were shipped to Newport aboard the frigate *Constitution,* although it is more likely that they made the passage aboard the transport *Baltic.* At Newport, the books apparently were stored for a while at Fort Adams, but in November, 1862, they were "unpacked, wiped, and repacked" into sixty-five cases one-half the size of the original containers. The new cases were then stored in the "lower room" of the Custom House of the city; although at the time 1,380 volumes were kept out for use by the officers and members of the academy's first class at their quarters, the "Atlantic House," a converted old summer hotel. Earlier, another ninety volumes on seamanship and gunnery had been secured from storage, presumably for instructional purposes. The unused packed books, and a few boxes of specimens from the academy's lyceum, however, were not forgotten. At regular intervals and on damp days, a fire was provided in the storeroom in an effort to inhibit the growth of mold, and on two other occasions before the war was over, the books were again unpacked, inspected, and carefully wiped clean. Further, steps were even advanced to insure the books for $21,000 in 1863.[22]

According to Park Benjamin's history of the Naval Academy, much of the training of the decimated academic classes of midshipmen at Newport took place aboard the practice ships *Constitution* and *Santee.* This mode

of teaching was also employed by the Confederate States Navy, which
readily adopted the old sea customs of the North, including the requirement that midshipmen furnish themselves with a copy of Bowditch's or
some other approved treatise upon navigation, and on marine surveying
and with blank journals. Aboard the Confederate schoolship *Patrick
Henry,* although a library was not specifically mentioned in the regulations governing her operation, books and other teaching materials
were selected and purchased by the seven-man academic board composing the ship's faculty.[23]

At the end of the war the Naval Academy returned to Annapolis with
its library (eleven boxes of it on the *Constitution* and seventy-two on the
Santee) under much less dramatic circumstances than it had departed.
The academy was moved in the summer of 1865, and in September,
Rear Admiral David D. Porter, a hero of the war, became the superintendent. His was an "epoch-making administration," which not only
reestablished the Naval Academy, but transformed it into a college and
set its course for years to come. The navy finally had its permanent professional academy, and its library was again accessible to midshipmen
and officers ashore.

Chapter VIII

Of Science, Lyceums, and Libraries

Come, bright improvement! on the car of Time,
  And rule the spacious world from clime to clime;
Thy handmaid arts shall every wild explore,
  Trace every wave, and culture every shore.

—Pleasures of Hope

Books came to be acquired and libraries formed in the navy as a result of another intellectual need which was separate from the learning of the naval officer's profession. This was in connection with the pursuit of scientific knowledge, both for its own sake and for its application to the maritime affairs of the new nation. The participation of the navy in the furtherance of pure and applied science, which called forth various libraries to support research, was in three areas: (1) the activities of naval officers as individuals in the formation of lyceums and libraries, and the organization of professional associations, (2) the mounting of worldwide naval expeditions by the government, and (3) the navy's organization of, or alliance with, scientific activities which developed into permanent shoreside establishments such as the coast survey, the Naval Observatory, and the Nautical Almanac Office.

The initiation or extent of encouragement of scientific endeavor at any one time in the navy's early history was largely determined by the policy of the federal government toward the support of science or the promotion of commercial expansion at that time, as well as the status of scientific development in general. During the period prior to the Civil War, Congress was somewhat reluctant to appropriate funds for

permanent scientific projects, having doubts as to the constitutional
validity for doing so, and having fears that the effects might be politically
adverse as well as costly for a democratic society. Nevertheless the
government did become increasingly involved in scientific activities.
At first it was only natural to utilize the readily available resources and
personnel of the army and navy in the execution of scientific projects
which were undertaken to promote the general welfare of the young
republic. For a time, the U.S. Military Academy produced the only professionally trained engineers; and some of the navy's young officers,
from association with the best mathematicians and scientists of the
country, developed a competency in marine surveying and astronomy,
and thereby acquired a taste for research. As time passed, however, a
class of professional scientists emerged within the civilian population
who were qualified to conduct full-time research, which itself became
more sophisticated as emphasis was placed more on the theoretical approach to scientific and technological inquiry. But as the reliance on the
armed forces to perform most of the nation's scientific and engineering
tasks diminished, some of the naval projects which had begun as temporary or unfunded operations remained.[1] The interest of individual
officers in science and in professional growth through association also
survived and developed; and the libraries which were formed to support
specific scientific activities flourished for varying periods of time.

LYCEUMS, LIBRARIES AND PROFESSIONAL ASSOCIATIONS.

Until recent times scientists relied a great deal upon the surface traveler
of land and sea to help extend the frontiers of knowledge by bringing
back data and specimens of scientific interest from remote regions of the
earth. Even as the missionary entertained the fervid hope that the mariner
would aid him in the dissemination of the gospel, the scientist called
upon the seafarer to aid in the cause of science. Most merchant and
naval seamen as a matter of course collected curiosities and items of
unique interest in order to present them to their friends upon their return home; and many a local museum "cabinet" or waterfront tavern
was also enriched by botanical, zoological, geological, and ethnological
objects brought from distant lands and oceans. A ship's captain might,
in magpie fashion, carry off such items as a Roman sarcophagus weighing
some 3,500 pounds, or a mummy disinterred in Egypt. Or he might
acquire smaller objects such as ancient coins, or a limb of one of the
cedars of Lebanon, and then donate them to various colleges or other
scientific and literary institutions. He also might bring back from a
voyage field and garden seeds or foreign strains of farm animals for
propagating purposes. Financial gain was another motive for collecting,
and merchants also encouraged the collecting habits of sailors. An ex-

ample of an inducement by the jewelry trade is evident in advertisements found in the appendix of the 1827 edition of Blunt's *American Coast Pilot*, where a ship's officer might have read that "Robert Gedney's Comb Manufactory," located on the corner of Pearl and Fulton Streets in New York, paid cash for "tortoise shell, ivory and horn."

More significantly, scientists attempted to interest mariners in the proper collection and preservation of natural history specimens. The first publication of the Academy of Sciences of Philadelphia was a small informational circular, printed in 1817, which contained practical directions for maritime voyagers on the art of scientific collection.[2] Other scientific societies also printed and distributed similar pamphlets over the years. The cooperation of the government in enlisting the services of naval officers to further the aims of science was also sought by the scientific community. The Navy Department complied by incorporating some of these requests into the sailing orders of vessels bound abroad. Printed material concerning the collection of museum specimens and items of potential agricultural import, prepared by the government and others, was also furnished to captains of naval vessels. When Commodore John Downes embarked upon a voyage of circumnavigation in the *Potomac* in June of 1831, Secretary Levi Woodbury mentioned in his orders to him:

> It may be in your power, while protecting the commercial, to add something to the agricultural interests of our country, by obtaining information respecting valuable animals, seeds, plants, &c.; and by importing such as you can conveniently, without expense to the government, or neglecting the more appropriate duties assigned you.
>
> The cultivation of the sugarcane has become an object of increasing importance and value, and you may be able to meet with different varieties in the course of your cruise, and procure directions as to the mode of culture. It is very desirable that this branch of agriculture should not be lost sight of in your inquiries.
>
> The copy of a resolution of Congress, of the twenty-fifth of January, eighteen hundred and thirty, upon this subject, and the collection of vegetables, grain, &c., is enclosed for your information and attention.
>
> There are many scientific, botanical, and agricultural institutions, to which your collections might be profitably intrusted, and by which, whatever you procure, would be applied to the greatest advantage; among them is the Columbian Institute of the city of Washington.

> This society, as well as the Treasury Department, has pre-
> pared directions for the preservation of articles, and requested
> that they might be distributed among our naval commanders.
> In compliance with their wishes, I send you a few copies.

The Columbian Institute for the Promotion of Arts and Sciences
was a private scientific society which began to flourish in the year 1816.
It was organized by various civilian and military residents of Washington
and was led for a time by Dr. Edward Cutbush, USN, a naval surgeon.
The membership hoped that the organization would develop into a
national institution which would serve to collect and disseminate scientific
information of benefit to the country, and would also provide the culturally devoid federal city with a scientific society worthy of the nation's
capital. After some years of activity, the Institute languished; its leader
left Washington; and its charter finally expired in 1838. Three years
later its remaining members were invited to join (and to transfer the
effects of the old Institute) a new and somewhat similar society, called
the National Institution for the Promotion of Science, organized in
1840. Upon incorporation in 1842, the new society was renamed the
National Institute. It was patterned after other local American scientific
societies of the time, but had some pretentions of becoming a national
society. It did succeed briefly in this goal in connection with the Wilkes
Exploring Expedition, as will be recounted later. Like its predecessor,
the National Institute hoped to further its aims by asking American consuls abroad and the armed forces to collect materials for it. In June, 1842,
Secretary Abel P. Upshur lent support to the Institute by issuing a circular to the Navy Department (which was still on the books of the navy in
1851) in which he quoted a resolution of the society soliciting the help
of the navy in carrying out its objects, and personally commented on the
usefulness of the organization and noted its national importance.
    Although many officers of the navy for years willingly promoted
knowledge by contributing collected specimens, etc., to scientific and
other organizations, including the marine museum maintained by the
American Seamen's Friend Society, a few of them, in 1833, felt the need
for a scientific institution within the service itself. Even though the Navy
Department provided ships and navy yards with libraries, and a library
existed at navy headquarters in Washington, a cultural deficiency was
apparent. What was really needed was a shore-based institution such as
the army had at West Point. Aside from its primary mission of training
officers, the Military Academy there provided a symbolic home for the
army: a library, a museum, a place for heroic portraits and monuments,
and for captured trophies. In a word, tradition was enshrined at West
Point. But Congress at this time was not ready to provide a similar in-

stitution for the navy, which by the very nature of its far-flung activities and mode of existence it would seem to need even more than the army.

The need for a professional home was first recognized by a group of naval officers at the New York Navy Yard who felt a desire to better themselves professionally and culturally through association. They also wanted to contribute directly to the scientific world of the day, for all about them advances were being made, and they longed to employ their talents and to use the unique opportunities available to them in the cause of knowledge. In the recent past, attempts had been made to form naval fraternal organizations in New York and in Boston, but the goals of these organizations did not aspire beyond the provision of mutual insurance or assistance for their members. The time had come again in the cultural history of the navy for the men themselves to provide for a need that the government was reluctant to recognize.

On November 27, 1833, a few officers of the U.S. Navy and Marine Corps attached to the navy yard at Brooklyn gathered to form "a Society for the object of Establishing a permanent Library, Reading Room, and Museum of Natural History, Curiosities, etc. . . . ," which they subsequently named the U.S. Naval Lyceum.[3] The choice of name was in keeping with the vogue of the day. Many local associations called lyceums had been formed in the United States during the latter part of the 1820s in response to a popular education movement led by Josiah Holbrook. In its pure form, the early American lyceum was dedicated to the practical education of adults, especially through the means of public lectures supported by those being taught. By 1829, Holbrook had enlarged his ideas, and he was able to cite eleven advantages that would accrue to a community that established a lyceum according to his plan. Only two or three of these aims were applicable to the U.S. Naval Lyceum. These pertained to the moral and intellectual self-improvement that could be derived from an educational environment, and to the establishment of a library and a museum of science. Although the U.S. Naval Lyceum began during the infectious stages of Holbrook's lyceum movement, and had a few characteristics and goals in common with it, it was from its inception a professional association.

At the organizational meeting chaired by Master Commandant Matthew C. Perry, it was resolved that a committee of seven nominate suitable candidates for the offices of president, vice-president, corresponding and recording secretaries, treasurer, librarian, and assistant librarian. Another meeting was convened the following day to elect the officers proposed by the nominating committee. Commodore Charles G. Ridgely, commandant of the navy yard, was elected president, *ex officio*. Perry was elected first vice-president, while Dr. Thomas L.

Smith, Assistant Surgeon, USN, was chosen librarian, to be assisted by
a Mr. John Bellingham. It was with a touch of emotion that Commodore
Ridgely communicated the news of the formation of the Naval Lyceum
to Secretary of the Navy Levi Woodbury on December 11, 1833. He
mentioned that he did not know when he had "ever made a communication to the Department with more sincere gratification," and that he was
assured that the Naval Lyceum "would meet with the approbation of
the President . . . and every Member of the Cabinet," in addition to
Woodbury. Enclosed with his letter was a copy of the hastily drawn up
constitution of the Lyceum, and a list of the thirty-four members and
officers of it. Sent jointly was a letter by a committee delegated to inform the secretary about the new organization. Of special interest is
their statement, "It is thought that this society, in its connection with
the Naval School, will have an important tendency to direct the younger
class of officers to the higher branches of professional Science, and
direct them from the habits of idleness and insubordination, so often
prevalent when large numbers are collected together."

At that time, so-called schools for midshipmen were conducted at
three of the navy yards, usually aboard the receiving ships attached to
the stations. Professor Edward C. Ward, who early became a member
of the administration committee of the Naval Lyceum, and also its
second librarian, was the instructor at the Brooklyn school. The concern
of the membership for the education and discipline of junior officers is
evident in their statement to Woodbury. In order to help provide for this
problem, novice midshipmen were invited to use the facilities of the
Naval Lyceum, while full membership was made available to those who
had achieved the rank of passed midshipman.

Secretary Woodbury replied almost immediately to Commodore
Ridgely's letter, stating that he would be happy to lend any aid in his
power to promote the objects of the Naval Lyceum. He soon demonstrated his good intentions by allowing the association to become privately incorporated, and wisely advised, on March 13, 1834, that it be
done through the New York legislature rather than the U.S. Congress,
for he doubted that it would succeed before the latter body. Through
the efforts of Charles A. Livingston and two other members of the legislature, the U.S. Naval Lyceum received a charter of incorporation from
the State of New York, authorizing it to hold $25,000 in property, in May
of 1835.

The first year of the Naval Lyceum was one of rapid physical growth.
In order to accomplish its ambitious plans, the members met once a
week, and sometimes even more frequently. From the very start, the
association received support from the local community in the form of
donations of books and other materials. One of the first resolutions of

thanks recorded in the minutes of meetings was to some twenty persons, mostly from New York and New Jersey, who had extended their patronage to the institution. Among those listed was the navy's old friend, William Wood. He again must have offered to collect books for the new library and reminded the Naval Lyceum of the *Franklin's* library which was in their very midst. The library was taken over, and its fate finally assured, at least for another half-century. This collection was reported to be the nucleus of the intended new library, and "a public spirited gentleman" was daily adding to its number.[4] Apparently William Wood again employed his well-tried methods of direct solicitation on the liberal citizens of the city. For his efforts in behalf of the Naval Lyceum, its grateful membership elected William Wood its first corresponding member—a category of membership that in practice was awarded to persons who were not quite illustrious enough to be honorary members.

However, some corresponding members were elected from the world of scholarship. John Torrey, Alexander Dallas Bache, and Edmund Blunt were among those accorded this status. Other corresponding members selected were officers of the U.S. Army, foreign navies, certain members of the diplomatic service, and those who had rendered some singular contribution to the Naval Lyceum. Honorary membership was bestowed upon the president and vice-president of the United States, the cabinet officers, the Board of Navy Commissioners, and other personages, such as James Fenimore Cooper, Washington Irving, General Lafayette, Benjamin Silliman, and former Presidents James Madison and John Q. Adams. All apparently accepted the honor and each received a diploma of membership. Some of the corresponding members actually did correspond on matters of specific interest to the society, while a few honorary members were kind enough to visit the Naval Lyceum when business brought them to New York.

For many years, the Naval Lyceum occupied rent-free quarters on the third floor of Building No. 1, which was the office building of the successive commandants of the navy yard from 1833 to 1910. Eventually, with the increased renown of the society, the entire structure became known as the Lyceum building. It was located in an attractive area of navy yard, with shade trees and cannon at the front of the building providing a proper setting for this unofficial repository of the navy's prestige. Nearby, on a well-kept lawn, was a bandstand from which concerts were given at certain regular intervals.[5] No doubt the contemporary visitor was impressed with what he saw and experienced there and went away with some pride in his country's navy.

Frequent mention was made in the minutes of the Naval Lyceum to the purchase of glass and lumber for the construction of cabinets to exhibit the many specimens of natural history, ethnological objects, and various artifacts that accumulated. At almost every meeting the latest donations from members and other interested parties were reported. The encyclopedic variety of the items which were accepted was indicated in an inventory of donations presented at the December 31, 1834, meeting. Shells, insects, ancient vases, lamps and "marbles," fish, birds, animal skins, mineralogical specimens, and other "Natural Curiosities" from all parts of the world were enumerated in quantity. Additionally, 508 specimens of coins and medallions of silver, gold, brass, and plaster were inventoried along with several oil paintings, engravings, drafts, and "autographs of a great variety." The curators of the "cabinets" hoped that during the coming year those members who had the leisure and disposition to do so would devote themselves to organizing this typical nineteenth century *omnium gatherum*. If there were volunteers for the project, they perhaps soon found themselves to be in unfamiliar waters, for later, in 1837, the curators thought it best to recommend the employment of a competent person to organize a collection of birds and other specimens lately received from the officers of the sloop-of-war *Peacock*. In 1855, the collections were classified and listed in an "Iconographic Catalogue of the U.S. Lyceum, at the Navy-Yard, Brooklyn, N.Y." The catalog, compiled by the librarian, appeared in several monthly issues of the *United States Nautical Magazine and Naval Journal.* The preface to the catalog, in the October number, attempted to point out the superior and unique character of the museum, referring to it as "Well-filled cabinet-cases of the handsomest specimens in Natural History [which] fitly illustrate the life and tastes of the sailor . . . eminently checkered as it is with originality."

The Naval Lyceum also engaged in other publishing activities, especially during its beginning years. One of the first items to appear under its auspices was an eleven-page pamphlet in 1834 with the title, *General Directions for Collecting and Preserving Articles in the Various Departments of Natural History.* It was reprinted from a pamphlet published in 1829 by the Franklin Society of Providence, Rhode Island, and was distributed as a guide for "public officers and agents and all others disposed to aid in promoting the objects of the institution." The curators of the Naval Lyceum's museum were of the opinion that little had been done by naval officers in the way of collecting specimens of scientific value, and they hoped that their brethren would become interested in participating in this activity for the Lyceum. Their little pamphlet was intended to provide the necessary information for handling and preserving collected animal and plant materials in the field.

Instructions for performing two other scientific activities (meteorological observations and shell collecting) were also published by the Naval Lyceum as articles in its short-lived periodical, the *Naval Magazine.*

This bimonthly publication, edited by Chaplain Charles S. Stewart, was launched with hopes for its self-supporting success in 1836. But even with a boost from the Navy Department in the form of a pledge for thirty-two subscriptions, it survived only two years. The magazine contained general naval intelligence, articles on professional subjects, fiction, travel sketches, and other miscellaneous pieces. Among its contributors were James Fenimore Cooper, Alexander Slidell Mackenzie, and well-known naval officers of the day, many writing under *noms de plume*. On the whole, the *Naval Magazine* was one of quality in content and format, but due to an insufficient number of subscribers and to unanticipated high production costs, the journal suspended publication in 1837. It was never revived, for the Naval Lyceum nearly depleted its treasury in paying off the magazine's bills. Subsequent Lyceum publications were limited to a few catalogs of the library and similar small pamphlets.

External to its own affairs, the Naval Lyceum had contact with other scientific and cultural societies. The nearby Brooklyn Lyceum may have provided inspiration or served as an example for the Naval Lyceum during its initial period of organization, for it had held its first public meeting and lecture only a fortnight or so before the Naval Lyceum was founded. Frequent invitations were extended to the members of the Naval Lyceum to visit, attend lectures and exhibitions, or to participate in activities there, as well as at the Lyceum of Natural History of New York, the New York Atheneum, Columbia College, and other local cultural institutions. Invitations were also received to appoint delegates to attend annual meetings of a national organization that grew out of Josiah Holbrook's ideas, called the American Lyceum, which was devoted to the advancement of education, especially in common schools, and to the general diffusion of knowledge. The Naval Lyceum sent delegates to at least three of these meetings where they reported on the activities of their society. Chaplain Stewart on his return from one such meeting in 1835 "handed to" the Naval Lyceum five pamphlets that the secretary of the American Lyceum had given him. One wonders whether any of the members even looked at these reports and essays written on the education of female teachers and the deaf and dumb. Nevertheless, the Naval Lyceum took these and other meetings seriously, and was itself respected. When, in 1837, preliminary considerations were being made concerning an expedition to the South Seas, Secretary of the Navy Mahlon Dickerson formally asked the Lyceum's advice in recommending what researches should be followed.

In 1834 the membership donated $147 for relief of the Poles, and in 1854, sent a contribution to the fund for the erection of the Washington Monument. The Naval Lyceum also performed empirical tests on certain materials and pieces of apparatus brought to its attention, and the members of the investigating committees reported their findings to the membership. While most of the communications submitted to the Lyceum were in the form of papers read at the meetings, outside lecturers did on occasion address the group by invitation. No doubt the resident members derived benefit from their exposure to the active local world of learning, or from their amateur dabblings in science, yet it was the library they assembled that provided the main source for their professional self-improvement.

The library collection, while not exclusively devoted to naval topics, naturally became strong in this area. In addition to the books from the *Franklin's* library, many others were acquired almost simultaneously with the founding of the Naval Lyceum. The marine insurance companies of New York donated $500 for the purchase of books. The organized merchants of South Street, and those of Pine and Pearl Streets, contributed toward the library, and individual firms donated a few costly items. Current reading matter was supplied by the local newspapers in the form of free subscriptions. In 1834, an attempt was made to acquire the remainder of the *North Carolina's* library, then thought to be at the Depot of Charts and Instruments. Vice-president Matthew C. Perry probably remembered it, for he had been first lieutenant aboard the *North Carolina* when she sailed to the Mediterranean in 1825. It is not clear whether the library was eventually secured, but Lieutenant William L. Hudson, prior to leaving for Washington, was instructed at the November 11 meeting "to endeavour to obtain for the Lyceum" what was left of it, "other than such books as may be duplicates" of those already in possession of the association.

Over the years, many persons either gave, or deposited on loan, books which were valuable in content or were unique because of their association or intrinsic value. Former President James Madison presented a sixteen-volume edition of Conrad Malte-Brun's *Geographie mathematique, physique et politique* . . . published in Paris, in 1803. Both James Fenimore Cooper and Washington Irving gave copies of their works, as did authors of less renown. Commodore Isaac Hull deposited 200 to 300 volumes from his personal collection, and the official library allowed to the navy yard by the Navy Department was loaned permanently to the Naval Lyceum.

Library matters appeared frequently before the membership, even though there was a library committee appointed to assist the librarian in policy decisions. Some of the problems that were experienced in the operation of the library were just as common then as they are now: the disposal of duplicates (very early there was mention of selling them at auction), the refusal of unwanted gifts or loans, overdue books, growth of the collection, binding, the preparation of catalogs, and maintaining

order in the reading rooms. A present-day librarian, however, would wel-
come the nature of the latter problem and the ease in which it was settled.
During the meeting of Tuesday, November 4, 1834, it was resolved that
members be enjoined from wearing their hats while in the rooms of the
Lyceum in order to preserve proper decorum; and no further mention had
to be made about this matter over the years. Another problem of a recurring nature involved the unauthorized removal of the latest newspapers
from the library. At the meeting of December 15, 1835, the librarian was
directed to observe who was responsible for taking away the newspapers
and report them to the membership, so that they could be fined. Apparently one of the alleged offenders was the Lyceum's president, Commodore Ridgely, although the librarian thought he should be excepted from
the rule. The administration committee agreed and quickly offered a
resolution which allowed the president this privilege, legally.

One of the benefits that absent members enjoyed, in addition to paying
a dollar less in dues, was having newspapers, letters and packages
forwarded to them through the library. After certain newspapers had
been in the library for a period of at least two weeks, they were sent to
the various squadrons of the navy for distribution among the members.
In the year 1839, for instance, several thousands of letters and newspapers were forwarded by the assistant librarian with the aid of the
society's porter. The office of assistant librarian was a paid position as
of April 1, 1837, from which date twenty-five cents daily, including
Sundays, was to be paid for his services; and in 1856, he was reported
to receive $500 per annum.[6] The assistant librarian was responsible
for the day-to-day operation of the library, while the librarian provided
the administrative direction and authority. At regular intervals a special
committee was appointed to take an inventory of the collection, and the
finance committee reviewed the library's fiscal books. Both library
positions were important ones in the Naval Lyceum because of the high
place that the library held in the structure of the society. A more or less
static museum could be left to run itself, but a dynamic library needed
constant supervision and daily care.

The library's operation was in keeping with the times. Many general
books were not allowed to circulate, while several valuable books could
not be consulted without the librarian's permission; and relatively severe
fines were imposed for various infractions of the library's rules. The
library was, in effect, a gentleman's library. In order to keep the large
volumes from chafing as they were withdrawn from the shelves, the
shelves were lined with baize, the better to protect the bottom edges of
the bindings. No rough substitutes were employed by these men, experienced as they were with shipboard chafing gear. They knew libraries
well enough to provide the proper furnishings for their own. And al-

though it might be necessary to communicate their orders in a loud, clear voice when afloat, they took pains to write into the constitution of the Naval Lyceum that "indulgence in loud and general conversation, or in any practices calculated to disturb the pursuits of members or visitors who may be present [in the library] is strictly prohibited."

An idea of the content and size of the library in its various stages of growth can be gained from checking the few remaining catalogs of the collection. The earliest and most useful is a manuscript catalog, dated 1841. It contains almost complete bibliographic descriptions of many of the original books, and is arranged in a classified order. The terminology employed in this catalog, and the number and relationship of the classes used throughout its scheme of classification, was similar to that used by the Library of Congress at the time. Possibly the 1831 edition of *The Catalogue of the Library of Congress* was used as a model for classifying the Lyceum's library. This catalog and *The Catalogue of the Boston Atheneum* (1827) were the only two catalogs of libraries published before 1833 owned by the Naval Lyceum in 1841. When the librarian was charged with the responsibility of organizing the collection on January 14, 1834, perhaps he and the library committee already had these and other local sources at hand. Later printed catalogs, intended only as listings of the books owned by the Lyceum, do not tell much about the organization of the library. The books listed in these catalogs were grouped under broad subject classifications, which were themselves usually arranged in an alphabetical order. The holdings of the library as listed in these subject categories appear largest in "Naval and Military," "History," Voyages and Travels," "Belles Lettres," "Natural History," and "Biography." American and foreign periodicals of professional and literary interest (procured by subscription or exchange) were also well represented. Among the more rare and costly individual books in the collection were examples from each century since the invention of the printing press. Over a period of forty-seven years, the library steadily grew in size from 1,134 volumes in 1835, to 5,000 in 1881 (the "Iconographic Catalogue" had already listed the holdings as "nearly 5,000 valuable volumes and pamphlets in 1855). However, the membership of the organization appears never to have been very large. Some thirty-four members were enrolled in 1834, about ninety-eight in 1856, and still ninety-eight in 1881.

A foreshadowing of the Civil War is recorded in the minutes of the meeting of January 5, 1836, when a resolution was passed directing the librarian to prevent the newspapers *Human Rights,* the *Emancipator,* and the *Liberator* from being laid on the reading room table. As the years passed, the meetings of the Lyceum became more infrequent—bimonthly in 1838, to intervals of several months, to finally a half-year between some meetings. Then, for the duration of the conflict, the Naval Lyceum did not meet from June 1, 1860, until February 1, 1864. But it was not until 1871 that regular meetings were again resumed. A report by the librarian in 1871 on what had been accomplished toward re-organization since December 15, 1870, mentioned, "The books of the library have been collected, as far as possible, rearranged according to their classification; and a new catalogue written out." He indicated that it would cost not less than $80 to have a new library catalog printed outside the navy yard, and that there was not sufficient type at the printing press aboard the receiving ship to do the job. Also, he noted that a number of the missing books appeared to be charged against the names of clerks and employees of the navy yard who had left and could not be traced.

The Naval Lyceum flourished in its reorganized state for at least an-other eleven years. On June 30, 1882, the last meeting to be recorded was held, and no written indication that the society's life was coming to an end was evident. In fact, just a year before, an article about the Naval Lyceum, published in Hamersly's *Naval Encyclopedia* (1881), described it as a vigorous and prospering organization. Nevertheless, within a few years its final dissolution was to take place. The last member was enrolled in 1885, and by 1888 the Naval Lyceum ceased to exist. The remaining books and artifacts were transferred to the U.S. Naval Acad-emy where at first they apparently created a problem. In November of 1890, Superintendent Robert L. Phythian was ready to give them up, on Rear Admiral Stephen B. Luce's suggestion, to the navy's struggling in-fant War College at Newport, Rhode Island, because there was no "suit-able place to stow the books and exhibit the relics."[7] Fortunately, the surviving representatives of the Naval Lyceum had arranged the dona-tion in such a manner that it could not be easily dismissed, and the ma-terials remained at Annapolis. Today many of the original books of the Lyceum, associated as they were with their donors—beginning with William Wood and the *Franklin's* library, and with the illustrious offi-cers who founded the society—still survive. Others have disappeared, some, no doubt, during periods of their neglect at the Lyceum and the Naval Academy. Yet those that remain serve to perpetuate the aspira-tions of the Naval Lyceum at the very institution which many of its members hoped would someday be established for the betterment of the navy.

Eight years after the founding of the U.S. Naval Lyceum, a similar organization was instituted at the navy yard in Charlestown, Massachu-setts. The success of the Brooklyn association was noted at a meeting of naval officers and civilians at the Tremont House in Boston on February 25, 1842. It was decided there to adopt and extend the organizational plan of the U.S. Naval Lyceum and establish locally a "Naval Library and Institute" which was to have for its objects: "to form a collection of works on General and Naval Literature and Science; to supply a place of deposit for paintings, engravings, maps and charts—for cabinet curiosities of Natural History;—of models of Naval Architecture and machinery connected with the Naval profession . . . ," and to exhibit objects related to the nautical sciences. At the following meeting on May 27, 1842, a proposed constitution was accepted, and a slate of officers was elected. The commandant of the navy yard, Commodore John Downes, became president, *ex-officio*; Mr. William Sturgis, of Boston, was installed as first vice-president; and Dr. William Whelan, USN, was elected librarian. Unlike the U.S. Naval Lyceum, the Naval Library and Institute admitted officers of all the armed services and civilians on equal terms as members. From the very beginning, hoping to derive assistance from local citizens, the Naval Library attempted to have civilians as active members. The election of Mr. Sturgis, a former merchant ship captain, prominent businessman, and philanthropist, as a presiding officer of the association was perhaps more politically designed than coincidentally arranged. Also, the membership was not content to form a library in name only. One of the first orders of business was to define the priorities concerning the purchase of books. The librarian, curator, and corresponding secretary were charged as a committee "to form a catalogue of three classes of books: 1st. Those which are necessary. 2d. Those which are desirable. 3d. Those which are acceptable, in order that the funds of the Society, when any shall be raised, may be appropriated to the purchase and collection of a Library adapted to the object of the institution." Another committee was chosen to solicit donations of money, books, models, and other articles. This time, it appears that William Wood was not present among the benefactors or solicitors for this library in his native Boston. By December 5, there were enough funds on hand to subscribe to several foreign and American literary reviews, *Silliman's Journal,* and one Boston and two Washington newspapers. It was further resolved that such newspapers as could be procured would be forwarded to absent members. Within a year of its founding, the Naval Library and Institute was completely established and set on its long career of providing educational benefits to its members.

While the minutes of its meetings were not as detailed as those of the U.S. Naval Lyceum, many of the same kinds of activities and problems were noted in its record and in a brief twenty-five-year published history of the society.[8] Over the years, the Naval Library did not attempt to publish anything more ambitious in scope than this historical sketch, and except for an annual report dated 1868, it appears not to have published anything else. The apparent reason for this was a lack of expendable funds. It is of interest to note that in order to meet the expenses of printing and distributing the historical account, duplicate volumes were sold from the library. A manuscript catalog of the library, prepared in 1875, provides some information about the composition and arrangement of the book collection at this time.[9] It consisted of some 3,037 volumes, and was divided into eleven broad categories, with those in "Reviews and Novels," "Naval and Military," "Historical Works," "Religious Works," and "Lives, Travels and Memoirs" having the largest numbers of books. Two other artificial groups, "Political Works" (which was composed mostly of government documents), and "Magazines," accounted for about one-third of the total collection. The classification used at this date was rather simple, and may have been derived from the scheme in use at the Naval Academy in 1860. No descriptive bibliographical data other than titles, size, and number of volumes were given in the manuscript catalog. It served merely as a finding list, giving book location by bookcase and shelf number, and was still being used as late as 1901.

The Naval Library and Institute was held together during the Civil War by virtue of a few meetings, at which little business was transacted. The only notable event recorded for this period pertains to the loan of certain museum articles to the National Sailors' Fair held in Boston in November of 1864. The fair, organized to raise money for the benefit of Union sailors, was chronicled by a publication, edited by Julia Ward Howe, called the *Boatswain's Whistle*. Prominent New England literary figures contributed original pieces to its pages in an effort to attract additional subscribers and funds. This souvenir newspaper also served to describe many of the events that took place at the fair, but no mention of the Naval Library or its intended exhibit found its way into it. Understandably, Captain John A. Winslow and the USS *Kearsarge,* recently returned from victorious battle with the CSS *Alabama,* were the attractions that visitors wanted to see or read about most.

In 1866, the Naval Library and Institute appears to have been in a reflective, but assertive, mood. It paused briefly to review its past and to take stock of its immediate condition, and then proceeded on its course with renewed vigor. This resurgence of interest by the membership was evident for the next few years, during which time the library and museum expanded into an additional room in the Institute's government-furnished quarters. The librarian in his report of 1867 remarked that more volumes had been added to the library for the year past than in any previous year since the founding of the organization, and that the library had never been in better condition. The size of the book collection was stated to be 1,872 volumes, "many of the books [being] rare and costly, and nearly all valuable as works of reference and instruction."

At the same time, of the 275 annual members who had joined the society since 1842, eighty were still active. It was hopefully believed that if this small group were expanded, and if each member would promptly pay his assessments, the organization could remain financially solvent.

Unfortunately, this was not the case. By May, 1873, the Institute was short of funds and needed to urge its delinquent members to remit their dues if the organization was to continue its useful purposes. For the next twelve years, the society met more or less regularly. New members were enrolled, elections were held, but not much in the way of business appears in the minutes of the meetings. Between June, 1874, and March, 1875, there was concern over the loss of books by theft; and in February of 1876, the Naval Library authorized its president to lend any museum articles he saw fit to the United States Centennial Exhibition in Philadelphia. The members resolved not to incur any debts unless there were funds to meet them in April, 1879; but a moribund condition had already seized the corporate body, and in June, 1882, the members were again concerned about reviving interest in it. Even though some positive actions were contemplated between 1882 and 1885, such as glazing the doors of the bookcases to protect the books, printing additional diplomas, selling duplicate volumes, and again lending two museum items (this time to the local Sailors' Home Carnival), the Naval Library was bravely experiencing a living death.

A hiatus of twelve years appears in the ledger of minutes, when no meetings took place. Then in November, 1897, some interested persons, Rear Admirals Luce and George E. Belknap among them, took steps to revitalize the Naval Library for the second time. They noted the loss of valuable articles and the poor condition of the quarters. After five monthly meetings, the society did not meet again until November 30, 1900, at which time hopes were expressed that the Navy Department would make needed repairs to the building, and perhaps assign someone to be librarian and curator of the collections. On January 30, 1901, Rear Admiral William T. Sampson announced that the secretary of the navy had a retired naval officer in mind for the position. No further mention of such a position was made in the minutes of the four subsequent meetings in 1901. The end had finally come. Three more meetings were to take place, one each in years 1914–1916, before all plans for survival were abandoned. Concern about having to move the library and museum to another location was evident at the 1915 meeting, and may have precipitated serious thought about the practicality of continuing the society. The book of minutes ends, on May 15, 1916, with a resolution to send a circular to the entire membership requesting its opinion on the disposal of the effects of the organization. By 1921, the Naval Library and Institute was disbanded. Its considerable remains were, like those of the

U.S. Naval Lyceum at Brooklyn, sent to the United States Naval Academy, where less than one-tenth of the library collection was retained. Only about 313 out of the 5,000 or so volumes found their way into the Naval Academy Library as reported in the library's log, dated March 10, 1923.[10] About one-half of the collection constituted government publications. These were returned to the Superintendent of Documents in Washington; other volumes were distributed to the city library, several colleges, and several academic departments of the Naval Academy, or were otherwise disposed of. The Naval Academy Library still had space problems, and still needed to broaden its collecting interests beyond its immediate needs.

In reviewing the histories of the Brooklyn Naval Lyceum and the Boston Naval Library and Institute, it is apparent that certain organizational weaknesses limited their growth and continued success. Chief among them was the inability of the societies to raise and retain money. The collection of a small assessment fee from a membership which was itself small and widely dispersed was hardly adequate to sustain operations. Delinquency in dues payment, an apparently persistent problem, further reduced the sources of income. As the years passed, lessening enthusiasm, and a lessened interest in the two associations by their members became increasingly evident. Although they survived the Civil War, the Naval Lyceum, and the Naval Library did not change their basic goals or procedures when they each reorganized. During the postwar period there was still an urgent need for the dissemination of scientific and professional knowledge among the entire officer corps of the navy; however, the old provincial lyceum approach of lecture, library, and museum soon proved that it was no longer adequate to satisfy the modern needs of the profession.

In October, 1873, a group of naval officers met at the U.S. Naval Academy in Annapolis and formed a new professional association which they called the U.S. Naval Institute. The founders recognized that the navy needed a publication such as the *Journal of the Royal United Service Institution* to serve as a professional forum. They accordingly provided that their organization publish a journal in which significant communications could be presented. This periodical, the *Proceedings of the U.S. Naval Institute,* quickly gained a high rank among other professional journals of the world, after being launched in 1874. Although meetings of the Institute were at first held at branches of the association (which were established at various shore and sea stations), in about fifteen years' time all the branches appear to have dissolved and the work of the organization became concentrated with the parent body at Annapolis. Less attention then was also given to the reading of papers. In the late 1890s this method of dissemination was all but abandoned. Papers no longer had to be read to the membership before publication, and the regular stated meetings gave way to one annual business meeting. The Naval Institute had evolved a formula for success which was not unlike other flourishing professional societies. Its membership grew, while the organization prospered. Today, after a century of existence, the association enjoys a secure and respected position in the community of science and letters.

The path to success for the Naval Institute was not entirely smooth, to be sure. Yet through its wider appeal and more modern approach it was able to overcome some of the recurring problems which plagued the two older associations. In its early years, the Institute, in an effort to gain additional members, attempted to merge with the U.S. Naval Lyceum, and with the Naval Library and Institute, and to use their facilities as branches of the Institute. Branches were established in New York and Boston, but no mergers with the existing societies occurred. The U.S. Naval Lyceum foundered just about the time the Naval Institute was hoping to absorb it; and it appears that the Naval Library and Institute chose to continue its separate, though precarious, existence.[11]

The task of providing for the professional self-improvement of naval officers was soon effectively assumed by the more viable U.S. Naval Institute. Along with the change of emphasis to publication as a better means of communication, the business of the profession privately supporting a gentleman's library, museum, and reading room to accomplish the same ends became more or less a thing of the past. Yet, the older associations had in their better days exerted a beneficial influence upon the educational outlook and development of their members. A quotation from a ten-year summary of the activities of the Naval Lyceum which appeared in the minutes of the September 24, 1844, meeting perhaps best illustrates the contemporary value of the institution: ". . . Some of its Members through its means . . . are enabled to unravel the hitherto apparent maze of Natural History and the Sciences. The nomenclature of these pursuits no longer startle[s] the ear on Shipboard, as unheard of and unpronounceable sounds, the unmeaning affectations of learning." Thus, a respect for universal knowledge, along with a precedent for free inquiry and association sanctioned by the Navy Department, was the intangible legacy that these organizations left to the American naval profession.

NAVAL EXPEDITIONS. In chapter I, mention was made of a few famous naval expeditions of the early periods of European exploring activity, and of the collection of books or libraries that were carried on these voyages. Although, during one phase of this activity, Commodore David Porter engaged in some exploration of the Pacific Ocean when not otherwise occupied with the capture of prizes and the destruction of British whalers in the War of 1812, the United States did not attempt to organize an exploring expedition in the grand tradition of the Old World maritime powers until the era of great geographic discovery was almost drawing to a close. But once the nation entered into the spirit of exploration, it sent out several successive and overlapping naval expeditions of varying sizes and importance between the late 1830s and the beginning of the Civil War. Like their European predecessors, the leaders of the larger American expeditions had need to assemble often uniquely specialized libraries for the use of the scientific and naval personnel attached to the expeditions. These libraries as entities had a transitory existence, and often vanished after they had fulfilled their purpose. Indeed, some few even met tragic ends before their respective expeditions were finally disbanded.

The first scientific expedition to be organized by the United States came about during the third decade of the nineteenth century when the apparent necessity of the government to support scientific endeavor was linked to its interest in aiding commercial expansion. Since the time of Commodore Porter's raiding voyage in the Pacific, whatever progress had been made in American maritime discovery was due mostly to the activities of intrepid Yankee whalers. Many whaling ship captains in the course of their quests for whales and seals, and while seeking more profitable hunting grounds in the Pacific and Antarctic Oceans, reported finding uncharted islands, shoals, and reefs. As it became increasingly apparent that more information about these remote regions of the world was needed in order to gain commercial advantage and to navigate in safety, pressure was exerted upon Congress to have the navy organize an expedition to investigate certain areas of the South Seas. On the strength of a House resolution in 1828, the navy made an abortive effort to organize its first scientific expedition to the Pacific. Commodore Thomas ap Catesby Jones was ordered to the command of it, and an available sloop-of-war, the *Peacock,* was selected for outfitting. Other preparations were made to the extent that Lieutenant Charles Wilkes was sent to New York to purchase suitable scientific instruments. While there, he also purchased about $127 worth of books for use on the expedition to augment the ship's library which Secretary Southard intended for the *Peacock.*[12] The navy's plans were soon scuttled by the Senate when it learned of the preparations that had taken place without its sanction. With the defeat for reelection of President John Quincy Adams, who had earlier proposed unsuccessfully several visionary government-sponsored scientific institutions, interest in the expedition waned and support in Congress for it was not forthcoming for several more years. But the stage had been set and a few of the major *dramatis personae* the books, instruments, and other articles that had been purchased by everyone connected with the expedition, Jones had countered by asking

By 1836 the way had been cleared for the mounting of an ambitious "South Seas Survey and Exploring Expedition," which was finally charged with the responsibility for "the promotion of the great interests of commerce and navigation" as well as "to extend the bounds of science and promote the acquisition of knowledge." Having passed the legislative hurdles that had posed the question, "why?," the project now faced the equally hard question of how to implement it. Partly due to the dilatory actions of Navy Secretary Mahlon Dickerson and to the department's inexperience in handling an enterprise of this nature, preparations dragged on for two years. While the nation's patience was wearing thin, the promotor of the idea, Jeremiah Reynolds, was writing ever-increasingly critical and near-hysterical public letters about the management of the project.[13] Reynolds, at first, had been attached to the expedition as the commander's secretary, and had made several significant contributions to it, including the formation of a civilian scientific corps to which many of the country's new breed of scientists were attracted. But before the squadron was outfitted, he had succeeded in making himself *persona non grata,* and was left behind, along with several other disappointed persons, who for one reason or another had hoped to share in the adventure.

Books were again included among the first items to be obtained for the proposed expedition. On July 22, 1836, Lieutenant Wilkes, after reporting that he was unable to procure suitable charts and instruments in Baltimore, Philadelphia, and New York, was furnished with $20,000 and ordered to proceed on the first packet to Europe in order to secure whatever in his judgment was needed. He was also reminded that it might be in his power while in England and France to obtain "a well selected collection of the best books and charts," and to visit the hydrographic bureaus of these two countries, well experienced as they were in naval exploration, in order to obtain "much valuable information respecting the discoveries already made in the Pacific." Soon after, Commodore Jones asked that Wilkes purchase about thirty-six titles of voyages and travel books which he believed were indispensable in the formation of "a complete library for the exploring expedition." Many of the works, he stated, could not be bought in the United States, "and none of them except in abridged form and of little use.[14]

In January, 1837, Lieutenant Wilkes reported that he had obtained the best collection of charts from the two foreign hydrographic bureaus and a small collection of standard works comprising all that he deemed "would be useful in the different scientific departments of the expedition." The critic Reynolds, of course, took exception to this statement and declared, as far as the scientific books were concerned, that he did not know how an equal number of more useless volumes could have been selected. He maintained that the scientific corps had not been consulted, and that many "working books, manuals, and models" were still required. Further, as a result of the secretary's delay, Reynolds reported that the corps was then actively "ransacking public and private libraries" to remedy the evils occasioned by the tardy arrangements. The truth of the matter appears that members of the corps had been consulted as early as the autumn of 1836. They at least had made some domestic book purchases and had resorted to borrowing some unavailable items. At that time, the secretary of the navy had also asked the advice of a few learned institutions (including the Naval Lyceum) about the goals and needs of the expedition, and had received in reply a list of thirty-eight titles of recommended books (one-third voyages and travels, two-thirds scientific) along with a wealth of suggestions from the American Philosophical Society. In August, 1837, a comprehensive list of books was prepared in Philadelphia. It represented the books that already had been procured, and others that were on order from Europe, or were to be ordered or to be obtained on loan. Moreover, the names of the individuals who recommended the books were noted in the margins along with the status of each book. Among those of the portion of the scientific corps assembled at Philadelphia whose names appeared with their choices of books were James Eights, Asa Gray, Joseph P. Couthouy, Charles Pickering, James D. Dana, Titian R. Peale, and Horatio Hale. The book list ran to twenty-two leaves, and comprised about 600 titles in the natural sciences and in the category of voyages and travels.

Certain members of the corps had been authorized to purchase the necessary books for their departments and had placed orders in Europe, but plans were still being made to borrow some of the books. Asa Gray had hoped to get a few titles from the Library of Congress, but was told by the secretary of the navy that the navy had no authority to request them inasmuch as Congress was not then in session. The book collection grew in size. In January, 1838, it was reported that arrangements for the accommodation of the corps had been completed aboard the frigate *Macedonian* at the New York Navy Yard and that space had been allowed for a library of at least one thousand volumes of "rare and valuable works on the whole range of sciences" in octavos, quartos, and folios.

In the fall of 1837 a difference of opinion between Secretary Dickerson and Commodore Jones over who should be the librarian of the collection helped the exasperated and ailing commodore decide to ask to be relieved of his command. When Dickerson requested him, on October 31, to transmit a "classified and systematically arranged" catalog of all

were on hand to take part in a larger scaled production which was to
follow at a more auspicious time.

that a librarian be appointed. He suggested a person whom he considered
suitable for the position, stating that a competent librarian was then
needed to "receive, arrange, and appropriately dispose" of the books
aboard the frigate. But Dickerson had already appointed the Reverend
Walter Colton as chaplain to the expedition and had given him the extra
duty of being "historiographer," or chronicler of the expedition. Jones
was now told on November 9, 1837, that Colton would also have the
duties of librarian. However desperately the commodore might have
thought he needed a librarian, it appears that he was more disgruntled
by having to take Chaplain Colton than by not having the librarian's
position approved. This prospect probably hastened his decision to
relinquish the assignment.

In the long run, neither Jones, nor his choice as librarian, nor Chaplain Colton, nor the *Macedonian* went on the voyage. Secretary Dickerson also fell ill in early 1838, and the final organization of the expedition
was taken over by Secretary of War Joel R. Poinsett. He succeeded in
giving it the needed direction, and at the same time placed more emphasis on its scientific goals. By the time of the expedition's departure from
Hampton Roads, Virginia, in mid-August, 1838, the scientific corps
had been reduced from thirty-two to nine civilians, Lieutenant Wilkes
had been appointed its commander (without an increase in rank), and a
squadron of six vessels was finally outfitted. The Reverend Jared L.
Elliott took over the controversial chaplain's billet on August 2. Within a
day after reporting aboard Wilkes's flagship, the sloop-of-war *Vincennes,*
he was busy with library work, for the collection of books that had been
purchased and assembled for the expedition aboard the *Macedonian*
still was not recorded. Chaplain Elliott began by first making a list of
the books on the *Vincennes,* and then spent the afternoon of the next
day employed in the same task aboard the sloop *Peacock.* On August 6,
he apparently finished and sent a copy of his listing to Lieutenant Wilkes,
who then was in Washington. The larger vessels to which the scientific
corps was attached (*i.e.,* the sloops *Vincennes* and *Peacock*, and the *Relief* and *Porpoise*) definitely had portions of the scientific library aboard.
The size and content of the library on each ship varied as the voyage
progressed, for there was naturally some shifting back and forth of
scientific personnel and of various stores and equipment over the four-
year duration of the expedition.

At sea, Lieutenant Wilkes soon had to issue an order in writing per-
taining to the scientific library on the flagship. He noted on November 1,
1838, that there was some misunderstanding in relation to the use for
which the forward cabin, or reading room was intended, and thought to

clear it up by addressing the order to his first lieutenant. Wilkes's action, brought about by the old problem of inconsiderate users of library facilities, also tells something additional about the customary ship's library and its quarters, for Wilkes wrote that he viewed the reading room "in the same light as the ship's library." It was a place where "everyone" could be free of interruption when using the books. In order to keep it that way, Wilkes observed that "the accommodations, though not large, will with due respect and consideration for each other's views, be found to be ample, and will naturally prevent any one from appropriating exclusively its small conveniences to himself; or using its table for writing (intended for books and the facility of reference to them), as there no doubt exists sufficient room in the several apartments appropriated to the different officers for that purpose, without incommoding any one." He ended the order by telling Lieutenant Thomas T. Craven to confine the use of the cabin to its proper purposes, and "not permit the issue of slops, &c., to take place in it."[15]

When the *Relief* was detached from the squadron in order to return home in 1839, Chaplain Elliott went aboard her on the Fourth of July, and with the help of Alfred T. Agate, artist to the expedition, selected some books which were transferred to the *Vincennes*. Afterward, a part of this collection was sent to the *Peacock*. Two years later, the portion of the expedition's scientific library aboard the *Peacock* was lost when the sloop grounded and broke up, on July 18-19, 1841, near the Astoria that Washington Irving had written about some years earlier. A few sentences worthy of Irving—or Cooper, even more so—written by a member of the crew, described vividly the last hours aboard the stranded *Peacock,* and serve to remind the reader that libraries at sea are apt to perish under dramatic circumstances. Augustus S. Baldwin, acting sailing master of the sloop, wrote as part of his official report:

> Between 1 and 2 a.m. of the 19th, the tide having ebbed considerably, she re-commenced thumping so violently that it was thought she would go to pieces before daylight. The quick repeated shocks—the rattling of masts—crackling of timbers and beams—rushing of water down every hatchway, fore and aft, added to the pitchy darkness of the night—rendered the scene truly forlorn, dimly lit up by lanterns as it was; yet not the slightest sign of insubordination, panic, or alarm, did I observe.

The library, originally consisting of about 150 titles at the beginning of the voyage, had to be left behind when the crew abandoned the *Peacock* at daybreak. All that was saved were the manuscript scientific journals and the ship's papers which were sent ashore enclosed in india-rubber bags, along with the navigational instruments and charts, in the first boat that left the stricken sloop. The following day the crew had hoped to return to salvage more, but the *Peacock* was by then gone. The library with her had found a sailor's grave.

In the course of its four-year career, the expedition surveyed a part of the Antarctic continent and hundreds of Pacific islands, and dispatched an exploring party on an overland journey from the Oregon Country to California as well. The scientific specimens which were collected on the voyage and sent back were turned over to the National Institute at Washington, which for a time, because of them, took on the status of a quasi-official institution. Upon the return of the vessels to New York, all or parts of their libraries were ordered removed by Lieutenant Wilkes to be delivered to the Washington Navy Yard and then to the Institute, ostensibly to be used in the writing up of the narrative of the expedition. Wilkes, although ordered to deliver all of the scientific journals to the Depot of Charts and Instruments by Secretary of the Navy Abel P. Upshur on July 28, 1842, stubbornly kept them. As a result, the secretary, who wanted the Navy Department to retain custody of them, had to correspond with Wilkes and others over a period of time in order to find out where they were. Lieutenant Matthew F. Maury at the Depot of Charts and Instruments reported on October 11, that although some of the instruments had been returned, none of the collection of "600 or 700 volumes" of scientific books had. A few days later, Upshur learned that the National Institute had the library and wrote to Dr. Charles Pickering, its new curator, about it. In reply, Pickering in a letter dated November 24, 1842, mentioned that six unopened boxes were indeed there. They were marked as containing logbooks, notes, and charts, and instruments from the *Porpoise* and the schooner *Flying Fish*. But more significantly, the curator sent along a copy of what he called "the List of Books belonging to the Library of the Late Exploring Expedition received from Capt. Wilkes." It comprised thirteen leaves, on which some 250 titles of books were recorded, including a separate listing of the small collection of books from the *Porpoise*. Also listed separately were many titles of books and manuscripts that the expedition had sent back previously, having collected them from South America and Pacific islands. Most of these titles apparently were concerned with current topics and written in the vernacular of the places from which they were obtained.[16]

On November 30, 1842, Secretary Upshur directed Dr. Pickering to send the boxes of official data books to his office and the instruments to the Depot of Charts and Instruments but said nothing about the library or the collected books. It appears that he wanted the library to remain at the Institute, at least at that time, for in April, 1842, he attempted to have the New York navy agent locate a set of books that had been received too late to go out with the expedition and to send it to the Institute. As an entity the library, as it was described by Dr. Pickering, becomes impossible to trace further in the confused aftermath of the expedition and the early history of the National Museum.

The publication of the scientific results of the expedition by the government proved to be involved and costly and much more protracted than the preparations for the voyage had been. In the process of administering the publication of the report, entitled *United States Exploring Expedition During the Years 1838-1842,* Charles Wilkes became involved in petty political and scientific controversy. But because of his perseverance and uncompromising standards, an enduring scientific work, worthy of the time, anguish, cost, and effort put into the expedition, was produced. Various portions of the report prepared by Wilkes and renowned American scientists appeared over a thirty-year period. When it was finally suspended in 1874, most of the then-proposed set of twenty-four volumes had been published.[17] The five-volume narrative portion of the report, written by Wilkes, was requested by ship commanders for their libraries as soon as it appeared in 1844, and for years afterward. And one hundred years after the expedition had first skirted the Antarctic continent, American scientists were still to value its contributions to knowledge.

Following in the wake of the Wilkes expedition, the government dispatched several other naval expeditions overseas for scientific or political purposes in the 1840s and 1850s. Some of the excursions involved little in the way of preparation, funds, ships, or personnel, and resembled somewhat the exploring and information-collecting activities which were being carried out at that time by the army within the American frontier. The naval officers selected for overseas exploring assignments usually had access to some kind of library or prepared themselves for their missions in advance by reading in the manner of the many illustrious explorers before them. In 1847, Lieutenant William F. Lynch proposed, and was allowed to undertake, the exploration of the River Jordan and the Dead Sea. Prior to sailing with his detachment of thirteen men on the *Supply,* a storeship which would convey the expedition across the Atlantic and at the same time bring supplies to the Mediterranean Squadron, Lieutenant Lynch occupied his time simply "collecting materials and procuring information."[18] Similarly, Lieutenant William L. Herndon, aboard the *Vandalia* at Valparaiso, in 1850, received orders to disembark and await further instructions concerning an assignment to explore the valley of the Amazon. Lieutenant Herndon later mentioned in his report that while waiting ashore, he used the resources at hand to learn more about the region he was about to venture into. The

commander of the British naval forces of the Pacific took an interest in
Herndon's mission and searched "through his valuable library, for all
that had been written" about the Amazon for him. Several members
attached to the Chilean Navy also loaned the lieutenant books and maps
so that he could prepare his plans and choose the best route of travel.

Another expedition to a foreign country was less casual in its preparations, and because its mission was primarily for astronomical purposes,
some of the books needed for the intended observations were already at
the Naval Observatory. The commanding officer, Lieutenant James M.
Gilliss, formerly chief of the observatory, was given permission in November, 1848, to withdraw from it certain books and instruments that
he requested, and was allowed to purchase others which were not available in the collection. Upon setting out, Lieutenant Gilliss (his assistants
and equipment had already been embarked) was treated to the novelty
of being a passenger aboard a commercial steamer on the first leg of his
expedition (the Naval Astronomical Expedition to Chili) from New
York to Panama. His observations, at least on human nature, began
immediately, for Gilliss found himself at sea with a shipload of California-
bound gold-seekers, the majority "adventurers whom the eastern portion
of the United States could well spare!" Despite its irregular beginning, the
expedition, which was abroad for four years, collected valuable data on
stars visible in the Southern Hemisphere as well as other unique scientific
information.

Three other overseas expeditions of the period, involving naval personnel, fitted more closely the classic pattern of naval exploring activities.
Each expedition was fitted with a library especially suited to the mission,
which was chosen by its commanding officer or the scientists attached to
it. When Lieutenant Thomas J. Page was given command of the brand-
new steamer *Water Witch* in order to explore and survey the waters of
the Rio de la Plata estuary, he was allowed to purchase about fifty titles
of books on the subjects of Paraguay and South America, and on nautical surveying. Four months prior to Page's departure from Norfolk
on February 8, 1853, Commodore Matthew C. Perry sailed from New
York aboard the steamer *Mississippi* in the van of his expedition to
Japan. This expedition, largely diplomatic in its mission, overshadowed
all others in its importance to world history. In preparing for his delicate role as the negotiator of a treaty which would open Japan to
Western intercourse, Perry built up a serviceable library on all aspects
of the Japanese nation and people. Works not readily available in the
United States were purchased in Europe, as had been done for the Wilkes
expedition. The interest generated in Perry's preparations caused a London publisher to reprint one of the hard-to-find items.[19] The commodore
took the library with him, and while at Hong Kong, borrowed other

books on the subject of Japan from the library of the sinologist Samuel W. Williams, whom he also employed as his interpreter.

Simultaneous with the political Japan Expedition, the United States sent out a scientific expedition in 1854 to survey the North Pacific Ocean, the Bering Straits, and the China Seas, and incidentally to implement, while doing so, the treaty which Perry negotiated with Japan in 1854. The North Pacific Exploring Expedition, as it was called, carried civilian scientists, who in the manner of the Wilkes expedition, had selected books in the natural sciences for use on the voyage. The *Vincennes* and the *Porpoise,* veterans of the Wilkes expedition, were again used as exploring vessels, but this time it was the *Porpoise* and her library that never returned from the three-year cruise, for the unlucky brig was lost in the China Sea.

While the expedition to the North Pacific engaged in limited Arctic exploration on the Western side of the continent, the disappearance of Sir John Franklin on the Eastern side set in motion two other successive polar expeditions in 1850 and 1853. These were the first American expeditions to be organized and supplied through private funds, although the government assumed the responsibility for the expeditions and allowed naval volunteers to be detailed to them. Henry Grinnell, a wealthy New York businessman, defrayed the major expenses so that the expeditions could search for the missing Franklin expedition, and also engage in scientific exploration in the Arctic. The second Grinnell expedition was led by Dr. Elisha Kent Kane, USN, a veteran of the earlier Grinnell exploring adventure of 1850. Kane took with him aboard the brig *Advance,* "a large well-chosen library," which was furnished partly by Grinnell, and partly by the government.[20] In his attempt to find Sir John Franklin's party, Kane pushed too far north along the Greenland coast. With the rapid approach of winter in 1853, the *Advance* was trapped in the ice. The brig was not freed the following spring, and the expedition spent another winter in the region before it was decided to abandon the *Advance.* In May, 1855, the valuable library aboard her was left to the mercy of the elements and the shipboard rats when Kane's scurvy-ridden party left Rensselaer Harbor and groped its way south by boat and sledge to the nearest settlement. A last vestige of the library, in the form of the *Penny Cyclopedia,* served to sustain the retreating mariners in a manner not originally intended by its publisher, the Society for the Diffusion of Useful Knowledge, for "sundry volumes" of the *Cyclopedia* were used as fuel in order to bake the last of the explorers' flour into bread. And when the fire that consumed the many pages of uplifting knowledge finally died, these modern-day mariners had, in a sense, also retreated across the centuries and assumed in every respect the status of the earliest seafarer. They were alone with nature still untamed, and were without books.

SHORESIDE AGENCIES AND THEIR LIBRARIES. In the course of its administrative development, certain permanent agencies evolved within the Navy Department which came to be devoted solely to scientific inquiry. The origins of these agencies sprang from the practical need of the government to provide for the survey of the nation's coasts and from the specific needs of the service itself, especially as these needs were interpreted by the several strong-willed officers and civilians who at one time or another were in a position to influence the direction of scientific endeavor in the navy. As part of the resources required to conduct research, books and libraries, of course, were essential. They were either supplied when necessary, or else the personnel of the scientific activity in need of books had ready access to them.

Some of the books and equipment, and above all, the proper instruction and spirit necessary to undertake research were initially provided to the navy by the Swiss-born scientist Ferdinand R. Hassler. In 1807, when the government decided to implement a survey of the nation's coasts, Hassler's plan was selected as the most suitable, and he was hired to conduct the coast survey. At the time, the survey was established within the purview of the Treasury Department. Congress appropriated $50,000 for the project, which it anticipated would be terminated in a matter of a few years. Hassler was authorized to journey to Europe in order to purchase the necessary instruments and books, but the War of 1812 delayed his return. He did not get into the field to begin surveying until 1816–1817. Soon after, Congress passed a law that allowed only military and naval officers to participate in the survey, and Hassler was let out of its service. The Reverend Cheever Felch, who, at this time, was also engaged in working up his "System of Studies for Midshipmen," had told Congress that he could perform the survey in a shorter time and do a better job. He was initially detailed to the project and stayed with it awhile. But after twelve years of indirection, and as a result of a high turnover in personnel, the navy did not accomplish much while conducting the program.

Hassler returned to the survey again in 1832. Although he insisted that it remain under civilian control, he had as his assistants many military and naval officers to whom he taught the proper use of instruments in scientific surveying and chart making. He also provided them with books and encouraged their educational development. Hassler had brought his scientific library of several thousands of volumes with him when he emigrated to the United States in 1805; and in later years carried certain books with him into the field in a specially built carriage. The carriage was so constructed as to provide a smooth ride for the delicate instruments that were needed on station, as well as to serve as an office, wine cellar, and library for the eccentric superintendent.[21] Serving on the coast survey was a popular and a personally rewarding duty for many young naval officers, and it continued to be such even after Hassler's death. In 1851 there were as many as sixty-six naval officers attached to it, who were thus able to get scientific training at a time when the Naval Academy had little to offer in this regard.

About the time that the coast survey was reactivated under Hassler, the navy established the Depot of Charts and Instruments in Washington, upon the suggestion of Lieutenant Louis M. Goldsborough and with the recommendation of the Board of Navy Commissioners. Its original purpose was to provide a centralized location for the proper storage of astronomical instruments, charts, and nautical books, which had hitherto been allowed to stock-pile and deteriorate at the various navy yards. Lieutenant Goldsborough, the first superintendent of the depot, also assumed the responsibility of correcting and modifying the various foreign and commercial charts that were acquired by the navy. It was not long before he installed certain astronomical instruments in a rented building which enabled him to ascertain the errors and rates of the chronometers in his custody and to determine accurate time for the purpose. In 1833, Lieutenant Charles Wilkes relieved Goldsborough, and a year later installed a transit instrument (obtained from England in 1815 by Hassler) in a small observatory building that he constructed at his own expense. When Wilkes took command of the United States Exploring Expedition, Lieutenant James M. Gilliss was put in charge of the depot. He was also given the responsibility of making certain corresponding astronomical observations for the expedition at home. Although this additional assignment enabled Gilliss to obtain a larger telescope and other needed instruments, it became apparent that the facilities for this kind of work were inadequate, and that it was absolutely necessary to build a suitable observatory.[22] The Navy Department recommended that an appropriation for a permanent building be made in 1841, but it was delayed in Congress. Through the persuasive efforts of Lieutenant Gilliss, however, an act was subsequently passed that provided for the construction of a new facility for charts and instruments, and which included an adequate observatory.

Lieutenant Gilliss had the pleasure of supervising its design, selecting its equipment, and furnishing the library. He sought the advice of American and European astronomers in the phases of planning, including the selection of books for the library. The astronomer Sears C. Walker, founder of one of the first astronomical observatories in the United States (the High School Observatory at Philadelphia), provided Gilliss with a basic list of books which were contained in the observatory's library. Other suggestions of essential books for the beginning collection were made by the European astronomers, George Airy, Heinrich Schumacher, Johann Encke, and Johann von Lamont. While on an official visit to the principal observatories of Europe in 1842, Gilliss acquired nearly a thousand volumes for the intended library. He reported that many of the costly books on the list of recommendations were obtained at second-hand book stores at a fraction of their original prices. A considerable number of valuable books were also presented to him "by the distinguished *savans*" of the observatories "in token of their gratification at the establishment of an institution by the United States, where science will be prosecuted." In addition, the new depot was placed on the exchange lists of a dozen or so observatories, which helped insure the future growth of the library. It is of particular note that a number of the books originally obtained by Hassler in 1815 eventually found their way into the collection, and that it was also enriched later by a gift of desiderata from the widow of James M. Gilliss.

In 1844 the new building was completed and the facility was given the official name of the U.S. Naval Observatory. However, its new superintendent, Lieutenant Matthew F. Maury, chose to stress hydrography and meteorology rather than astronomy. His predilection toward these fields won him fame abroad. But it did not win him friends in the coast survey (where more astronomical support was expected from the observatory), nor among other American scientists, particularly at the Smithsonian Institution, who were attempting to coordinate the collection of meteorological data, and with whom Maury failed to cooperate.

In part, Maury's lessened emphasis on the role of astronomy at the observatory determined the choice of location of the Nautical Almanac Office, which was provided for by an act of Congress in 1849. Although the new agency was technically part of the Naval Observatory, it came directly under the secretary of the navy, and he allowed its first head, Lieutenant Charles H. Davis, to set up the office at Cambridge, Massachusetts. Since the earliest days of the Republic, there had been appeals to the national pride for the publication by the government of an ephemeris and nautical almanac such as was prepared by foreign maritime powers. This desire coupled with the actual need for an American ephemeris, as demonstrated through the work of the coast survey, was successfully advocated by Lieutenant Davis in particular. Not only did Davis hope to advance the standing of the country within the scientific community of nations by the publication of a superior almanac, but he sought to promote the cause of astronomy itself. Rather than attempt to prepare the almanac at the Naval Observatory, Davis chose to work among the mathematicians and astronomers of his alma mater, Harvard

University. Here he associated with men of the stature of Benjamin Peirce and Sears C. Walker of the Harvard Observatory, and with others of the coast survey engaged in work on longitude.[23]

The proximity of the university library and the availability of the late Nathaniel Bowditch's private library on mathematics, astronomy, navigation, and linguistics were also important inducements to locate in Cambridge. The Bowditch library consisted of over 2,500 volumes, 500 pamphlets and hundreds of maps and charts by the time of his death in 1838. It was given to the Boston Public Library in 1858 and has been actively maintained there since. It might also be mentioned, inasmuch as another aspect of the relationship of libraries and the sea is elicited, that as a young man Bowditch had access to the Philosophical Library of Salem. This library had been formed around a collection of scientific books seized as a prize of war by an American privateer in the Revolution. The books, which were part of the library of Dr. Richard Kirwan, an eminent chemist of the day, were being shipped across the "Irish Channel" when the vessel carrying them was captured. They were taken to Beverly, Massachusetts, where a "company of gentlemen" purchased them and founded the Philosophical Library, which later became the Salem Atheneum. Afterwards, an offer of renumeration was made to Dr. Kirwan for his library, but he declined it, expressing his satisfaction that his valuable library had found such a good home. The grateful Nathaniel Bowditch, however, left $1,000 to the Atheneum when he died as a token of his appreciation for having been allowed to use its resources during his formative years.

The university library at Harvard was available to workers of the Nautical Almanac Office, but it was not without its formalities. Simon Newcomb, who began his famous career as an astronomer at the office in 1857, recalled in his autobiography how, on one of his first days on the job, he was denied a book that he wanted at the Harvard library because he made the mistake of simply asking for it in the name of the Nautical Almanac Office. Before Newcomb left the library empty-handed, he was lectured on "the law governing the borrowing of books from the library of Harvard College" by "the most crusty and disobliging old man" he thought he had ever encountered. He and the chief librarian, John S. Sibley, so described, later became good friends, and Newcomb subsequently learned that Sibley had thought of him at the time as "the most presumptuous youth that had ever appeared in the library."

With a reorganization of the Navy Department in 1862 (Matthew F. Maury departed the Naval Observatory in April, 1861, in order to join the Confederate States Navy), the Nautical Almanac Office and the Naval Observatory were brought closer together. The Nautical Almanac Office was moved to Washington in 1866. Over the years, it

developed a separate library; and it consisted of 4,000 volumes at the time
it was consolidated with the library of the Naval Observatory in 1909.

The Navy Department Library, 1828-1860. The second quarter century
of the Navy Department library's existence appears to have been no
more eventful than its first. Routine correspondence of the department
concerning gifts, purchases, loans and other transactions involving books
provides some information about the scope and use of the library, if not
about noteworthy occurrences in its history. Whether all of the items
received as gifts or as purchases were intended for the library or were
actually added to it is not always clear. Some materials were sent for the
edification of the secretary of the navy, and may have found their way
into the collection as a result. Such items as pamphlets on improvements
in the Royal Navy (*e.g.,* a report on a gun carriage; another on the use
of a chain messenger for anchors; etc.), sent by Lieutenant Uriah P. Levy
in 1829, and a pamphlet forwarded by Commodore James Barron the
same year were gratefully received. Geographical works and navigational aids were also acquired in a random manner. In 1832, Lieutenant
A. B. Pinkham sent a two-volume set of *Histoire d'un voyage aux isles
Malouines* which he had "met with at a Bookseller's stall on one of the
Bridges of Paris," and thought might be rare and of interest to the government. Secretary Levi Woodbury was happy to accept it on December
15, and indicated that he would avail himself of whatever useful information the work might contain. In a like manner Woodbury acknowledged the receipt of twenty valuable charts and plans which Captain
Philip F. Voorhees may have presented to the department in person in
the spring of 1834.

The American vice-consul in London also thought of forwarding to
Washington appropriate books that were given to him, such as the
Nautical Almanac of 1834 and a recent edition of *Mechanical Improvements Connected With the Royal Navy,* by Joseph Bothway. These
items and seven numbers of the *Nautical Magazine* were sent for the
use of the Board of Navy Commissioners in 1832 and 1833.[24] Navy
authors, notably Maury, Brady, Totten, Chauvenet, Dr. Ruschenberger,
J. H. Ward, and Commander John A. Dahlgren, were also among those
who sent copies of their books to the Navy Department, or otherwise
made known the fruits of their literary labors, or hoped for some form
of recognition or patronage in their endeavors.

The correspondence between James K. Paulding, when he was a navy
agent, and Secretary of the Navy Levi Woodbury illustrates some of the
kinds of materials that were acquired by purchase. While many ordinary
domestic publications were probably purchased without difficulty, the

department's interest in British publications is mostly indicated in the letters due to the problems encountered in their purchase. In 1831 Paulding was to acquire for the secretary the British *Navy List* and Falconer's *Dictionary of the Marine*; and in 1833 the periodical *Court Journal*, along with the latest *Navy List,* the *Naval Chronicle,* and the "Red Book" (*i.e.,* the *Royal Kalendar*) were to be supplied.[25] Six volumes of another periodical, the *Mirror of Parliament*, were sent by railroad car from New York in April, 1841, by navy agent P. C. Wetmore, and a parcel containing the *Annales maritimes et coloniales* was forwarded to the navy commissioners from an overseas firm by the New York agent in July of 1842.[26] About this time, the Washington book firm of Franck Taylor seems to have kept the department informed about the latest foreign publications. Several British and French books on naval topics were sent to the Board of Navy Commissioners on approval just before the date of its dissolution, and Secretary George Bancroft selected a foreign title on the exploration of Oregon from a lot sent to him under similar conditions in 1845. It also appears that at this time other firms sent book catalogs to the department, from which items were selected for the various needs of the navy, such as books for the use of the commander of the Pacific Squadron in 1846, and for the ship's library aboard the sloop *Jamestown* in 1847.

The department, as in earlier years, continued to send ship commanders materials for their information and for regulatory purposes. Peter Force's *National Calendar* (1820–1836), and the usual revised regulations and registers, annual reports, and compilations of laws were standard issue. Other regulatory or reference materials not furnished either by distribution or in the ship's library, when requested, might be loaned to a commanding officer from the department. The loan procedure seems to have been quite informal. Items such as books on courts-martial and diplomatic relations, or items that could not be readily purchased, were made available to officers and to other governmental agencies for indefinite periods. A knowledge of the books available in the department for distribution or loan was displayed by Commodore Jesse D. Elliott, when he requested several books to be sent to him at Pensacola on July 11, 1830. After listing them by title, he knowingly remarked that they were all in the Navy Department. He was requested on August 18, to return only one of them when he was finished with it. As in the past, not all of the books could be found for loan when requested. An instance of a signal book being missing was noted in a letter of January 14, 1837, to Commodore James Barron. He was informed that the book he had inquired about a year or so previously had been found in the office of the navy commissioners, but had since been sent to the Naval Committee of the Senate so that it could be compared with another then in use. Despite the seeming casualness of operation, efforts were made at times to remind borrowers to return materials. In November, 1849, the bureau chiefs and the officer in charge of the Naval Observatory were asked to return any books or pamphlets that belonged to the library of the department that might have been in their offices.

Naval officers apparently also used the library facilities of other government agencies over the years. In 1839, Captain William C. Bolton borrowed several "imperfect and duplicate" books from the War Department for use on the *Brandywine,* and still had them four years later, intending to give them to the U.S. Naval Lyceum, when he was asked to return them; and Captain Thomas W. Wyman on May 29, 1843 inquired whether the Navy Department could secure permission for him to borrow books from the Library of Congress prior to his working on the tables of allowances list of 1844.[27] Books were also loaned to officers by the Board of Navy Commissioners. In 1839, the board offered to loan certain books to Captain Matthew C. Perry aboard the steamer *Fulton,* if he would personally assume the responsibility "for their being returned to the Office, when required."

From 1815 to 1842, in a sense, two book collections existed in the Navy Department: that of the department itself, and that of the Board of Navy Commissioners. It appears that the former was more general in content, and that the latter contained mostly technical and professional works. This was a practical working arrangement which reflected the administrative needs of the department, but it did not contribute to the development of a strong central library. The situation was not helped by the reorganization of the department in August, 1842. At this time a collection of books which "were in a case in the late Office of the Navy Commissioners" were simply removed and made available to the several chiefs of the new bureaus.[28] Although the secretary of the navy asked for an extra clerk to take care of the department's library in 1843, by 1849 three of the bureaus had libraries which either individually or in sum were greater than the department's library. In Charles Jewett's report on public libraries of this date, it was noted that the Navy Department had "no regularly organized library," but that there were "valuable collections of books in the office of the chief clerk, in the Bureau of Ordnance and Hydrography, in the Bureau of Yards and Docks, and in the Bureau of Construction." The total of these collections, including "Congressional documents," was estimated at 3,000 volumes.

The subordination of the Navy Department's library to those of the bureaus during this period is brought out in a letter to the secretary of the navy, dated June 26, 1851, in which Alexandre Vattemare mentioned that he was sending to him a collection of books and documents on behalf of the Ministère de la marine et des colonies. These items, he explained, were for the most part, "wanted by several bureaus of your Department," as determined on his previous visit to Washington. In thanking Vattemare for sending "the valuable collection of books and documents relative to Naval Affairs," Acting Secretary of the Navy Charles M. Conrad enclosed another list of desiderata, on October 18, this time for materials needed by the Bureau of Construction, Equipment and Repair.

For some reason, neither the Navy Department nor its bureau libraries were mentioned in William J. Rhees's survey of libraries, published in 1859, although several other libraries of naval interest rated a paragraph or more in the report. The "National Observatory" library was listed as having 1,000 volumes in 1855, the "United States Coast Survey," 3,017 volumes (1857), the U.S. Naval Lyceum, 4,500 volumes (1856), and the library of the U.S. Naval Academy, "open daily three hours, for the use of the officers and students," 4,600 volumes (1855). For comparative purposes, it is of interest to note that on the eve of the Civil War, the library of the War Department, "founded in 1832," was recorded as having 8,000 volumes (1857), and the Treasury Department library as having 4,256 (1857).[29] Some years after the war, the Navy Department library had not yet attained the size of the pre-war library of the War Department, and was said to have "contained some 7,000 printed volumes, chiefly relics of ships' libraries," in 1882. The library that year, however, experienced a rebirth when the secretary of the navy placed it in the newly created Office of Naval Intelligence in the Bureau of Navigation, and provided for its direction. The present-day Navy Department library dates from this action.[30]

Chapter IX

Reading at Sea

We . . . followed our course . . . all which time, we had no night, but that easily, and without any impediment, wee had when wee were so disposed, the fruition of our bookes, and other pleasures to passe away the time: a thing of no small moment, to such as wander in unknowen seas, and long navigations, especially, when both the windes and raging surges, do passe their common and wonted course.

—Martin Frobisher

The mariner has always been subject to loneliness at sea. This state was yet another inherent hardship of his occupation that had to be endured. From the poem of the anonymous Anglo-Saxon *Seafarer,* wistfully meditating upon his fate on the icy winter seas, to the utterances of Andrew Furuseth fighting for maritime trade unionism in twentieth century America, the lonely life of the sailor has at times been poignantly described by those who followed the sea for their livelihood. Both proud of his hardiness and yet sorry for himself, the mariner in his lament did not overlook the rueful thought that the landlubber, living a normal existence safely ashore, little realized the hazards he faced on the deep, or the disagreeable living conditions he endured there. Indeed, the opinions landsmen formed of the sailor during the age of sail were mostly gained by observing his behavior ashore. Here, released from the confinement of the ship and the restraints of severe discipline and hard work, the sailor usually made up for his deprivations by abandoning himself, with the help of the small wages he had accumulated, to a hedonistic spree in port. This mode of life of the sailor ashore was proverbial; whether the reputation he gained thereby was deserved or not, it was perpetuated in stories which depicted "Jack" as a happy, carefree, generous, but dissolute individual. Also, in eighteenth- and nineteenth-century iconography, sailors were usually shown either ashore carousing, or aboard their ships in port engaged in a variety of convivial amusements in the presence of women, happily at drink and play. Yet in a few of these scenes, amidst the confusion of revelry, a sailor or two might be seen reading a book or a letter, or writing.

With a book in his hands, the seaman assumes a more positive character, at least at sea, for there books played an important part in the recreations of the sailor. Reading helped dispel the loneliness and boredom of a hard existence, and provided one of the few intellectual pastimes available on shipboard. To a few seamen, a sailing ship was "my Yale College and my Harvard"; to others it was the first opportunity to acquire the skill of reading. The place of books and reading in the routine of the ship—the conditions that promoted or prevented reading, and its competition with other shipboard recreations—will be the subject of this chapter.

Many contemporary accounts and observations about life aboard sailing ships and the habits of seamen mention reading in passing, but few reveal anything quantitative about the ability to read among seamen. Whatever information exists is mostly subjective and contradictory, having usually been written either to deplore the general lack of education among sailors, or else to acclaim their capability to absorb learning. Statements by various writers have been made which implied a state of almost universal illiteracy among some crews—that, for instance, it was expected that a seaman would "touch the pen" or make his mark when signing a ship's articles. Other observations have ranged from the admission that a few or several men in a crew could not read or write, to reports that indicated seamen were a "reading people," and that as a group they read more than others in similar circumstances when ashore.

In the early years of the nation, when native-born Americans made up most of the crews of U.S. vessels, the illiteracy rate among seamen was probably the same as that for the country as a whole. Unfortunately, no data on illiteracy in the United States exist for the years 1790–1830; and the data collected between the censuses of 1840 and 1860 are not uniformly comparable. Further, since the compilation of the census of 1870, the definition of literacy in the United States (as in most foreign countries) is based on the ability of an individual to write in any language, rather than to read, as had been the criterion for literacy in the previous three decades.[1] Nevertheless, the data collected in the censuses of 1840, 1850, and 1860 give a rough indication of the percentage of the population which was defined as illiterate at those times. During this period the average percentage of illiterates in the total population of the United states was 21.4 percent, and the average percentage of illiterates among the white population was 9.5 percent. Aboard ship in 1834–1837, Chaplain Charles Rockwell reported that he found about forty seamen including boys who could not read, or who read poorly.[2] This would amount to about a 10 percent illiteracy rate (assuming a crew of 400 seamen and marines on the frigate *Potomac*), which was within the lower range of the 1840 census figures of the U.S. population, as well as comparable to the earlier informal census taken by the agent of the Merchant Seamen's Bible Society at Gravesend, England, mentioned in chapter II, if, indeed, they are at all comparable. While the meager evidence of illiteracy aboard the frigate *Potomac* seems to indicate agreement with the national situation, other factors, such as the presence of a higher proportion of foreign-born among a ship's crew (*i.e.,* the frigate *Constitution* in 1844–1847 carried 46 percent foreign-born crew members, while the white male population of the country was only 15 percent foreign-born in 1850) may tend to make such correlations questionable.

The desire to read and to learn at sea is evident in various accounts. Books for beginners and for children—spellers, grammars, and arithmetic books—were at times requested by sailors for use at sea in otherwise barren educational situations. Other instances are recorded of sailors learning to read on their own from the Bible or from other simply written materials taken or found aboard ship. The example of literate sailors reading to themselves must have been an inducement for at least a few seamen to learn to read; and the frequently reported practice of reading aloud to an audience of shipmates probably had a like effect. Richard H. Dana, who in *Two Years Before the Mast* often mentioned books and reading aboard the two merchant vessels he sailed on in 1834–1836, told how one day on the California coast, when the crew could not be worked, he read Scott's *Woodstock* to six or eight attentive sailors for about ten hours continuously (fig. 10). He further remarked about the intellectual capabilities of his audience: "Many things which, while I was reading, I had a misgiving about, thinking them above their tastes, I was surprised to find them enter into completely."

The living conditions and routine aboard ship were at once both conducive and prohibitive to reading. At times ample opportunity existed for sailors to indulge in leisurely pursuits, but at other times adverse weather, darkness, and physical tiredness brought on by hard work, prevented reading. Dana again is a reliable source to quote in this regard. On a weekday, whatever reading sailors enjoyed was done in the watch below (*i.e.,* when they were not on duty or working), but on Sunday, the only day off from work (other than that necessary to sail the ship), if the day was pleasant, the sailors dressed in their best clothes and brought their sewing and other work and books on deck, where they employed "themselves in reading, talking, smoking and mending their clothes." Dana also noted "On board some vessels Sunday is made a day of instruction and of religious exercises; but we had a crew of swearers, from the captain to the smallest boy; and a day of rest, and of something like quiet, social enjoyment, was all that we could expect."

A storm could upset a sailor's use of his free time, for then, in Dana's words, "it was vain to think of reading or working below, for we were too tired, the hatchways were closed down, and everything was wet and uncomfortable, black and dirty, heaving and pitching." At anchor the crew had more leisure time for themselves at night, inasmuch as they stood watch only about two hours; but then they had no time for themselves in the day, for they worked from sunrise to sunset, "so that reading, mending clothes &c." had to be put off until Sunday. Although Dana managed to find time to read aboard the small brig *Pilgrim*, he found the living conditions aboard the larger ship *Alert* comparatively better. Her clean forecastle was "large, tolerably well lighted by bull's-eyes," and was "far better than the little, black, dirty hole" in which he had lived for many months on the *Pilgrim*. On his first visit to the *Alert*, Dana found some of her crew "quietly at work in the forecastle, either mending and washing clothes, or reading and writing." A part of the crew also slept in a spacious and cleanly kept 'tween decks area almost in the manner of a frigate.

The forecastle of the whaler *North America* was described in 1839 by Francis Olmsted (an alumnus of Yale, who like Dana went to sea for his health) as "a *receptacle* for sailors, where twenty-one men are *stowed away*. . . ." Apparently it was much larger than the forecastles of most ships of the *North America's* tonnage. It was kept clean, and was furnished with a lamp and table, so the seamen had the "conveniences for reading and writing," if they chose to use them, which many did. Some seamen practiced writing every day, while others were learning how to write. They bought their stationery from the ship's slop chest, and came to Olmsted or one of the officers "for copies, or to have their pens mended."

Aboard warships there appeared to be frequent opportunity to read, if a seaman was disposed to do so. Professor Joshua Henshaw reported that on the *Columbia* in 1838–1839, the seamen who were not on watch read books while others sat on deck and plied their sewing needles in the making of hats, or else played games. In 1844–1847 aboard the *Constitution*, another contemporary observer mentioned that the watch below was occupied in almost the same manner during the forenoon, and that the gun deck was "quite a library" with the "idlers" reading. The afternoon passed with "reading, working, etc., until four o'clock." In the evening, there would again be time to read and write, especially for officers, after six o'clock.[3] However, at certain hours (8 or 9 P.M. for the ship generally, and 9 or 10 P.M. for the wardroom) all lights and fires were extinguished, except for binnacle and sentry lights. In addition, the 1841 naval regulations stated that "no person must be permitted to read in bed by the light of a lamp or candle," so this luxury was denied an officer, if the regulation was enforced aboard his ship. Sunday was also a day of rest on a man-of-war, as on a merchant ship. It was more likely to begin with religious services in the navy, but afterwards, the day was given over to leisurely activities. At anchor, according to Nathaniel Ames, there was abundant time during the day for some seamen, between drills and housekeeping duties, to read, sleep, or to do nothing.

The books that seamen owned were kept in their sea chests along with whatever possessions they had taken to sea with them. Dana mentioned how he "overhauled" the chests of his new shipmates, looking for books, after he transferred to the *Alert*. He found nothing to suit his taste until a sailor produced a copy of Bulwer-Lytton's *Paul Clifford* from the bottom of his chest. The Bible was often among the belongings of a sentimental or permanent nature which were found in sea chests. Its ubiquity at sea is perhaps best illustrated in the well-known story of the *Bounty* mutineers. A Bible that a member of the crew took aboard HMS *Bounty* in 1789 ultimately may have been the only book on Pitcairn Island for many years. It was from this Bible that the patriarch of the colony, John Adams, was supposed to have taught the mutineers' children to read.[4] Nathaniel Ames mentioned that he had frequently known men to keep the straggling leaves of a worn Bible in their chests for years; and Chaplain Walter Colton had the disconcerting experience to find that a seaman, who, although he had a well-thumbed Bible in his chest, reserved a special place in the chest for his religious tracts— right next to an eye-gouger, a weapon that he intended to use on some future enemy. One day Colton's own private library, which was in his small room aboard the *Congress,* was set adrift and drenched in a gale as the frigate was buffeted by heavy seas. The often damp and wet conditions aboard a wooden sailing vessel did not offer an ideal storage situation for books to either seamen or officers.

Books as private property were borrowed, loaned, given away, and sold among seamen on the same ship or among other vessels. Whenever there was contact between the crews of two ships, opportunity to exchange books was likely. As Dana observed after a visit to a whaler on the California coast, "They gave us pieces of whalebone, and the teeth

and other parts of curious sea animals, and we exchanged books with
them,—a practice very common among ships in foreign ports, by which
you get rid of the books you have read and re-read, and a supply of new
ones in their stead, and Jack is not very nice as to their comparative
value." But a desired book could bring a fair price at sea. A gunner aboard
the sloop-of-war *Cyane* paid $5 for one that he bought from the whaler
Barnstable when on the same coast in 1843.[5] On the other hand, if a
statement from an account of life at sea in the 1850s is to be believed, a
seaman-guest aboard a ship might be given a book by his sailor-host
merely because he expressed an interest in it; and to have refused the
gift or to have offered to pay for it would have been "an unpardonable
offence" against the forecastle etiquette of that day. Among messmates
in the same crew, it could be another story. If one seaman did not return
the books of another, a sarcastic reminder, such as recalled by Henry J.
Mercier in *Life in a Man-of-War,* was, no doubt, unhesitatingly directed
to the delinquent borrower. Books aboard some ships also helped overcome some of the social barriers between officers and seamen. As
already noted from the accounts of Nathaniel Ames and William
McNally, naval officers loaned both their own books and books from
the officers' libraries to certain seamen. Captains and mates on merchant ships, at times, also loaned their personal books to crew members
of their vessels.

If the quantity of books accessible to seamen varied somewhat from
ship to ship, the quality of reading materials did not differ a great deal
from that available to landsmen. Much of the cheap and popular literature of the day found its way aboard ship in the sea chests of sailors; but
in the climate of nineteenth century uplift, this was regarded as deplorable by the reformer. In his eyes, there were just two kinds of literature
on shipboard—good, and bad. The good consisted of the religious and
"worthwhile" materials which he attempted to supply, and the bad included practically everything else. By identifying and condemning the
components of the latter category in magazine articles and elsewhere,
the reformer recorded for posterity yet a few more examples of reading
matter sailors had aboard ship.

One of the chief aims in providing Bibles, tracts, and religious books
and libraries to seamen was to supplant the so-called "bad" books sailors
had available to read; and though reformers in general advocated the
promotion of education among seamen, some of them feared that if
seamen were not led to "useful reading," more injury than good would
result in their being educated, for then sailors would be enabled "to
imbibe the poison of immoral and blasphemous publications."[6] The
conversion of seamen was thought to have been made more difficult because
they were furnished with books of an "infidel" character, such as "Hume,

Gibbon, Paine, and the Arabian Nights." These works were cited along with the singing of "vain and profane songs" and the "study of the jest book" as evil influences which made up part of the common amusements of sailors, at the time of Richard Marks's *Retrospect.*

In later years it was stated, "there are no forecastles entirely destitute of books, but in many cases, these books consist chiefly of the lower class of novels, such as retail the daring feats of pirates and robbers, and such as lead the reader through the dens of infamy, or accounts of the infamous." Comparing novels to alcoholic "bottles of liquid ruin" which poisoned the soul, another writer also believed this "untold amount of trash . . . , the refuse of a glutted market at home," hindered the work of religion among seamen. But perhaps the best description of "the corrupt literature of the sea" was contained in a plea for good books which originally appeared in the American Tract Society's *American Messenger.* It mentioned that at the head of almost every wharf an exhibition of "trash" selected especially for seamen was for sale. This material consisted of "song books, dream books, extravagant romances, licentious stories and pictures, the 'Pirate's Own Book,' 'Horrible Murders,' 'Mysteries of Paris,' and mysteries of the pit," and that almost every sea chest was "supplied with some of the scum of the 'polite literature.' " The writer also maintained that these materials when read filled the imagination with "scenes of debauchery and blood," and that young Philip Spencer, the ringleader of the attempted mutiny aboard the U.S. brig *Somers,* had begun his infamous career, which was "so ignominiously finished" with his hanging at the yardarm, by reading *The Pirates Own Book.* This book, which Herman Melville depicted a sailor as owning in *Redburn,* and which Daniel Noble Johnson mentioned being furtively read and discussed by a group of apprentices at "school" aboard the *Delaware* in 1842, was an anthology of pirate stories. Today it is a valuable source on the history of pirates, and could hardly be thought of as a book that would incite murderous passions in a reader. Nevertheless, the writer of the *Messenger* article believed that books had a direct influence on behavior, for he went on to state that had the rebellious Spencer read John Angell James's *Young Man From Home* instead, he might have become a minister of the gospel! The writer was probably unaware of the fact that the *Somers* had a ship's library (which before the notorious voyage might have been augmented at the request of her captain, Alexander Slidell Mackenzie, possibly because the *Somers* was to serve as a model school ship), and that this resource of books did not change the young Spencer into an ideal seamen.[7] Neither, it might be added, did the presence at sea of the Bible and the very same titles that Abraham Lincoln had taught himself from as a boy ever produce a man of his stature from the forecastle, steerage, or cabin.

A large portion of the reading diet of seamen was doubtlessly comprised of the cheap, ephemeral literature of the streets which consisted of bizarre, lurid and sensational stories, political pamphlets, and books of amusement. Indeed, some of it might have been especially prepared for the seaman's consumption (as in the James Catnatch and Thomas Tegg era of publishing in England); but materials of more substantial fare were also obtained and read by seamen. As previously mentioned, in the accounts of Ames and Dana the works of Sir Walter Scott were noted as prevalent aboard ship. This was no wonder, for they were to be found on some of the remote frontiers of America, where they even presumably circulated among Indians. Dana found part of a copy of *The Pirate* in a storehouse for hides in San Pedro, and Ames some years before was caught reading *Woodstock* when he should have been more attentive to duty.

Other popular authors, of course, were read at sea. Dana mentioned Bulwer-Lytton, and William Godwin, and he had pressed an unfamiliar flower between the leaves of Cowper's *Letters*. McNally reported reading Cooper's novels, as did Chaplain Stewart note the popularity of Irving aboard the *Congress*. Again, on the West Coast, another young merchant seaman read *Astoria*, studied Spanish, and read educational books, for the studious always seem to find the time and materials to read. For those who did not bring their own books with them, there were likely to have been newspapers and stray issues of magazines to borrow and read. On long voyages and in remote settlements, previously unread old newspapers and magazines were as eagerly sought after as new books. Sailors and settlers avidly read old newspapers for news of home and ships, and were willing to buy or exchange them at sea and in such far-off places as the pueblo of Los Angeles in the 1830s.[8]

In addition to the general literature of landsmen that was carried aboard ship, there were certain other books that were still being specifically written for the seaman, which were mostly intended to help him in his occupation or in his personal life. These materials comprised religious, legal, medical, professional, and other works. Enough has already been said in this study about the plethora of religious literature that was directed toward the seaman. There were limits to the effectiveness of reaching the seaman through the printed page which even the evangelist must have recognized. Nevertheless, books such as Josiah Woodward's *Seaman's Monitor* were still being distributed in the 1830s. By mid-century, efforts toward saving the juvenile, more impressionable, seaman from the evils of the sailor's life had been stepped up. It was thought that the young, at least, might be taught Christian ways through more entertaining religious reading and by precept. This idea was expressed in the preface of *The Cabin Boy's Locker* (1853), a collection of inspirational stories for juvenile readers that had previously appeared as a regular feature of the same title in the *Sailor's Magazine.* The hope was expressed that the cabin boy aboard passenger ships would one day find his employment changed for the better. Instead of having to serve wine, ale, and strong liquors to those who set him a bad example, the "Cabin Boy's Locker" looked forward to the time when the boy at sea would "be courteously requested to select and hand their books" to passengers from the former liquor cabinet, which was by then to have been transformed and elevated into a book case (fig. 11).

Didactic writing such as this, directed as it often was to both juvenile and adult audiences, could not escape some measure of deserved criticism. Herman Melville, for one, poked fun at the religious sailors' magazines in *Redburn,* where the autobiographical character Wellingborough Redburn stated he had read about pious seamen who never swore, who gave their wages to the poor heathen of India, and who were preparing themselves for a Christian death. But to the less critical, or to those seamen who skipped the sermonizing parts, the *Sailor's Magazine* provided valuable maritime news and naval intelligence as well as a forum where many of the ills that beset the seafaring community were aired.

An example of a legal book for mariners was attorney William Sullivan's *Sea Life; or What May or May Not Be Done By Ship-owners, Shipmasters, Masters, Mates and Seamen,* which was published in Boston in 1837. But better known is Richard H. Dana's *Seaman's Friend* of 1841. In writing this book, Dana combined the knowledge he had gained at sea with that of his profession as a lawyer to produce a practical manual for seamen and others who were in need of information on ships and shipping. The last part of the book contained a treatise on contemporary maritime law, and a goodly portion of it was devoted to the rights and duties of merchant seamen. This section of Dana's book was probably the only understandable legal text available to seamen of his day. By comparison, another work, George T. Curtis's *Treatise on the Rights and Duties of Merchant Seamen,* published the same year, ran to 456 pages. Dana's book was popular for several years, and was also published in London as *The Seaman's Manual.*

Medical books to be used at sea were mostly written for masters of merchant vessels who needed advice on how to treat sickness and injury among their men. *The Sailor's Physician,* by Dr. Usher Parsons, was an early American work that was sold extensively. Between 1824 and 1867 it passed through five revised editions, and underwent a change of title to *The Physician for Ships.*[9] And books, such as Thomas Ritter's *Medical Manual and Medicine Chest Companion,* were written to be used in conjunction with proprietary medicine chests. For convenience,

CHAPTER XXIX

10. "Reading *Woodstock*." Richard Henry Dana and his shipmates in the shade of the *Alert's* studding-sail, as drawn by E. Boyd Smith for the 1911 Houghton Mifflin edition of *Two Years Before the Mast*.

11. The cabin boy as librarian. An engraving from the 1830s showing an artist's conception of "the after part of an elegant ship's cabin." The cabin boy has opened his literary locker and is depicted as providing books to four passengers.

the contents of the chests were keyed by number to the prescriptions for the ills described in the book.

The availability of various kinds of professional books that were intended for mariners has already been touched upon in other chapters. These books included works on mathematics, astronomy and navigation, the narratives and reports of voyages of science and discovery, and various treatises and manuals on seamanship and related topics. Perhaps indicative of both a wider literate audience and the relatively greater availability of books, the latter-day sailing ship manuals were mostly addressed to young apprentice officers and seamen in need of guidance and encouragement, rather than to shipmasters.

Other materials of a specialized nature for mariners included magazines such as the British *Naval Chronicle* (London, 1799–1818), and the later American titles, *Military and Naval Magazine* (Washington, 1833–1836), which merged into the *Army and Navy Chronicle* (1835–1842) and had a rebirth as the *Army and Navy Chronicle and Scientific Repository* (1843–1844); the *Naval Magazine* of the U.S. Naval Lyceum, and possibly the *Military Magazine* (Philadelphia, 1839–1842). It might also be mentioned that two general American literary magazines, the *Analectic Magazine* (Philadelphia, 1813–1821), and the *Southern Literary Messenger* (Richmond, 1834–1864), for a time in their histories took an interest in naval affairs (James K. Paulding and Matthew F. Maury were associated, respectively, with them), and thus may have been sought out and read by officers and seamen for this reason.

Reading was just one of several activities that claimed the free time of seamen aboard ship. First priority was given over to such domestic and personal chores as the washing and mending of clothing, but after, there was usually time for the seaman to take part in several amusements, games, hobbies, and other pastimes that provided mental or physical diversion. Akin to reading aloud was the sailor's art of story telling and recitation in the tradition of the skalds and joungleurs of yore; and there was also just plain yarn telling. The private learning, teaching, and tutoring of a variety of subjects were also intellectual recreations.

Another form of creative exercise that some seamen participated in aboard warships was the staging of theatrical performances. These productions, often on an elaborate scale, were financed in the U.S. Navy by the subscription of a vessel's entire crew, much in the manner of subcription libraries. At times a sum as great as $700 might be collected in order to purchase costumes and materials for constructing and painting scenery and props.[10] Stagestruck crew members volunteered their time so they could learn and also rehearse the various male and female roles of published plays (or even original works) which were later performed to the delight of the rest of the crew. Some ships' "thespian corps" performed a series of farces, tragedies, recitations, and masquerades while at sea; but the more memorable theater was usually presented when on station, anchored in a foreign port. On these occasions the after end of a frigate or a ship-of-the-line was converted into a theater, complete with music furnished by the ship's band, stationed in an improvised orchestra pit. The "house" was lit with nautical lanterns and decorated with flags and playbills, and the quarterdeck served as the stage. Usually, dignitaries and members of the *beau monde* of the port, as well as officers from other ships in the harbor, were invited to the performances. Afterwards a collation might be served to the guests, who were always reported to have been well entertained. Theater by subscription in the U.S. Navy may have lasted longer as a continuously crew-sponsored activity than did subscription libraries. It appears to have been established sometime before 1824, while earlier instances of acting aboard foreign ships have been recorded from the seventeenth century onward. Although Contre-amiral Joseph Casy recommended that the French navy provide for the organization of *troupes dramatiques* aboard its ships-of-the-line in 1840, most of the responsibility and expense of providing amateur theatricals on United States naval vessels was still borne by their crews well into the period of steam. The custom, carried out even in subzero temperatures in the Arctic wilderness, helped maintain an *esprit de corps* and dispel the monotony of shipboard life.

In a warmer clime, sea baptism at the equator, another old custom that had a beneficial effect on morale, was often performed aboard ship with the more aggressive seamen hastily cast in the roles of the various stock characters of Neptune and his court. This well-known ritual is, of course, still practiced today on ships and aircraft crossing the line.[11] Its origins are remote, as are the parallel initiation rites, no longer practiced, of certain ancient landsmen's occupations. The earliest record of the ceremony at sea dates back to a French vessel in 1529; and 1792 is the date given for its introduction aboard American ships.

Usually as part of the festive line-crossing occasion, the routine of a ship was further suspended after the ceremony so that a celebration or frolic of sorts could be held. At this time, the crew might have participated in physical games and sports, such as occurred aboard the privateer *Yankee* in 1812, when the remainder of the day and evening was "devoted to fencing, boxing, singing, dancing, drinking, laughing, and every species of mirth and fun." These and additional amusements were also enjoyed during the more normal periods of daily life aboard ships in general. Fishing, chess, checkers, backgammon, cards, and the playing of musical instruments were some of the other common activities that helped sailors pass their free time at sea. Among the amusements of seamen as captives on icebound ships in 1821, or in Dartmoor prison in 1815, were the viewing of magic lantern exhibitions in the former instance, and the making of ship models from beef bones (as well as fashioning the tools needed for the task) in the latter.[12] The value of recreation was recognized by a few early naval officers and doctors. In 1814, Dr. William P. C. Barton observed that music and dancing helped to "beguile the time and make the sailor more contented with his situation," and thus recommended that the two amusements be promoted among the men of the U.S. Navy.

While shipboard leisure was conducive to reading and the pursuit of many amusements, it was also productive of writing, or at least the gathering of materials for later publication. More than one seafaring author modestly confessed in the preface of his book that it was written from a diary or journal kept at sea and excused the need for his book and its flaws with a statement to the effect that he had had no intention of publishing it, but upon his return home his friends had induced him to. Happily, of the many works that followed this pattern, at least one had high literary merit. Mankind is much the richer in many ways for the words that Richard Henry Dana put on paper while his experiences as a seaman were still fresh in his mind. His *Two Years Before the Mast* eloquently exposed the hard life of the sailor to his contemporaries ashore, and captured the flavor of life at sea and under sail for all time. Dana's book was also chosen for shipboard reading, apparently because of its timely appeal, in the navy's seamen's libraries of 1841–1843, and in the "Sailor's Library" of the American Seamen's Friend Society. There is little doubt that from Dana's day to the present, his work has inspired innumerable voyagers to take pen in hand and attempt to write books about their travels while afloat.

Other writing at sea was in the form of letters which were sent home by sailors who told of their experiences on the deep to a more limited audience. Still other mariners were content to write, paint, and draw for their own or their messmates' pleasure, or whenever the sea-muse beckoned. Their private works, however, if seen by other eyes were not always appreciated. In the case of a deceased shipmaster and his legacy of poems, when his old sea chest was opened it was found to contain his personal books and papers along with some logbooks and a half-dozen manuscript-books of poems, many of them evidently original. The books of verses and the logs then suffered the singularly inappropriate fate of being slowly cut up over a period of weeks and made into gun cartridges on a ship bound for New Zealand.[13] In this connection, it might be observed that the very subject of the misunderstood or misfit artist aboard ship was celebrated by the sea-poet, John Masefield, in his poem "Dauber" some years later.

The opportunity or necessity for writing on the part of sea officers was also present in the routine keeping of shipboard journals and logbooks. Especially on voyages of discovery, almost everyone in some position of responsibility was required to keep a record of events and observations. This was done so that as much information as possible could be obtained and compared from the several journals in order that a true and complete account of the voyage might be prepared. The seventh of the ordinances of Sebastian Cabot, written for an intended voyage in 1553, spelled out this daily obligation in detail. Years after, in the U.S. Navy the custom of keeping an individual journal in which to record nautical observations was one of the few continuous educational exercises demanded of midshipmen at sea.

The fireside voyager Daniel Defoe was not too charitable in his opinion of the professional writing which was generated by those who commanded voyages of discovery, for he testily observed:

> So as soon as men have acted the sailor, they come ashore and write books of their voyage, not only to make a great noise of what they have done themselves, but, pretending to show the way to others to come after them, they set up as teachers and chart-makers to posterity. Though most of them have had this misfortune, that whatever success they have had in the voyage, they have had very little in relation; except it be to tell us that a seaman, when he comes to the press, is pretty much out of his element, and that a very good sailor may make but a very indifferent author.[14]

Notwithstanding the aptness, even today, of Defoe's remarks, the sailing ship, of course, did breed many successful authors who contributed to both the professional and romantic literature of the sea, and to literature in general, to say nothing of those who, thankfully, pretended "to show the way to others to come after them."

Aboard some warships and passenger vessels, occasionally crew members pursued the avocation of journalist, by preparing and distributing a newspaper wherein news of shipboard interest appeared, and where the written contributions of others might see the light of day. The *North Georgia Gazette and Winter Chronicle,* published first in manuscript, and later printed ashore, set the example for other Arctic newspapers put together aboard ship. It was distributed weekly aboard the *Hecla* and *Griper,* the two Royal Navy vessels under command of Lieutenant William E. Parry on a voyage for discovery of a northwest passage to the Pacific Ocean in the years 1819–1820.[15] The newspaper carried quite a bit of gossip about various theatrical performances aboard ship, but did not mention the presence of any kind of library; and books in general were apparently referred to only once—in a humorous want-ad.

A similar newspaper in 1821 was edited aboard the *Constellation* by DeWitt Clinton's midshipman son, James. The weekly manuscript "Gazette" was published by the frigate's midshipmen, "by way of filling up the blank of life, & killing ennui, on their tedious passage" to South America. For the same reasons, passengers aboard certain merchant ships from about the same date were also treated to the luxury of a local newspaper, and a few of these shipboard newspapers still survive. A printed one, the *White Star Journal* of 1855 (which was reproduced in facsimile some years ago) had, incidentally, several items about the ship's library, which was available to all classes of passengers. One item reported that a female saloon passenger had "kindly consented to act as librarian" during the emigrant ship's passage from Liverpool to Melbourne.

Although the results of shipboard journalism (either in a manuscript or printed state) provided amusement at sea, printing itself was also undertaken by the seafarer for more serious purposes. Proclamations and leaflets were printed at an early date aboard warships, and other printing presses at sea, including one supposedly in operation in 1564, were responsible for the printing of books and other materials afloat.[16] But more significantly, the establishment and continued existence of printing presses in the remote regions of the world accessible only by ship depended upon seamen to deliver the wherewithal of the trade; for just as the mariner helped the evangelist and the scientist in the promotion of their causes, he also acted as an agent in the dissemination of printing, and hence, in the advancement of learning and culture throughout the world.

With mention of the mariner as giver rather than receiver of the fruits of the printing press, our study has come full circle. It is perhaps appropriate to end it with a vignette that depicts the mariner in his inverted role of pioneer printer-publisher and cultural innovator. How well he performed the part is exemplified in the actions of Chaplain Walter Colton ashore in California in 1846–1848. When the chaplain arrived in Monterey Bay on July 15, 1846, aboard the frigate *Congress* (on a subsequent leg of the same voyage that had brought the Joel Turrill family to Hawaii), he little realized that he soon would be officiating as the *alcalde* or justice of the peace for the immense area of "the middle department of California."

The Stars and Stripes was flying above Monterey courthouse on the day that the *Congress* stood in from sea, for the town had fallen a week previously to U.S. naval forces under the command of Commodore John D. Sloat. Within a few days Commodore Sloat sailed for home, and

Commodore Robert F. Stockton on the *Congress* assumed command of the Pacific Squadron. Stockton, himself, soon departed aboard his flagship in order to proceed down the coast to San Pedro in a planned attempt to capture the pueblo of Los Angeles. But he left Chaplain Colton behind as his appointee in the important post of *alcalde*, which since the fall of the local government had been occupied by a purser and a surgeon from the sloop-of-war *Cyane*.

In office, Colton introduced the concept of trial by jury to his jurisdiction, and in partnership with one of the settlers, started the first newspaper in the territory. During the times his partner was absent on other business, Colton "cheerfully endured all the toil of getting out" their newspaper, the *Californian,* "with only the assistance of a typesetting sailor," Joseph Dockrill. Thus the talents of the seagoing chaplain and the skill of his seaman-printer made possible the beginnings of American culture in California. And in this instance as in others, the bread cast upon the waters for the benefit of seamen was again, in some measure, returned by them to the land.[17]

Appendixes

Explanatory Note

The books contained in the lists of four U.S. Navy libraries and one religious library (figs. 5-9) are bibliographically identified in the following appendixes. The editions of the books described in the navy libraries (Appendixes A, C, D, E) are representative of those which were likely to have been available at the time the individual lists were in use. However, the descriptions for some of the books in the religious library (Appendix B) are not as specific, especially in those instances where the older or more common titles had been published by various publishers or in several editions.

The bibliographic and other sources (*e.g.,* Karpinski, Naval storekeeper's inventory, etc.) referred to in the notes to the navy library lists are identified in the Bibliographic Notes, under "Appendixes."

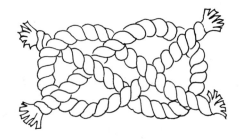

Seamen's Library List of the U.S. Navy, 1841-1843

The first "List of Books to be allowed for the Libraries of seamen on board vessels of the Navy" was issued jointly with the list of books for navy yards and vessels of the navy (Appendix E) on October 13, 1841, and it apparently was never subsequently altered or revised. The following list (and fig. 5) is from RG 45(*464*), Subject file NE: "Vessels' Libraries, etc., March 7, 1843, Chief Clerk of the Bureau of Construction, Equipment & Repair."

[1] *Dana's two years before the mast*
> Dana, Richard Henry. Two Years Before the Mast. A Personal Narrative of Life at Sea . . . New York, Harper & Bros., 1840. 1 v.
>> Harper's Family Library, no. 106.

[2] *Oracle of the Arts*

>Although this title was listed on the 1845 List of books contracted for by the Norfolk Navy Yard as having been furnished at a unit price of 25¢, it does not appear as such on other available contemporary lists or in catalogs of books used in the navy, including the Naval storekeeper's inventory of books for "Libraries for Seamen" of 1846. A copy was reported sold to the *Warren*, Oct., 1842 for 50¢

[3] *Robinson Crusoe*

Defoe, Daniel. The Life and Adventures of Robinson Crusoe . . . New York, Robinson & Franklin, 1839. 2 v.

[4] *Brannans official letters (late War)*

Brannan, John, comp. Official Letters of the Military and Naval Officers of the United States During the War with Great Britain in the Years 1812-15 . . . Washington, Pr. by Way & Gideon for the editor, 1823. 1 v.

[5] *Various narrations of imprisonment, shipwreck, perils and captivity*

>Among the seventy-nine titles of books for "Libraries for Seamen" in the Naval storekeeper's inventory at the New York Navy Yard in 1846, about ten titles could be considered in this category, especially if works on seafaring, exploration, and voyages were included (*e.g,* Charles S. Stewart's *Visit to the South Seas,* Nathaniel Ames's *Mariner's Sketches,* Samuel Leech's *Thirty Years from Home,* Colton's works, etc.). Also, several titles from the Harper's Family Library ([13] below) could be considered here.

[6] *Gardens Anecdotes of the Revolution*

Garden, Alexander. Anecdotes of the American Revolution, Illustrative of the Talents and Virtues of the Heroes and Patriots Who Acted the Most Conspicuous Parts Therein . . . 2d series. Charleston [S. C.], Pr. by A. E. Miller, 1828. 1 v.

[7] *Naval Monument*

Bowen, Abel, comp. The Naval Monument, Containing Official and Other Accounts of All the Battles Fought Between the Navies of the United States and Great Britain During the Late War, and an Account of the War with Algiers . . . rev. & corr. Boston, G. Clark, 1836. 1 v.

[8] *Sketches of Naval life in the Constitution & Brandywine*

Jones, George. Sketches of Naval Life with Notices of Men, Manners and Scenery on the Shores of the Mediterranean in a Series of Letters from the Brandywine and Constitution Frigates. By a "Civilian." New Haven, H. Howe, 1829. 2 v.

[9] *Pauldings Journal in the Dolphin*

Paulding, Hiram. Journal of a Cruise of the United States Schooner Dolphin Among the Islands of the Pacific Ocean . . . New York, G. & C. & H. Carvill, 1831. 1 v.

[10] *Picture of Australia*

    Mudie, Robert. The Picture of Australia; Exhibiting New Holland, Van Dieman's Land, and All the Settlements, from the First at Sydney to the Last at Swan River. London, Whittaker, Treacher, & Co., 1829. 1 v.

[11] *Sewards narrative of his Shipwrecks and discovery of certain Islands*

    Porter, Jane, ed. Sir Edward Seaward's Narrative of His Shipwreck, and Consequent Discovery of Certain Islands in the Caribbean Sea . . . London, Longman, Rees, Orme, Brown, & Green, 1831. 3 v.

[12] *Penny Magazine (bound)*

    [a] The Penny Magazine, v. 1-14. London, Society for the Diffusion of Useful Knowledge, 1832-45.

        Series 2, v. 1-2, 1846 as Knight's Penny Magazine.

    [b] The Penny Magazine, v. 1-16. Boston, S.D.U.K., 1832-46.

        The American edition was published from plates sent overseas from London. Both editions were probably supplied to the navy. A run of the magazine (v. 1-9, 1832-40) formerly belonging to the Naval Library and Institute, Boston, and now in the USNA Library, is of the more widely distributed London edition. One volume of the set bears the inscription in ink: "U.S. Ship Cumberland," on its flyleaf.

[13] *Selections from Family Library*

Harper's Family Library

    This was a publisher's series of small, cheaply priced, nonfiction books, published by Harper and Brothers in New York. In 1839 the series consisted of 84 volumes, in 1840, 105 volumes, and in 1844, 171 volumes. The books were sold individually or in sets (see Eugene Exman, *The Brothers Harper,* pp. 21, 381-83 for the listing of the completed library of 187 titles). In 1846, there were about 56 titles in the Family Library listed as on hand (including *Two Years Before the Mast*) in the Naval storekeeper's inventory of books for "Libraries for Seamen" at the New York Navy Yard. The titles were mostly in the categories of history, biography, and travel; and a few miscellaneous works were also included.

[14] *Cities and principal Towns of the Cabinet Cyclopedia*

The Cities and Principal Towns of the World. Vol. 1. London, Longman, Rees, Orme, Brown & Green, 1830. 1 v.

    The Cabinet Cyclopaedia. Conducted by . . . D. Lardner . . . Geography, v. 133. No more published.

Seamen's Library of the American
Seamen's Friend Society, 1843

The listing of the "No. 1 Sailor's Library, selected under the supervision of the American Seamen's Friend Society" given below (and fig. 6) is from the *Sailor's Magazine and Naval Journal,* 15 (May, 1843), 281. The American Tract Society, New York, is abbreviated as "ATS" where appropriate.

[1] *Abbot's Young Christian*
> Abbott, Jacob. The Young Christian. Rev. ed. New York, ATS, 1835. 1 v.
>> Christian Library, v. 32.

[2] *Alexander's Biblical Dictionary*
> Alexander, Archibald. A Pocket Dictionary of the Holy Bible. 25th ed. Philadelphia, American Sunday School Union, 1832. 1 v.

[3] *Bunyan's Pilgrim's Progress*
   Bunyan, John. The Pilgrim's Progress . . . ATS, 1830. 1 v.
      Evangelical Family Library, v. 4.

[4] *Baxter's Call with Chalmer's Preface*
   Baxter, Richard. A Call to the Unconverted . . . With an Introductory Essay by Rev. Thomas Chalmers, D.D. . . . ATS
   [1835]. 1 v.
      Evangelical Family Library, v. 6.

[5] *Buck's Religious Anecdotes*
   Buck, Charles. Anecdotes, Religious, Moral and Entertaining . . .
   New York, J. C. Riker, 1831. 2 v. in 1.

[6] *Brown's Concordance*
   Brown, John. A Concordance to the Holy Scriptures of the Old
   and New Testaments . . . New York, Harper & Bros., 1842.
   1 v.
      Another possibility for this entry is Brown's *A Brief Concordance to the Holy
      Scriptures.*

[7] *Bancroft's Life of Washington, 2 vols.*
   Bancroft, Aaron. Life of George Washington . . . Boston,
   Littlefield, 1839. 2 v.

[8] *Benevolent Merchant*
   The Benevolent Merchant. New York, M. H. Newman & Co.,
   [18—].

[9] *Cowper's Poems, 3 vols.*
   Cowper, William. Poems of William Cowper . . . Boston, E.
   Littlefield, 1841. 3 v.

[10] *Circumnavigation of the Globe*
   An Historical Account of the Circumnavigation of the Globe . . .
   New York, Harper & Bros., 1842. 1 v.
      Harper's Family Library, no. 82; and in the Cabinet Library (see Sabin 32050).
      Also on 1839 U.S. Navy library list.

[11] *Charles Morton*
   Shindler, Mary Dana. Charles Morton, or The Young Patriot. A
   Tale of the Revolution. New York, Dayton & Newman, 1843. 1 v.

[12] *Doddridge's Rise and Progress*
   Doddridge, Philip. The Rise and Progress of Religion in the
   Soul . . . ATS, [184-]; New York, Robert Carter, 1843. 1 v.

[13] *D'Aubigne's History of the Reformation*
   Merle d'Aubigne, Jean Henri. History of the Reformation of the
   Sixteenth Century . . . ATS, [184-]. 4 v.

[14] *Dairyman's Daughter, &c.*
Richmond, Legh. The Dairyman's Daughter . . . ATS, [18—].
1 v.
    Also abridged as ATS publication, no. 9.

[15] *Early Navigators*
Lives and Voyages of Drake, Cavendish and Dampier . . . New
York, Harper & Bros., [1831]. 1 v.
    Harper's Family Library, no. 30 (Sabin 20833). Also on 1839 U.S. Navy
    library list.

[16] *Emma*
Emma; or the Lost Found . . . New York, Mark H. Newman &
Co., [18—].

[17] *Fool's Pence, &c.*
The Fool's Pence . . . New York, ATS, [18—]. 8 p.
    ATS publication, 308.

[18] *Florence Arnott*
McIntosh, Maria Jane. Florence Arnott; or Is She Generous? . . .
by Aunt Kitty . . . New York, M. H. Newman & Co., Dayton
& Saxton, 1841. 1 v.

[19] *Gray's Chemistry*
Gray, Alonzo. Elements of Chemistry . . . Andover, [Mass.],
Gould, Newman & Saxon, 1840; New York, M. H. Newman &
Co., 1843. 1 v.

[20] *Gurney on the Sabbath*
Gurney, Joseph John. Brief Remarks on the History, Authority,
and Use of the Sabbath . . . Andover, Flagg, Gould & Newman, 1833. 1 v.

[21] *Great Secret*
Judson, Emily Chubbuck. The Great Secret; or How to be Happy.
New York, Dayton & Newman, 1842. 1 v.

[22] *Hale's History of the United States*
Hale, Salma. History of the United States . . . New York,
Harper & Bros., 1841. 2 v.
    Harper's Family Library, no. 119-20. See Sabin 29662-3.

[23] *Hitchcocks Geology*
Hitchcock, Edward. Elementary Geology . . . 3d ed. M.H.
Newman & Co., [c. 1842]. 1 v.

[24] *Jay's Prayers*
Jay, William. Prayers for the Use of Families; or The Domestic

Minister's Assistant . . . New York, Leavitt & Allen Bros.,
[184-]. 1 v.

[25] *Life before the Mast*
Dana, Richard Henry. Two Years Before the Mast . . . New
York, Harper & Bros., 1842. 1 v.

Binder's title on the Harper's Family Library (no. 106) edition was *Life Before
the Mast.* Also in U.S. Navy seamen's library.

[26] *Life of Columbus*
Irving, Washington. The History of the Life and Voyages of
Christopher Columbus. Philadelphia, Carey & Lea, 1840. 2 v.

See Sabin 35169-83. Also in U.S. Navy libraries of 1832-1843. Another similar
title published in New York, in 1832, listed in Sabin as 41026.

[27] *Memoir of Harlan Page*
Hallock, William Allen. Memoir of Harlan Page, or The Power
of Prayer . . . ATS, [1835]. 1 v.

[28] *Memoir of Gordon Hall*
Bardwell, Horatio. Memoir of Rev. Gordon Hall . . . Andover,
Flagg & Co., 1834; New York, Dayton & Saxon [etc.],
1841. 1 v.

[29] *Martyr Lamb*
Krummacher, Friedrich Wilhelm. The Martyr Lamb. 3d ed. New
York, R. Carter, 1841. 1 v.

[30] *Meditations on Prayer*
Bonnet, Louis. Meditations on the Lord's Prayer . . . New
York, R. Carter, [18—].

Another work by the author available from Carter's was his *The Family of
Bethany, or Meditations on the Eleventh Chapter of St. John.*

[31] *Michael Kemp*
Woodroofe, Anne Cox. The History of Michael Kemp, the Happy
Farmer's Lad . . . From 6th London ed. New York, R. Carter,
1841. 1 v.

[32] *Missionary's Daughter*
Thurston, Lucy Goodale. The Missionary's Daughter: A Memoir
of Lucy Goodale Thurston of the Sandwich Islands . . . ATS,
[c. 1842]. 1 v.

Youth's Library, no. 20.

[33] *Nevin's Practical Thoughts*
Nevins, William. Practical Thoughts . . . ATS, [c. 1836]. 1 v.

Evangelical Family Library, v. 13.

[34] *Nelson on Infidelity*
Nelson, David. The Cause and Cure of Infidelity . . . 2d ed. ATS, [1841]. 1 v.

[35] *Old Humphrey's Addresses*
Mogridge, George. Old Humphrey's Addresses. New York, R. Carter; London, The Religious Tract Society, 1842. 1 v.

[36] *Old Humphrey's Observations*
_____. Old Humphrey's Observations. 3d ed. New York, R. Carter, 1842. 1 v.

[37] *Old Humphrey's Thoughts for Thoughtful*
_____. Old Humphrey's Thoughts for the Thoughtful. New York, R. Carter, 1843. 1 v.

[38] *Paley's Natural Theology*
Paley, William. Natural Theology . . . Boston, Gould, Kendall & Lincoln, 1838 (1 v.); New York, Harper & Bros., 1840. 2 v.
Harper's Family Library, no. 96-97.

[39] *Polar Seas*
Leslie, John. Narrative of Discovery and Adventure in the Polar Seas and Regions . . . New York, Harper & Bros., 1840. 1 v.
Harper's Family Library, no. 14 (Sabin 40201). Another similar title described in Sabin (105518) is Ferdinand P. Wrangel's *Narrative of an Expedition to the Polar Sea . . .* , various publishers, including Harper's Family Library edition, no. 148.

[40] *Pitcairn's Island*
Barrow, John. A Description of Pitcairn's Island and Its Inhabitants . . . New York, Harper & Bros., 1840. 1 v.
Harper's Family Library, no. 31.

[41] *Retrospect*
Marks, Richard. The Retrospect: or Review of Providential Mercies, with Anecdotes of Various Characters. From 17th London ed. New York, R. Carter, 1841. 1 v.

[42] *Shepherd of Salisbury Plain, &c.*
More, Hannah. The Shepherd of Salisbury Plain . . . ATS, [184-]. 24 p.
ATS publication, no. 10.

[43] *Sargent's Temperance Tales. 6 vols.*
Sargent, Lucius Manlius. The Temperance Tales. Boston, Whipple and Damrell, 1838-40. 19 nos. in 6 v.

[44] *Seamen's Friend*
The wording, the "seaman's," or "sailor's," or "seamen's friend" was used in the titles of several publications during the age of sail. Richard H. Dana's *Seaman's Friend,* or more unlikely, the ATS publication no. 96, *The Sailor's Friend* (See [46] below) may have been intended as the entry here.

[45] *Smith's Geography and Atlas*
Smith, Roswell C. Smith's Geography; Geography on the Productive System . . . Hartford, Pub. by John Paine, 1843. 1 v. & atlas.

Sabin 83925-6 lists editions with atlas. Smith's *Atlas* as a separate work is described in Sabin 83928-30.

[46] *Tracts for Seamen*

Between the years 1826 and 1859, at least seventeen tracts of the ATS were prepared for distribution among seamen. The "Tracts for Seamen" were identified as such in the "Index to the Subjects of the Tracts" included in v. 11 of *The Publications of the American Tract Society* collected and published at this time. Reprints of tracts by George C. Smith, Richard Marks, and other clergymen were represented in the collection.

[47] *Uncas and Miantonomoh*
Stone, William Leete. Uncas and Minantonomoh . . . New York, Dayton & Newman, 1842. 1 v.

Sabin 92153.

[48] *Views of the Saviour*
Views of the Saviour . . . New York, M. H. Newman & Co., [18—].

[49] *Widow's Son*
The Widow's Son. ATS, [18—]. 20 p.

ATS publication, no. 35. A juvenile work by the same title was also written by Mary A. Welsford (1842).

[50] *Zebulon, or Claims of Seamen*
Harris, John. Zebulon, or The Moral Claims of Seamen Stated and Enforced . . . 1st American from 3d London ed. Boston, Gould, Kendall & Lincoln, 1837. 1 v.

Originally published in England as *Britannia* . . . .

Appendix C

1832 Library List: Books for Officers of the U.S. Navy

The listing of books to "be furnished for the use of vessels of war when on a cruise, and for the use of Yards" was originally issued for vessels on January 28, 1828. It was subsequently modified and printed (as reproduced in fig. 7) in *Rules of the Navy Department Regulating the Civil Administration of the Navy of the United States* (Washington, 1832), pp. 27-28.

[1] *Elements of Trigonometry*
    Hassler, Ferdinand R. Elements of Analytic Trigonometry, Plane and Spherical. New York, The Author, 1826. 1 v.
[2] *Euclid's Elements*
    [a] Simson, Robert. The Elements of Euclid . . . [published at Philadelphia between 1803 and 1838 in eleven editions].

[b] Playfair, John. Elements of Geometry, Containing the First Six Books of Euclid . . . [published at Philadelphia and New York between 1806 and 1850 in twenty-nine editions].

Either of these two texts was usually purchased to fulfill the authorization for "Euclid's Elements." According to Karpinski, editions of Playfair's *Euclid* gradually displaced Simson's work as the text most commonly used in the United States (Karpinski, pp. 149-50, 163-65; see p. 632 for his listing of other works based upon Euclid, and upon Simson and Playfair).

[3] *Bowditch's Navigation*

Bowditch, Nathaniel. The New Practical Navigator. 7th stereotype ed. New York, Blunt, 1832. 1 v.

[4] *Douglas on Marine Artillery*

Douglas, Howard. A Treatise on Naval Gunnery. 2d ed. London, J. Murray, 1829. 1 v.

Title as listed was reported as unavailable by Navy Agent James K. Paulding in 1828. Also on 1827 List of books for navy yards.

[5] *Marshall's Hand Book on the equipment of guns*

Marshall, George. Marshall's Practical Marine Gunnery . . . Norfolk, C. Hall, 1822. 1 v.

Title as listed was reported as unavailable by Paulding in 1828.

[6] *Ramsay's Universal History*

Ramsay, David. Universal History Americanised. Philadelphia, M. Carey & Son, 1819. 12 v.

[7] *History of Rome*

Ferguson, Adam. History of the Progress and Termination of the Roman Republic. New ed., rev. & corr. Edinburgh, Bell & Bradfute [etc.], 1825. 5 v.

[8] *Milford's Greece*

Mitford, William. The History of Greece. New ed. London, Pr. for T. Cadell, 1829. 8 v.

[9] *Rollin's Ancient History*

Rollin, Charles. The Ancient History of the Egyptians [etc.]. From 15th London ed., rev. & corr. Philadelphia, H. Adams, 1829. 8 v.

[10] *Gibbon's Decline and Fall of the Roman Empire*

Gibbon, Edward. The History of the Decline and Fall of the Roman Empire. London, T. Cadell [etc.], 1828. 8 v.

[11] *History of England*

Lingard, John. A History of England from the First Invasion by the Romans. London, J. Mawman, 1819-30. 8 v.

Thomas Keightley's *History,* and Hume, Smollet, and Bisset's *History* were also purchased.

[12] *Marshall's Life of Washington*
Marshall, John. The Life of Washington. 2d ed., rev. & corr. Phila-
delphia, J. Crissy, 1832. 2 v. and atlas.
Abridged from 1st Philadelphia ed. of 1804-07.

[13] *Botta's American Revolution*
Botta, Carlo G. G. History of the War of Independence of the
United States of America. 2d ed., rev. & corr. Boston, H. Gray,
1826. 2 v.

[14] *Modern Europe*
Russell, William. The History of Modern Europe. Philadelphia,
A. Small, 1822. 6 v.

[15] *Vattels Law of Nations*
Vattel, Emmerich de. The Law of Nations. Northampton, Mass.,
S. Butler, 1820. 1 v.
Also on 1827 List of books for navy yards.

[16] *American Atlas, compiled on the plan of Le Sage*
A Complete Historical, Chronological and Geographical Ameri-
can Atlas . . . to the Year 1826. 3d ed. Philadelphia, H. C.
Carey & I. Lea, 1827. 1 v.

[17] *La Voisne's Atlas*
Lavoisne, C. V. A Complete Genealogical, Historical, Chronological, and Geographical Atlas. From the last London ed., 3d
American ed., rev. & corr. Philadelphia, M. Carey & Son, 1821.
1 v.

[18] *Pair of Globes*
A pair of terrestrial and celestial globes (12 inches in diameter, and mounted)
was furnished to the sloop-of-war *St. Louis* in 1828 at a cost of $30.

[19] *Jacobson's Sea Laws*
Jacobsen, Friedrich J. Laws of the Sea. Baltimore, Edward J.
Coale, 1818. 1 v.
Also on 1827 List of books for navy yards.

[20] *Charnock, and others, on Naval Architecture*
Charnock, John. An History of Marine Architecture. London, Pr.
for R. Faulder [etc.], 1800-1802. 3 v.
Reported as unavailable by Paulding in 1828.

[21] *State Papers*
State Papers and Publick Documents of the United States. 3d ed.
Boston, Thomas B. Walt, 1819. 12 v.
The American State Papers, compiled by Gales & Seaton, also began publica-
tion in 1832.

[22] *Federalist*

> The Federalist on the New Constitution, Written in the Year 1788, by Mr. Hamilton, Mr. Madison, and Mr. Jay. New ed. Hallowell, [Me.], Glazier, Masters & Co., 1831. 1 v.

[23] *Walsh's Appeal*

> Walsh, Robert. An Appeal from the Judgments of Great Britain Respecting the United States of America. 2d ed. Philadelphia, Mitchell, Ames, & White, 1819. 1 v.

[24] *Ledyard's Travels*

> Sparks, Jared. The Life of John Ledyard, the American Traveller. Cambridge, Hilliard & Brown; New York, G. & C. Carvill [etc.], 1828. 1 v.

[25] *Vanconver's Voyages*

> Vancouver, George. A Voyage of Discovery to the North Pacific Ocean and Round the World. New ed., corr. London, Pr. for J. Stockdale, 1801. 6 v.
>
> Reported as unavailable by Paulding in 1828.

[26] *Ross's Voyages*

> Ross, John. A Voyage of Discovery . . . for the Purpose of Exploring Baffin's Bay. London, John Murray, 1819. 1 v.

[27] *Parry's Voyages*

> Parry, William E. Journal of the First, Second, and Third Voyages for the Discovery of a North-West Passage . . . in 1819-25. London, John Murray, 1828-29. 6 v.

[28] *Franklin's Voyages*

> Franklin, John. Narrative of a Journey to the Shores of the Polar Sea, in the Years 1819-22; With a Brief Account of the Second Journey in 1825-27. London, John Murray, 1829. 4 v.
>
> *Note:* The respective editions of items [26, 27, 28] are listed only in order to identify the works. Each "voyage" was published in several editions, and various editions were probably purchased for yards and vessels as available. The sets of these works listed in the Naval storekeeper's inventory of books "For libraries of Ships" at the New York Navy Yard in 1846, were "Franklin's Voyages, F's Journey, F's Narrative, Parry's Voyages, Parry's Journal, Ross' Expedition, Ross' Voyage, Ross' Second Voyage." See Sabin for listing of various editions.
>
> The travels of the three explorers were also recounted in: John F. Dennett's *The Voyages and Travels of Captains Parry, Franklin, Ross and Mr. Belzoni . . .* London, 1826. 1 v.

[29] *Life and Voyages of Columbus*

> Irving, Washington. A History of the Life and Voyages of Christopher Columbus. New York, G. & C. Carvill, 1828. 3 v.
>
> Later editions were published with title: *The Life and Voyages of Christopher Columbus* (see Sabin 35169-83).

[30] *Encyclopedia Britannica with its supplement*
Encyclopaedia Britannica; or A Dictionary of Arts, Sciences, and
   Miscellaneous Literature. 6th ed., enl. & imp. Edinburgh, Pr.
   for Archibald Constable, 1820-23. 20 v.
Supplement to the Fourth, Fifth, and Sixth Editions. Edinburgh,
   A. Constable, 1815-24. 6 v.

[31] *North American Sylva*
Michaux, François A. The North American Sylva. Philadelphia,
   Sold by T. Dobson, 1817-19. 3 v.

> Reported as unavailable by Paulding in 1828. Was continued by Thomas
> Nuttall in 1842 (see Sabin 48694-5, 56351). Another work also purchased by the
> navy with a similar title was Daniel J. Browne's *Sylva Americana*. Boston, W. Hyde
> & Co., 1832. 1 v.

[32] *Work on conversion and preservation of timber*

> Paulding reported that he was unable to find a work by this title in 1828. How-
> ever, Peter *"Barlow's essay on the stress and strength of timber, 1826"* was specified
> on the 1827 List of books for navy yards, and *"Barlow on Timber"* was listed in the
> Library of the New York Yard in 1846.

[33] *Hutton's Tracts*
Hutton, Charles. Tracts on Mathematical and Philosophical Subjects. London, F. C. & J. Rivington [etc.], 1812. 3 v.

[34] *Arnot's Natural Philosophy*
Arnott, Neil. Elements of Physics; or Natural Philosophy. 2d
   American from 4th London ed. Philadelphia, Carey & Lea, 1831.
   2 v.

[35] *Nicholson's ditto*
Nicholson, William. An Introduction to Natural Philosophy. 5th
   ed. London, Pr. for J. Johnson, 1805. 2 v.

[36] *Bible and Prayer Book*

> Secretary of the Navy John Branch added the "Bible and Prayer Book" to the
> original 1828 list during his tenure of office. The American Bible Society apparently
> was the chief source of the Bible for the navy, at least in the early years (see Strick-
> land, *History of the American Bible Society*, pp. 98-102, and Clifford M. Drury,
> *The History of the Chaplain Corps*, v. 1, pp. 59, 74). *The Book of Common Prayer*
> of the Protestant Episcopal Church, or similar books for other denominations, were
> furnished as prayer books. The Naval storekeeper's inventory of books "for libraries
> of Ships" at the New York Navy Yard in 1846 listed three copies of the Bible, and
> two copies of "Common Prayer" on hand at that date.

Appendix D

1839 Library List: Books for Officers of the U.S. Navy

The listing of books to "be furnished for the use of Vessels of War when on a cruise, and for the use of Navy Yards," issued June 10, 1839, and given below (and fig. 8) is from RG 45(*464*), Subject file NE.

[1] *Nicholson's Mathematics*

> Not in Karpinski. In 1846, editor William Nicholson's *British Encyclopaedia*, and Peter Nicholson's *Principles of Architecture* (1836; 3 vols.) were among the books in charge of the naval storekeeper for issue to ships' libraries at the New York Navy Yard. According to Karpinski, editions of Nicholson's *Encyclopaedia* (1818-21; 12 vols.) contained fairly extensive articles on the various branches of mathematics.

[2] *Euclid's Elements*

> See [2] 1832 List.

[3] *Bowditch's Navigation*

> Same title as [3] 1832 List: 11th stereotype ed., New York, Blunt, 1839. 1 v.

[4] *Maury's   do.*
Maury, Matthew F. A New Theoretical and Practical Treatise on Navigation . . . Philadelphia, Key & Biddle, 1836. 1 v.

[5] *Ramsay's Universal History*
Same as [6] 1832 List.

[6] *Gibbon's History—Decline & Fall of Rome*
Same title as [10] 1832 List: 5th American ed. from last London ed. New York, Harper & Bros., 1836. 4 v.

[7] *Ferguson's History of Roman Republic*
Same as [7] 1832 List.

[8] *Gillies' History of Greece*
Gillies, John. The History of Ancient Greece . . . Philadelphia, J. Marot, 1829. 1 v.

[9] *Rollin's ancient History*
Same title as [9] 1832 List: From Latest London ed., rev. & corr. New York, G. Long, 1837. 4 v.

[10] *Lingard's History of England*
Same as [11] 1832 List.

[11] *Constitution of the U.S. & the different States*
The American's Guide: Comprising . . . the Constitution of the United States, and the Constitutions of the Several States Composing the Union . . . Philadelphia, Towar & Hogan [etc.], 1832. 1 v.
Sabin 1270. Also 16086 *et seq.*

[12] *Marshall's Life of Washington*
Same as [12] 1832 List: 1839. 2 v.

[13] *Botta's American Revolution (until Bancroft's is completed)*
Same title as [13] 1832 List: 9th ed. rev. & corr. New Haven, T. Brainard, 1839. 2 v.

[14] *Hallam's constitutional History*
Hallam, Henry. The Constitutional History of England . . Boston, Wells & Lilly, 1829. 3 v.

[15] *Vattel's Law of Nations*
Same title as [15] 1832 List: 5th American ed. Philadelphia, T. & J. W. Johnson, 1839. 1 v.
Also on 1827 List of books for navy yards.

[16] *Bradford's Atlas*
Bradford, Thomas G. An Illustrated Atlas, Geographical, Statistical, and Historical of the United States and Adjacent Countries. Boston, Weeks, Jordan & Co., 1838. 1 v.

[17] *Jacobson's Sea Laws*

Same as [19] 1832 List.
Also on 1827 List of books for navy yards.

[18] *Gordons Digest, or Ingersoll's abridgement of U.S. Laws*
 [a] Gordon, Thomas F. A Digest of the Laws of the United States
   . . . 2d ed. Philadelphia, The Author, 1837. 1 v.
 [b] Ingersoll, Edward. Abridgement of the Acts of Congress Now
   in Force . . . Philadelphia, Towar & Hogan, 1825. 1 v.
   Gordon's Digest was also on the 1827 List of books for navy yards.

[19] *Treaties with foreign Powers*
 Elliot, Jonathan. The American Diplomatic Code Embracing a
 Collection of Treaties and Conventions Between the United
 States and Foreign Powers . . . Washington, Pr. by J. Elliot,
 1834. 2 v.

[20] *Federalist*
 Same title as [22] 1832 List: Hallowell [Me.], Glazier, Masters & Smith, 1837. 1 v.

[21] *Ledyard's Travels*
 Same as [24] 1832 List.

[22] *Astoria*
 Irving, Washington. Astoria, or Anecdotes of an Enterprise Be-
 yond the Rocky Mountains . . . Philadelphia, Carey, Lea,
 & Blanchard, 1836. 2 v.

[23] *Voyage of the Potomac*
 Reynolds, Jeremiah N. Voyage of the United States Frigate
 Potomac . . . New York, Harper & Bros., 1835. 1 v.

[24] *Porter's Voyage, 2d Edtn published by Wiley, N.Y.*
 Porter, David. Journal of a Cruise Made to the Pacific Ocean . . .
 2d ed. New York, Wiley & Halsted, 1822. 2 v.

  First edition, Phila., 1815; another shorter version published as *A Voyage to the
  South Seas* . . . London, 1823.

[25] *Ross', Parry's & Franklin's Voyages*
 See [28], note, 1832 List.

[26] *Life & Voyages of Columbus*
 Same title as [29] 1832 List: New ed., rev. & corr. Philadelphia, Carey, Lea, & Blanchard, 1838. 2 v. in 1.

[27] *Bancroft's History of the U. States*
 Bancroft, George. A History of the United States . . . Boston,
 Little, Brown & Co., 1834-37.

  Only two volumes were published before 1839. See Sabin for later volumes
  and dates.

[28] *Prescott's Ferdinand & Isabella*
Prescott, William H. History of the Reign of Ferdinand and Isabella the Catholic . . . 6th ed. Boston, C. C. Little & J. Brown, 1839. 3 v.

[29] *Cooper's Naval History of the U.S.*
Cooper, James Fenimore. History of the Navy of the United States. Philadelphia, Lea, 1839. 2 v.

[30]   *do.   Pilot*
The Pilot: a Tale of the Sea. . . .
First edition, 1824.

[31]   *do.   Red Rover*
———. The Red Rover. . . .
First edition, 1828.

[32]   *do.   Water Witch*
———. The Water-Witch; or Skimmer of the Seas. . . .
First edition, 1831.

[33]   *do.   Homeward Bound*
———. Homeward Bound; or, The Chase. A Tale of the Sea. . . . Philadelphia. Carey, Lea & Blanchard, 1838. 2 v.
First edition.

[34] *Encyclopedia Britannica*
Same as [30] 1832 List.
The seventh edition began in 1827 (Edinburgh, Adam Black) and was completed in 1842 in twenty-one volumes.

[35] *Hutton's Tracts*
Same as [33] 1832 List.

[36] *Arnott's Natural Philosophy*
Same as [34] 1832 List.

[37] *Wood & Bache's Dispensary*
Wood, George B., and Franklin Bache. The Dispensatory of the United States of America . . . 4th ed., enl. & rev. Philadelphia, Grigg & Elliot, 1839. 1 v.

[38] *Walsh's Appeal*
Same as [23] 1832 List.

[39] *Kent's Commentaries*
Kent, James. Commentaries on American Law . . . 3d ed. New York, The Author, 1836. 4 v.

[40] *Incidents of Travel in Egypt, Arabia & the Holy Land*
Stephens, John L. Incidents of Travel in Egypt, Arabia, Petraea, and the Holy Land. By an American . . . 4th ed. New York,

Harper & Bros., 1838. 2 v.

[41] *A Year in Spain*
Mackenzie, Alexander Slidell. A Year in Spain. By a Young American. 3d ed., enl. New York, Harper & Bros., 1836. 3 v.

[42] *Lives & Voyages of Drake, Cavendish & Dampier*
Lives and Voyages of Drake, Cavendish, and Dampier . . . New York, Harper & Bros., 1831. 1 v.
Harper's Family Library, no. 30.

[43] *Historical account of the Circumnavigation of the Globe from the Voyage of Magellan to the death of Cook*
An Historical Account of the Circumnavigation of the Globe . . . New York, Harper & Bros., 1839. 1 v.
Harper's Family Library, no. 82.

[44] *Plutarch's Lives*
Plutarch's Lives . . . Translated by John Langhorne and William Langhorne. New ed., rev. & corr. Baltimore, W. & J. Neal, 1836. 1 v.

[45] *Bible & Prayer book*
See [36] 1832 List.

1841-1843 Library Lists: Books for Officers of the U.S. Navy

The "List of Books to be allowed for the Navy Yards and vessels of War of the U.S." given below was promulgated October 13, 1841, along with the list of books for seamen's libraries (Appendix A). The 1843 list for yards and vessels was the same as the 1841 list except that four titles ([5, 20, 27, 30] denoted by an asterisk*) were to be omitted on the 1843 list, and one item ([56], denoted by a pair of asterisks**) was to be added. As illustrated in fig. 9, the books intended to be allowed to navy yards and to various classes of vessels were marked on the lists in four columns, indicated as:

    [A] "Navy Yards

    [B] Ships of the line, Frigates and large Steamers

    [C] Sloops of war and 2d class Steamers

    [D] Brigs & smaller vessels, over 6 guns."

But on March 7, 1843, the "List of Books" was also "altered so as to include brigs, in the column with sloops of war, and second-class steamers."

In the following list, the four allowance designations are given in brackets after each title as letters [A-D]. For example, "[1] *Euclid's Elements* [A-D]" means that this title was authorized for all four categories of yards and vessels. The source for this list (and fig. 9) is the same as given for the seamen's library list (Appendix A).

[1] *Euclid's Elements* [A-D]
> See [2], note, 1832 List; also [2] on 1839 List.

[2] *Bowditch's Navigation* [A-D]
> Same as [3] 1839 List; same title as 1832 List.

[3] *Maury's do.* [A-D]
> Same title as [4] 1839 List: 2d ed. Philadelphia, E. C. Biddle, 1843. 1 v.

[4] *Tytlers Universal History* [A-D]
> Woodhouselee, Alexander F. Tytler. Universal History . . . Ed. by an American. New York, Harper & Bros., 1839. 6 v.
>
> Harper's Family Library, no. 86-91.

[5] *Gibbons decline & fall Roman Empire** [A-C]
> Same as [6] 1839 List; same title as [10] 1832 List.

[6] *Fergusons History of [do] Republic* [A-C]
> Same title as [7] 1839 List and [7] 1832 List: Philadelphia, T. Wardle, 1841. 1 v.

[7] *Mitfords History of Greece* [A-C]
> Same title as [8] 1832 List: Rev ed. London, T. Cadell [etc.], 1838. 8 v.

[8] *Rollins ancient History* [A-B]
> Same as [9] 1839 List; same title as [9] 1832 List.

[9] *History of England by Jas McIntosh & continuation* [A-C]
> Mackintosh, James. The History of England . . . Philadelphia, Carey & Lea, 1830-33. 3 v.

[10] *Constitution of the U.S. & the different States* [A-D]
> Same title as [11] 1839 List: Philadelphia, Hogan & Thompson, 1841. 1 v.

[11] *Marshalls life of Washington* [A-C]
> Same as [12] 1839 List and [12] 1832 List: 1840. 2 v.

[12] *Botta's American Revolution* [A-D]
> Same as [13] 1839 List; same title as [13] 1832 List.

[13] *Vattel's Law of Nations* [A-D]
> Same as [15] 1839 List; same title as [15] 1832 List.

[14] *Bradford's Atlas—latest Editions* [A-C]
> Same as [16] 1839 List.
>
> Sabin notes: "Reproduced with new titles, 1839 and 1842; also with Philadelphia imprint."

[15] *Jacobsons Sea Laws* [A-D]
Same as [17] 1839 List and [19] 1832 List.

[16] *Gordon's Digest of U.S. Laws* [A-D]
Same as [18a] 1839 List.

[17] *Treaties with Foreign Powers or Elliots Diplomatic Code* [A-C]
Same as [19] 1839 List.

[18] *Federalist* [A-D]
Same title as [20] 1839 List and [22] 1832 List: New ed. Hallowell, [Me.], Glazier, Masters & Smith, 1842. 1 v.

[19] *Ross', Parry's & Franklin's Voyages* [A-D]
See [28], note, 1832 List; also on 1839 List.

[20] *Bancroft's History of the U.S.* * [A-D]
Same title as [27] 1839 List: Vol. 3 published 1840.

[21] *Life and Voyages of Columbus* [A-D]
Same title as [26] 1839 List and [29] 1832 List: New ed., rev. & corr. Philadelphia, Lea & Blanchard for G. W. Groton, 1841. 2 v.

[22] *Prescott's Ferdinand & Isabella* [A-D]
Same as [28] 1839 List.

[23] *Coopers Naval History of the U.S.* [A-C]
Same title as [29] 1839 List: 2d ed., corr. Philadelphia, Lea & Blanchard, 1840. 2 v.

[24] *An Encyclopedia (cheap Edition)* [A-B]

In addition to the *Encyclopaedia Britannica* authorized on the lists of 1832 and 1839, the *Encyclopaedia Americana* was currently published at this time. The Naval storekeeper's inventory of books "for libraries of Ships" at the New York Navy Yard in 1846 also listed the following encyclopedias on hand: *Edinburgh Encyclopaedia,* Nicholson's (*i.e., British Encyclopaedia. Cf.* [1] 1839 List), and the *London Encyclopaedia.* Also volumes of Dionysius Lardner's *Cabinet Cyclopaedia* were purchased individually, and no doubt parts or entire sets of other encyclopedias (*e.g., Encyclopaedia Metropolitana*) were acquired. See Robert Collison's *Encyclopaedias: Their History Throughout the Ages* (New York, 1964) for a discussion of these and other nineteenth century encyclopedias, and also James K. Paulding's comments on encyclopedias to the secretary of the navy in 1831 (Ralph M. Aderman, ed., *The Letters of James Kirke Paulding,* pp. 113-14).

[25] *Woods and Bache's Dispensatory* [A-C]
Same as [37] 1839 List.

[26] *Walsh's appeal* [A-D]
Same as [38] 1839 List and [23] 1832 List.

[27] *Kents Commentaries* * [A-C]
Same title as [39] 1839 List: 4th ed. New York, The Author, 1840. 4 v.

[28] *Plutarch's Lives* [A-C]
Same translation as [44] 1839 List: New York, 1841. 1 v.

[29] *Bible and Prayer Book* [A-D]
> See [36], note, 1832 List; also [45] on 1839 List.

[30] *Stories Commentaries on the Constitution* * [A-C]
> Story, Joseph. Commentaries on the Constitution of the United States . . . Boston, Hilliard, Gray & Co. [etc.], 1833. 3 v.

[31] *Simm's Treatise Mathl Instrs. 2d. Edtn 1836* [A-D]
> Simms, Frederick W. A Treatise on the Principal Mathematical Instruments Employed in Surveying, Levelling, and Astronomy . . . 2d ed. London, Troughton & Simms [etc.], 1836. 1 v.

[32] *Belcher on Nautical Surveying 1835* [A-D]
> Belcher, Edward. A Treatise on Nautical Surveying . . . London, P. Richardson, 1835. 1 v.

[33] *Edye, on displacement of Ships* [A-B]
> Edye, John. Calculations Relating to the Equipment, Displacement, etc., of Ships and Vessels of War. London, S. & R. Hodgson, 1832. 1 v.

[34] *Douglass on Naval Gunnery* [A-D]
> Same as [4] 1832 List.

[35] *Shermans British Gunner—1828* [A-D]
> Spearman, J. Morton. The British Gunner. 2d ed. Woolwich, Allen & Leadenhall, 1828. 1 v.

[36] *Writings of Washington, by Sparks* [A-B]
> Sparks, Jared, ed. The writings of George Washington . . . Boston, F. Andrews, 1839-40. 12 v.

[37] *Simmon's on heavy ordnance* [A-C]
> Simmons, Thomas F. Ideas as to the Effect of Heavy Ordnance . . . London, F. Pinkney, 1837. 1 v.

[38] *Clerk on Naval Tactics—Octavo* [A-C]
> Clerk, John. An Essay on Naval Tactics. 3d ed. Edinburgh, Adam Black [etc.], 1827. 1 v.
>> Also on 1827 List of books for navy yards.

[39] *Ekins Naval Battles* [A-B]
> Ekins, Charles. The Naval Battles of Great Britain . . . 2d ed. London, Baldwin & Cradock, 1828. 1 v.

[40] *La Hoste Naval Tactics—Engl. Translt.* [A-B]
> Hoste, Paul. A Treatise on Naval Tactics . . . Edinburgh, Bell & Bradfute, etc., 1831. 1 v.

[41] *Treatise on the Steam Engine (Lardner)* [A-C]
> Lardner, Dionysius. The Steam Engine Explained and Illustrated . . . 7th ed. London, Pr. for Taylor & Walton [1840]. 1 v.

[42] *Grier's Mechanics pocket Dictry. 2d Edn 1837* [A-D]

Grier, William. The Mechanic's Pocket Dictionary . . . Glasgow, Blackie & Son, 1837. 1 v.

[43] *Anthons Classical Dictionary* [A-B]
Anthon, Charles. A Classical Dictionary . . . New York, Harper & Bros., 1841. 1 v.

[44] *Jameson's mechanics of Fluids for pract'l men* [A-B]
Jamieson, Alexander. Mechanics of Fluids for Practical Men . . . London, W. S. Orr & Co., 1837. 1 v.

[45] *Hough on Courts Martial* [A-B]
Hough, William. The Practice of Courts-Martial. 2d ed., rev. & corr. London, Kingsbury, Parbury & Allen, 1825. 1 v.
   Also on 1827 List of books for navy yards.

[46] *Genl. Macomb do.* [A-B]
Macomb, Alexander. The Practice of Courts Martial . . . New York, Harper & Bros., 1841. 1 v.

[47] *Adye—on Courts Martial* [A-B]
Adye, Stephen P. A Treatise on Courts Martial . . . 8th ed. London, Vernor, Hood [etc.], 1810. 1 v.

[48] *Tytler—* [*do*] [*do*] [*do*] [A-B]
Woodhouselee, Alexander F. Tytler. An Essay on Military Law, and the Practice of Courts Martial . . . 3d ed. London, T. Egerton, 1814. 1 v.
   Also on 1827 List of books for navy yards.

[49] *McArthur* [*do*] [*do*] [*do*] [A-B]
McArthur, John. Principles and Practice of Naval and Military Courts Martial . . . 4th ed. London, Pr. by Strahan, 1813. 2 v.

[50] *Spectator* [A-D]
The Spectator. . . .
   Originally published as a periodical by Joseph Addison and Richard Steele in London between 1711-1712. Various editions were later published separately (including selections from it in the Harper's Family Library), or in collections with other similar essayists' periodicals (*e.g.*, [51, 52, 53] below) in such works as Alexander Chalmers's *British Essayists,* and James Ferguson's *British Essayists,* etc. Two complete sets of a multi-volume edition were listed in the Naval storekeeper's inventory of books "for libraries of Ships" at the New York Navy Yard in 1846, as well as an incomplete set which lacked vols. 4 and 5. Also at this time, a one-volume edition was reported in this navy yard's library; and the early USNA Library at one time had a six-volume edition.

[51] *Rambler* [A-D]
Johnson, Samuel. The Rambler . . . .
   Originally published in London, 1750-1752. Various editions, and in Chalmers's and Ferguson's collections (see note [50] above). One complete set of unspecified volumes was listed in the 1846 Naval storekeeper's inventory and a three-volume set was in the early USNA Library.

[52] *Idler* [A-D]
Johnson, Samuel. The Idler. . . .
> Johnson's essays from the *Universal Chronicle,* 1758-1760. Various editions; and in Chalmers's and Ferguson's collections (see note [50] above).

[53] *Adventurer* [A-D]
The Adventurer. . . .
> Periodical edited by John Hawkesworth and originally published in London, 1752-1754. Various editions, and in Chalmers's and Ferguson's collections (see note [50] above).

[54] *Stevens Central America* [A-D]
Stephens, John L. Incidents of Travel in Central America . . . New York, Harper & Bros., 1841. 2 v.

[55] *Totten's Naval Text Book* [A-D]
Totten, Benjamin J. Naval Text-Book . . . Boston, C. C. Little & J. Brown, 1841. 1 v.

[56] *Fordyce's Naval Routine* ** [A-D?]
Fordyce, Alexander D. Outlines of Naval Routine. London, Smith, Elder & Co. [etc.], 1837. 1 v.

* * * * *

On January 18, 1844, eleven additional books were allowed to the libraries of the sloops-of-war *Portsmouth, Plymouth, Albany, Germantown, St. Mary's* and *Jamestown.* These titles were numbers [27, 33, 40, and 49] on the 1841/43 Lists, and:

[i] *Webster's Dictionary. Octavo Edition.*
Webster, Noah. An American Dictionary of the English Language. 1st ed. in octavo. New Haven, The Author, 1841. 1 v.

[ii] *Falconer's Marine Dictionary*
Falconer, William. A New and Universal Dictionary of the Marine . . . London, Cadell [etc.], 1815. 1 v.
> Also on 1827 List of books for navy yards.

[iii] *Simmons on Courts Martial*
Simmons, Thomas F. Remarks on the Constitution and Practice of Courts Martial . . . 3d ed. with additions. London, F. Pinkney, 1843. 1 v.

[iv] *Marten's Law of Nations*
Marten, George F. The Law of Nations . . . 4th ed. London, W. Cobbett, 1829. 1 v.

[v] *Sheet Anchor*
Lever, Darcy. The Young Sea Officer's Sheet Anchor . . . 2d London ed. London [& Philadelphia], M. Carey, [1819]. 1 v.

Also on 1827 List of books for navy yards.

[vi] *Epitome of the Royal Naval Service*
  Miles, Edmund. An Epitome, Historical and Statistical, Descriptive of the Royal Naval Service of England . . . London, M. A. Nattali, 1844. 1 v.
[vii] *Raper's Navigation*
  Raper, Henry. The Practice of Navigation and Nautical Astronomy . . . 2d ed. London, Bate, 1842. 1 v.
        —Source: RG 45(*42*), Circular, Jan. 18, 1844.

Bibliographic Notes

Abbreviations

PERIODICALS

A &NC	—*Army and Navy Chronicle.*
A & NC & SR	—*Army and Navy Chronicle and Scientific Repository.*
CH & SM	—*Christian Herald and Seaman's Magazine,* v. 1-11 (1816-1824); as *Christian Herald,* v. 1-7.
NSM	—*New Sailor's Magazine and Naval Chronicle.*
SM & NJ	—*Sailor's Magazine and Naval Journal* (New York), v. 1-29 (1828-1857); v. 30-36 (1858-1864) as *Sailor's Magazine;* and as *Sailor's Magazine and Seamen's Friend* thereafter.
Proc. USNI	—*Proceedings of the U.S. Naval Institute.*
USNM & NJ	—*U.S. Nautical Magazine and Naval Journal.*

OTHER

RG 24—Record Group 24 of the U.S. National Archives: Records of the Bureau of Personnel.

RG 45—Record Group 45, National Archives: Naval Records Collection of the Office of Naval Records and Library.

The italicized numbers appearing in parentheses in citations for items in this record group denote a particular series of records. For example, R.G. 45(*1*) means that the entry "Letters to Officers . . ." sent by the Secretary of the Navy has been cited. The numbers assigned in the abbreviations, incidentally, conform to the record identification numbers that were used by the National Archives in the preparation of its preliminary inventory of this record group in 1945.

Letters Sent by the Secretary of the Navy (SN):
RG 45(*1*)   Letters to Officers, Ships of War.
   (*3*)   Miscellaneous Letters Sent.
   (*6*)   Letters to Commandants and Navy Agents.
   (*13*)   Letters to Bureaus of the Navy Department.
Letters Received by the Secretary of the Navy (SN):
   (*21*)   Miscellaneous Letters Received.
   (*22*)   Letters from Officers Below the Rank of Commander.
   (*23*)   Letters from Commanders.
   (*24*)   Letters from Captains.
   (*28*)   Letters from the Board of Navy Commissioners (BNC).
   (*32*)   Letters from Bureaus of the Navy Department.

* * * * *

(*41*) Directives ("Orders, Circulars, Instructions, Regulations"), Apr., 1776–Dec., 1863.

(*42*) Directives ("Circulars and General Orders"), May, 1798–July, 1895.

* * * * *

Letters Sent by the Board of Navy Commissioners (BNC):

(*212*) Circulars Issued.

(*213*) Letters to the Secretary of the Navy (SN).

(*214*) Letters to Officers.

Letters Received by the Board of Navy Commissioners (BNC):

(*221*) Letters from Officers.

(*222*) Letters from the Secretary of the Navy (SN).

(*229*) Letters from the American Consul in London.

* * * * *

(*326*) Selected Correspondence of the Superintendent of the U.S. Naval Academy; and "List of Books in the Library of the Academy, Feb. 10, 1852."

(*464*) Subject file NE (Drills, training and education). Box 1: 0-1859; and Subject file XS (Naval supplies ashore). New York Navy Yard envelope, July–Dec., 1842.

RG 181 —Record Group 181, National Archives: Records of Naval Districts and Shore Establishments.

RG 217 —Record Group 217, National Archives: Records of the U.S. General General Accounting Office.

RG 405 —Record Group 405, National Archives: Records of the U.S. Naval Academy.

USNA-L —Library, U.S. Naval Academy.

USNA-M—Museum, U.S. Naval Academy.

NOTES

Chapter I

Quotation at chapter head: Francis Bacon, *Advancement of Learning* (1605).

1. Books and reading of Columbus: Samuel E. Morison, *Admiral of the Ocean Sea* (Boston, 1942), v. 1, pp. 120-29, 224-27, 413-14; John B. Thacher, *Christopher Columbus, His Life, His Work, His Remains* (New York, 1904), v. 3, pp. 452-53; Douglas C. McMurtrie, *The Book; the Story of Printing and Bookmaking* (3d ed. New York, 1943), p. 320. Quote of Pigafetta: *The Philippine Islands, 1493-1898*, ed. by Emma H. Blair (Cleveland, 1906), v. 33, pp. 27-29.

2. About Hakluyt: Janet Hampden, *Richard Hakluyt, Voyages and Documents* (London, 1958), pp. 1-2; George B. Parks, *Richard Hakluyt and the English Voyages* (2d ed. New York, 1961), 158-59, 184. A facsimile edition of Hakluyt's voyages has recently been published in two volumes: *The Principall Navigations, Voiages and Discoveries of the English Nation . . . Imprinted at London, 1589* (Cambridge, 1965); hereafter cited as Hakluyt *facs.*

3. All references to Captains Fox and James are from Miller Christy, ed., *The Voyages of Captain Luke Fox of Hull and Captain Thomas James of Bristol* (London, 1894), v. 2, pp. 265-67, 606.

4. All references to John Aborough are from Dorothy Burwash, *English Merchant Shipping, 1460-1540* (Toronto, 1947), pp. 19-20, 32-34, 42-48.

5. Hakluyt *facs.*, v. 1, pp. 259-60; Gt. Brit. Admiralty, *Regulations and Instructions Relating to His Majesty's Service at Sea* (London, 1734), p. 97.

6. About Captain Frobisher: David W. Waters, *The Art of Navigation in England in Elizabethan and Early Stuart Times* (New Haven, 1958), pp. 144-46, 499, 530-31; Samuel E. Morison, *The European Discovery of America; The Northern Voyages, 500-1600* (New York, 1971), p. 502.

7. John Smith, *A Sea Grammar; With the Plaine Exposition of Smiths Accidence for Young Sea-men, Enlarged* (London, 1627), p. 83. Another edition of Capt. Smith's work was recently published with annotations by Kermit Goell (London, 1970). In it, the books recommended by Smith in 1627 are bibliographically identified by the editor on pp. 93-94; *cf.* also, Lawrence C. Wroth, *The Way of a Ship* (Portland, Me., 1937), pp. 69-70.

8. About Captain Sturmy: Cyril E. Kenney, *The Quadrant and the Quill* (London, 1947), pp. 67-68, 125-164. The publication of the Laws of Oléron in rutters is discussed in David W. Waters, *The Rutters of the Sea* (New Haven, 1967), and in Burwash, *op. cit.*

9. Books for recreation and sale: Fabri—Palestine Pilgrims' Text Society, *The Library of the Palestine Pilgrims' Text Society* (London, 1896), v. 7, pt. 1, pp. 150-52; Spanish books at sea—Irving A. Leonard, *Books of the Brave* (Cambridge, Mass., 1949), pp. 159-82, 270-71. About the barber-surgeon: John J. Keevil, *Medicine and the Navy, 1200-1900* (London, 1957), v. 1, pp. 68-69. About John Barlow: Basil Lubbock, ed., *Barlow's Journal of His Life at Sea* (London, 1934), v. 1, pp. 251-52.

10. Hakluyt, *facs.*, v. 1, p. 464. The gift books are also bibliographically identified in the "Modern Index" of this work, v. 2, p. 847.

11. Medicine: Keevil, *op. cit.*, pp. 152-53, 215-17. Education: Gt. Brit. Admiralty, *op. cit.*, pp. 136-37.

12. Henry Lyons, *The Royal Society, 1660-1940* (Cambridge, 1944), p. 111.

13. Colin A. Ronan, *Edmond Halley, Genius in Eclipse* (Garden City, N.Y., 1969), p. 164; Angus Armitage, *Edmond Halley* (London, 1966), p. 138.

14. John C. Beaglehole, ed., *The Journals of Captain James Cook on His Voyages of Discovery* (Cambridge, 1955), v. 1, p. cxxxvi; Edward Parry, *Memoirs of Rear-Admiral Sir W. Edward Parry, Kt.* (5th ed. London, 1858), pp. 67-68; Christopher Lloyd, *The Voyages of Captain James Cook Round the World* (London, 1949), p. xiii.

15. Jean François de Galaup La Pérouse, *A Voyage Round the World Performed in the Years 1785, 1786, 1787, and 1788* (London, 1799; New York, 1968 [facsimile]), v. 1, pp. 189-93.

Chapter II

Quotation at chapter head: *CH & SM,* v. 8 (July 7, 1821), 121-22.

1. Religion, the sea, and chaplains: Clifford M. Drury, *The History of the Chaplain Corps, United States Navy* (Washington, 1948), v. 1, pp. 1-2; Waldo E. L. Smith, *The Navy and Its Chaplains in the Days of Sail* (Toronto, 1961), pp. 1, 155.

2. Bray and the Annopolitan Library: Edgar L. Pennington, *The Reverend Thomas Bray* (Philadelphia, 1934), pp. 5-10; Charlotte Fletcher, "The Reverend Thomas Bray, M. Alexandre Vattemare, and Library Science," *Library Quarter-*

ly, 27 (Apr., 1957), 95-99; Anne W. Brown, "The Phoenix: A History of the St. John's College Library," *Maryland Historical Magazine*, 65 (Winter, 1970), 413-29.

3. Samuel Smith, *Publick Spirit Illustrated in the Life and Designs of the Reverend Thomas Bray, D.D.* (2d ed. London, 1808), pp. 22-25; Pennington, *op. cit.*, p. 34.

4. Austin B. Keep, *History of the New York Society Library* (New York, 1908), pp. 12, 16, 23; Bernard C. Steiner, "Rev. Thomas Bray and His American Libraries," *American Historical Review*, 2 (Oct., 1896), 59-75.

5. Thomas Bray, "Bibliothecae Americanae Quadripartitae; part IV, Parochialis, or Catalogues of the Libraries Sent to the Several Provinces of America, 1709." Photocopy of MS. in Scion College Library, at St. John's College Library, Annapolis, Md.

6. The S.P.C.K.: William K. L. Clarke, *A History of the S.P.C.K.* (London, 1959), pp. 78, 84; Henry P. Thompson, *Thomas Bray* (London, 1954), p. 41.

7. The S.P.C.K. and the Royal Navy: Waldo E. L. Smith, *op. cit.*, pp. 142, 152-53.

8. A chronological record of the distribution of the Bible in the army, navy, and among merchant seamen and boatmen by the American Bible Society from 1817 to 1855 is found in William P. Strickland's *History of the American Bible Society* (New York, 1856), pp. 86-102.

9. Reported in *CH & SM*, 6 (Apr. 17, 1819), 10, and (July 17), 218.

10. [Richard Marks], *The Retrospect, or a Review of Providential Mercies* (Philadelphia, 1821), pp. 80-81. The first edition of this little book was published in London, 1816.

11. Lawrance Thompson, "The Printing and Publishing Activities of the American Tract Society from 1825 to 1850," *Papers of the Bibliographical Society of America*, 35 (2d Quarter, 1941), 84-85.

12. The remainder of this chapter is based upon materials found in three early religious sailors' magazines (*CH & SM, NSM*, and *SM & NJ*) and other general sources. Specific sources used are cited as they occur in the text.

13. Waldo E. L. Smith, *op. cit.*, p. 155. At this time religious libraries were also advocated for civil prisoners confined to prison hulks, as noted in W. Branch-Johnson, *The English Prison Hulks* (London, 1957), pp. 129-30.

14. Boston Society for the Religious and Moral Improvement of Seamen, *An Address to Masters of Vessels on the Objects of the Society* (Boston, 1812), p. 3; Harold D. Langley, *Social Reform in the United States Navy, 1798-1862* (Urbana, Ill., 1967), p. 50.

15. John Pintard, *Letters of John Pintard to His Daughter, Eliza Noel Pintard Davidson, 1816-1833* (New York, 1940), v. 1, pp. 295-96.

16. Elmo P. Hohman, *Seamen Ashore* (New Haven, 1952), p. 283.

17. U.S. Public Health Service, *The Ship's Medicine Chest and First Aid at Sea* (Washington, 1955), pp. 1-10.

18. The S.P.C.K. libraries are discussed in Clarke, *op. cit.*, pp. 77-80, and an illustration there of a cabinet library faces p. 51.

19. *Library Association Record*, 3 (Oct., 1933), Supplement, vi.

20. American Seamen's Friend Society, *The Acts of the Apostles of the Sea* (New York, 1909), pp. 6-7.

21. A good capsule survey of religious work among seamen to World War I is contained in *The New Schaff-Herzog Encyclopedia of Religious Knowledge* (New York, 1911), v. 10, pp. 316-19; and the work of the American Seamen's Friend Society is reviewed in George Webster's *The Seamen's Friend* (New

York, 1932).

22. Edward Parry, *Memoirs of Rear-Admiral W. Edward Parry, Kt.* (London, 1858), pp. 186-88.

23. [Nathaniel Ames], *A Mariner's Sketches* (Providence, 1830), p. 241.

24. *The New Schaff-Herzog Encyclopedia,* v. 10, p. 316.

Chapter III

1. Background material concerning life in New York City and the status of its libraries is from general sources, but specific factual data and quotes are from: Thomas B. Macaulay, "On the Royal Society of Literature," *Knight's Quarterly,* 1 (June, 1823); John Pintard, *Letters From John Pintard to His Daughter, Eliza Noel Pintard Davidson, 1816-1833* (New York, 1941), v. 3, pp. 32, 100; Austin B. Keep, *History of the New York Society Library* (New York, 1908), pp. 307-18; [Joseph A. Scoville], *The Old Merchants of New York City* (New York, 1863), v. 1, p. 449, v. 2, pp. 56-57.

2. References to named packets and packet lines, maritime activity and news in the port of New York, and about ship versus stagecoach travel are mostly from Robert G. Albion, *Square Riggers on Schedule* (Princeton, 1938), pp. 38, 96, 146-48, 203, and from his *The Rise of New York Port* (New York, 1939), p. 339. Factual information about steamers is from Erik Heyl, *Early American Steamers* (Buffalo, 1953), v. 1, p. 369, and John H. Morrison, *History of American Steam Navigation* (New York, 1903), p. 339.

3. The notice of the bethel meetings aboard the *Cadmus* and the *Franklin* was recounted in *SM & NJ,* 3 (July, 1831), 338. Maury's account of the *Franklin's* library appeared as "Scraps from the Lucky Bag, No. III: Details of the School-Ship," *Southern Literary Messenger,* 6 (Dec., 1840), 786-800. The article was also reprinted in *A & NC,* 11 (Dec., 1840), 385-89.

4. About William Wood, Pintard, and John Kyrle: Pintard, *op. cit.,* v. 3, p. 27; Edward V. Lucas, "The Man of Ross," in *Adventures and Enthusiasms* (New York, 1920), pp. 71-84. A portrait of William Wood in his prime appears in *Ballou's Pictorial Drawing-Room Companion,* 13 (Sept. 19, 1857), along with a biographical sketch, "The Late William Wood, Esq.," on p. 188.

5. General information on workingmen's libraries is from Sidney Ditzion, "Mechanics' and Mercantile Libraries," *Library Quarterly,* 10 (Apr., 1940), pp. 197-219, and Jesse H. Shera, *Foundations of the Public Library* (Chicago, 1949), pp. 229-31. About Wood and the Boston Mechanic Apprentices' Library Association: *Annals of the Massachusetts Charitable Mechanic Association, 1795-1892* (Boston, 1892), p. 9; Mary Knight Lincoln, ed., *In Memoriam: Frederick Walker Lincoln* (Boston, 1899), p. 30; Boston Mechanic Apprentices' Library Association, *Report of the Committee of the Library* (Boston, 1859), p. 3; Charles C. Jewett, *Report on the Public Libraries of the United States of America,* Smithsonian Institution Annual Report, 1849 (Washington, 1850), pp. 27-28. Wood and the Mercantile Library Association: *A Catalogue of Books of the Mercantile Library Association of Boston* (Boston, 1850), p. 3.

6. About Lord Brougham: Henry P. Brougham, "Practical Observations Upon the Education of the People . . . ," in *The Works of Henry Lord Brougham and Vaux* (Edinburgh, 1872), v. 3, pp. 417, 453; Jewett, *loc. cit.;* William J. Rhees, *Manual of Public Libraries, Institutions and Societies in the United States* (Philadelphia, 1859), pp. 109-110; *Mechanics' Magazine,* 22 (Mar. 21, 1835), pp. 457-63.

7. General Society of Mechanics and Tradesmen of the City of New York,

*Some Memorials of the Late William Wood, Esq. . . . Presented in a Report
of the Apprentices' Library Committee . . . Dec. 2d, 1857* (New York, 1858),
pp. 15-28; idem, *Centennial Celebration of the General Society . . . November
16th . . . and 17th, 1885* (New York, 1885), p. 10.

8. Wood and Canandaigua: Albert G. Granger, *The History of Canandaigua;
An Address* (Canandaigua, 1876), pp. 13-14; "Eccentric Billy Wood," *Ontario
County Times Journal,* Feb. 18, 1891. The poem honoring William Wood is
quoted in Caroline Cowles Richards, *Village Life in America, 1852-1872* (new
& enl. ed. New York, 1913), p. 94.

9. Jonathan P. Miller, *The Condition of Greece in 1827 and 1828* (New
York, 1828), pp. 287, 290; Jerzy J. Lerski, *A Polish Chapter in Jacksonian
America* (Madison, 1958), p. 128.

Chapter IV

Quotation at chapter head: *CH & SM,* 8 (Sept. 1, 1821), 255.

1. The brief history of the Pacific station in relation to the *Franklin's* cruise
and Commo. Stewart's conduct in South America is from Robert E. Johnson,
Thence Round Cape Horn (Annapolis, 1963), pp. 1-7, 29-35. Charles Stewart
is yet to have a biographer; however, some published biographical information
about him exists. The sketch presented here is taken mostly from H. D. Smith,
"Rear-Admiral Charles Stewart," *United Service,* n.s., 1 (Mar., 1889), 277-78.

2. The source for a great deal of the information presented in this chapter
(as well as Chapters V-VIII) is Record Group 45 of the U.S. National Archives.
The various sub-groups or series of documents contained in RG 45 which were
consulted in the research for this book are listed in the Abbreviations. Whenever
a letter or other item from one of these series is referred to in the text, it is mentioned in such a manner (by officers' names and ranks, correspondents' names,
dates, etc.) that it should be evident to which series it belongs. Thus, no footnote
citation is made unless further clarification is necessary. All citations to records
of the National Archives appear in abbreviated form, *e.g.,* RG 45(*1*) to (*464*),
RG 181, etc.

3. Weaver's trial was reported in *Niles' Weekly Register,* 26 (Apr. 3, 1824),
72-75, and (Apr. 24), 119-21; 27 (Dec. 4, 1824), 216.

4. Daniel Henderson, *The Hidden Coasts, a Biography of Admiral Charles
Wilkes* (New York, 1953), pp. 23-25.

5. [William A. Weaver], *Journals of the Ocean and Other Miscellaneous
Poems* (New York, 1826).

6. Charles O. Paullin, *Paullin's History of Naval Administration, 1775-1911*
(Annapolis, 1968), pp. 200-201.

7. John W. Francis, *Old New York; or Reminiscences of the Past Sixty
Years* (New York, 1858), p. 351; Pintard, *Letters to His Daughter,* v. 2, p. 141.

8. Wiley's "Den" and the "bookish people" who frequented his store are
commented upon in *The First One Hundred and Fifty Years, a History of John
Wiley and Sons, Inc., 1807-1957* (New York: Wiley and Sons, 1957). Other information about the firm is from contemporary newspapers and general sources.

9. General Society of Mechanics and Tradesmen of the City of New York,
Some Memorials of the Late William Wood, p. 27.

10. Notices about the *Franklin* and her library in Valparaiso, Mrs. Stewart,
and sickness and death among the ship's crew appeared in *Niles' Weekly Register,* 22 (June 22, 1822), 272, (July 13), 320, (Nov. 30), 197-98; 25 (Feb. 14, 1824),

384; 26 (June 16, 1824), 264. The logbook of the *Franklin* is in RG 24(*218*).

11. *National Intelligencer,* Sept. 9, 1824.

12. RG 45(*24*) Stewart to SN, Oct. 19, 1824.

13. *Ibid.* (*3*) SN to Wood, Dec. 5, 1831.

14. *Ibid.* (*1*) SN to Chauncey, Dec. 17, 1831.

15. MS. at USNA-M.

16. "Catalogue of the Books Composing the Library of the U.S. Naval Lyceum, 1841" (MS. at USNA-L).

Chapter V

Quotation at chapter head: Timothy D. Hunt (See note 25 below).

1. RG 45(*21*), Wood to SN, Oct. 6, 1824; Dec. 3, 1831. See note 2 of Chapter IV for an explanation of the notation used for citing National Archives record groups in this study.

2. The voyages of the *United States* and *Dolphin: CH & SM,* 11 (Jan. 3, 1824), 28-29; Nathaniel Ames, *A Mariner's Sketches,* pp. 242, 252-59. About the riot in Hawaii: Bradford Smith, *Yankees in Paradise* (Philadelphia, 1956), pp. 130-34.

3. About the *Erie: CH & SM,* 10 (Dec. 6, 1823), 447-48; *New York National Advocate* and *New York Mercantile Advertiser,* Nov. 10, 1834. The *North Carolina: National Intelligencer,* Feb. 2, 1825. Byron and the *Ontario:* Leslie A. Marchand, *Byron, A Biography* (New York, 1957), v. 3, pp. 999-1000.

4. The *Potomac: SM & NJ,* 6 (July, 1834), 352; Francis Warriner, *Cruise of the United States Frigate Potomac Round the World* (New York, 1835); Jeremiah Reynolds, *Voyage of the U.S. Frigate Potomac . . . in the Years 1831-34* (New York, 1835); Charles Rockwell, *Sketches of Foreign Travel and Life at Sea* (Boston, 1842), v. 2, pp. 395-96; [George Jones], *Sketches of Naval Life* (New Haven, 1829), v. 2, p. 242.

5. The *Columbia*: Henry L. Burr, *Education in the Early Navy* (Philadelphia, 1939), pp. 124-25, 172-73; [Joshua S. Henshaw], *Around the World, a Narrative of a Voyage in the East India Squadron* (New York, 1840), v. 1, pp. 21-27, 170-71, 188-91. The *Delaware*: Mendel L. Peterson, ed., *The Journals of Daniel Noble Johnson (1822-1863), United States Navy.* Smithsonian Miscellaneous Collections, v. 136, no. 2 (Washington, 1959), p. 52.

6. "Old Ironsides": [Henry J. Mercier], *Life in a Man-of-War, or Scenes in "Old Ironsides"* (Boston, 1927), p. 108. Originally published in Philadelphia, 1841. The *Potomac:* Rockwell, *loc. cit.*

7. William McNally, *Evils and Abuses in the Naval and Merchant Service Exposed* (Boston, 1839), pp. 160-63. About soldiers' libraries: Jewett, *Report on the Public Libraries of the U.S.,* pp. 187-88.

8. About the Royal Navy: *A & NC,* 11 (Sept. 10, 1840), 162-63. Apprentices: Langley, *Social Reform in the U.S. Navy,* pp. 106-9; *A & NC,* 8 (June 13, 1839), 383. The two almost identical passages occurred in F. P. Torrey, *Journal of the Cruise of the United States Ship Ohio* (Boston, 1841), p. 10, and in Roland F. Gould, *The Life of Gould, an Ex-Man-of-War's-Man* (Claremont, N.H., 1867), pp. 48-49. It appears that Gould incorporated this information and a great deal else from Torrey's work into his own. Paulding's authorization: RG 45(*6*), SN order, Jan. 7, and May 27, 1840.

9. RG 45(*28*), June 15, 1841.

10. Eugene Exman, *The Brothers Harper* (New York, 1965), p. 21. About the

Portsmouth: Joseph T. Downey, *The Cruise of the Portsmouth, 1845-1847* (New Haven, 1958), p. 82.

11. Howard P. Vincent, *The Tailoring of Melville's White-Jacket* (Evanston, Ill., 1970), pp. 6-10, 117-20. Also, Melville's reading at sea has been examined by Merton M. Sealts in *Melville's Reading* (Madison, Wisc., 1966), pp. 10-15.

12. About the *United States's* charts: Charles R. Anderson, *Melville in the South Seas* (New York, 1939), p. 358; Walter Colton, *Deck and Port* (New York, 1856), p. 321. About her library: Anderson, *loc. cit.*; Jay Leyda, *The Melville Log: a Documentary Life of Herman Melville, 1819-1891* (New York, 1969), v. 1, p. 180.

13. RG 24(*218*), Logbook of the frigate *United States.*

14. Colton, *op. cit.*, pp. 19, 33, 323-24; Clifford M. Drury, "Walter Colton, Chaplain and Alcalde," *California Historical Society Quarterly,* 35 (June, 1956), 102; Elizabeth Douglas Van Denburgh, *My Voyage in the United States Frigate "Congress"* (New York, 1913), pp. 37, 43, 54-55.

15. RG 45(*22*), Chaplain Charles W. Thomas to SN, Jan. 31, 1855.

16. The *SM & NJ* was the source for all materials used in the remainder of this chapter unless specifically cited.

17. F. Allen Briggs, "The Sunday School Library in the Nineteenth Century," *Library Quarterly,* 31 (Apr., 1961), 166-67.

18. Charles S. Stewart, *Brazil and La Plata* (New York, 1856), pp. 198-99, 270-71.

19. *SM & NJ,* 31 (Sept., 1858, and other issues), inside front cover. The *Life Boat, Children's Work for Seamen,* was issued with the *Sailor's Magazine and Seamen's Friend* in 658 numbers between Jan., 1858, and Dec., 1912. Its pages were numbered consecutively with those of the parent magazine.

20. Webster, *The Seamen's Friend,* pp. 90-93; *SM & NJ,* 34 (June, 1862), 290-91.

21. The *North America:* Francis A. Olmsted, *Incidents of a Whaling Voyage* (New York, 1841; New York, 1969), pp. 52-53. A discussion of the validity of the *Acushnet's* library in relation to Melville's reading appears in Wilson Heflin's "Herman Melville's Whaling Years" (Ph. D. diss., Vanderbilt University, 1952), pp. 182-83. The contents of the library purchased for the Nantucket whaler of 1840 will be described in a forthcoming article by Heflin and Edouard Stackpole in *Historic Nantucket.* About absence of libraries: John Ross Browne, *Etchings of a Whaling Voyage* (New York, 1846), pp. 110-11; William F. Gragg, *A Cruise in the U.S. Steam Frigate Mississippi* (Boston, 1860), p. 26.

22. Webster, *op. cit.*, 73-74. The first YMCA libraries were also intended to shield against evil, as discussed in Doris M. Fletcher's "Read a Book and Sin No More: the Early YMCA Libraries," *Wilson Library Bulletin,* 31 (Mar., 1957), 521-22.

23. RG 45(*213*), Apr. 8, 1834, Oct. 26, 1836; (*42*), Sept. 30, 1843; (*1*), SN to Capt. Stringham, Nov. 18, 1844; Jewett, *Report on the Public Libraries of the U.S.,* p. 160.

24. Three pertinent studies concerning individual and institutional book ownership on the midwest and California frontiers are of interest here: Ralph L. Husk, *The Literature of the Middle Western Frontier* (New York, 1925), v. 1, pp. 67-69; Michael H. Harris, "Books on the Frontier: the Extent and Nature of Book Ownership in Southern Indiana, 1800-1850," *Library Quarterly,* 42 (Oct., 1972), 416-30; Doyce B. Nunis, *Books in Their Sea Chests* (Berkeley: California Library Association, 1964), pp. 3, 23.

25. John Harris, *Britannia; or The Moral Claims of Seamen* (London, 1837). Also published in the United States as *Zebulon; or The Moral Claims of Seamen,* and reprinted in part in *SM & NJ,* 10-11 (Apr.-Sept., 1838). T. D. Hunt's "Wants of Seamen" appeared in the *Honolulu Friend* prior to 1850, and was published in part in *SM & NJ,* 22 (Mar., 1850), 193-96, and as an appendix to the Reverend Henry T. Cheever's *The Whale and His Captors* (New York, 1853 and 1855 eds.), pp. 347-56.

Chapter VI

Quotation at chapter head: Auguste Levasseur, *Lafayette in America in 1824 and 1825; or A Journal of a Voyage to the United States* (Philadelphia, 1829; New York, 1970), v. 2, p. 258.

1. The history of the register is traced in Louis H. Bolander, "The Navy Register; Its Evolution," *Bull. New York Public Library,* 58 (July, 1954), 337-43.

2. RG 45(*1*), SN to Tingey, June 22, 1799. See note 2 of Chapter IV for an explanation of the notation used for citing National Archives record groups in this study.

3. RG 45(*24*), Morris to SN, Oct. 17, 1817, with enclosures dated Oct. 3.

4. *Ibid.* (*1*), Nov. 7, 1817; (*6*), Oct. 30, 1817; (*213*), Nov. 26, 1817, with enclosure Sinclair to BNC, Nov. 22.

5. The private ownership of charts by naval officers at the close of the Revolution is mentioned by Marion V. Brewington in "American Navigation During the Revolution," v. 2, pp. 803-5 of *Naval Documents of the American Revolution* (Washington, 1966). Also, the relationship of the British and American naval regulations is reviewed by Harry R. Skallerup, "Notes on Early Naval Regulations," in U.S. Navy Dept., *Naval Regulations, Issued by Command of the President of the United States of America, January 25, 1802* (Annapolis, 1970), pp. [37-43]. Truxtun's essay was appended to his book, *Remarks, Instructions, and Examples Relating to the Latitude and Longitude* (Philadelphia, 1794), pp. i-xiii.

6. RG 45(*221*), Francis H. Gregory to BNC, Aug. 16, 1825; U.S. Navy Dept. Board of Navy Commissioners, *Tables Showing the Masts and Spars and Stores, etc. . . . Allowed to the Different Classes of Vessels . . .* (Washington, 1826), p. 67.

7. An account of Blunt's life and activities is presented in Harold L. Burstyn's *At the Sign of the Quadrant* (Mystic, Conn., 1957); RG 45(*21*), Blunt, June 28, and Nov. 10, 1811; E. Millicent Sowerby, ed., *Catalogue of the Library of Thomas Jefferson* (Washington, 1955), v. 4, pp. 80-81.

8. The history of the various editions of the major works published by Blunt is traced in Burstyn, *op. cit.,* pp. 115-19. Blunt also sent a similar request and a printed list to the secretary of the navy on Apr. 17, 1826, and in it referred to another earlier letter written in January. The copy of the Bowditch from the *Franklin's* "Masters Department," dating from 1821, is located at USNA-L. The 1827 navy yard library list: RG 45(*212*), to Commandants, May 3, 1827.

9. Charles Francis Adams, ed., *The Works of John Adams* (Boston, 1854), v. 9, p. 47. The various moves of the Navy Department office are mentioned in *Paullin's History of Naval Administration, 1775-1911,* pp. 107-9, 157-58, and in *American State Papers . . . [Class VI], Naval Affairs* (Washington, 1834), v. 1, p. 320.

10. Christopher McKee, *Edward Preble, a Naval Biography, 1761-1807* (Annapolis, 1972), pp. 342-44; Henry M. Christman, ed., *Walt Whitman's New*

York (New York, 1963), pp. 121-27; Charles Morris, *The Autobiography of Commodore Charles Morris* (Annapolis, 1880), pp. 75-76; RG 45(*214*), BNC to Morris, Sept. 2, 1825.

11. About Jefferson and navigational items: Sowerby, *op. cit.,* pp. 80-81, 101.

12. Henry W. Dickinson, *Robert Fulton, Engineer and Artist, His Life and Works* (London, 1913), pp. 209-10; RG 45(*1*), May 4, 1810, and Apr. 6, 1811.

13. The executive departments reported their expenditures in *House Documents,* 17th Congress, 2d Session, Doc. 56 (Navy Dept.); Doc. 68 (War Dept.); Doc. 81 (State Dept.); Doc. 96 (Treasury Dept.). The two manuscript catalogs of the Navy Department library, dating from 1824 and 1829 are located in the Navy Department Library, Washington, D.C.

14. Imprisonment: *Philadelphia's* crew—Thomas Harris, *The Life and Services of Commodore William Bainbridge, USN.* (Philadelphia, 1837), pp. 84-87; Dartmoor prison—Josiah Cobb, *A Green Hand's First Cruise* (Baltimore, 1841), v. 2, pp. 164-67.

15. Morris, *op. cit.,* p. 34; Phineas C. Headley, *Life and Naval Career of Vice-Admiral David Glascoe Farragut* (New York, 1865), pp. 186-88, McKee, *op. cit.,* pp. 219-21; Alexander Slidell Mackenzie, *The Life of Commodore Oliver Hazard Perry* (New York, 1843), v. 2, pp. 140-41.

16. David Porter, *Journal of a Cruise Made to the Pacific Ocean* (2d ed. New York, 1822), v. 1, pp. 88-89, v. 2, pp. 140-41, 171; Nicholas B. Wainwright, *Commodore James Biddle and His Sketch Book* (Philadelphia, 1966), p. 11; Ruby R. Duvall, "Isaac Mayo—Officer and Gentleman of the 'Old Navy,'" *Shipmate,* 24 (May, 1961), 2-4; "Lieutenant J. P. Baker and Dr. Quarrier's Proposal for a Library on Board H.M.S. Leander," *Naval Chronicle,* 35 (Mar., 1816), 225-28.

17. Books on the Detroit frontier: RG 45(*21*), Lewis Bond to SN, Jan. 14, 1821. About Chaplain Felch: Burr, *Education in the Early Navy,* pp. 150-51; RG 45(*22*), Jan. 21, 1822; (*1*), Jan. 12, 1822; (*1*), SN to Commo. Charles Morris, July 19, 1831; Clifford M. Drury, *History of the Chaplain Corps,* v. 1, p. 30.

18. George Jones, *Sketches of Naval Life,* v. 2, pp. 240-41. Schools for midshipmen: Burr, *op. cit.,* pp. 129-30, 161-65. About West Point: Park Benjamin, *The United States Naval Academy* (New York, 1900), p. 109. An advertisement for E. C. Ward's school appeared in the 1821 ed. of Blunt's *New Practical Navigator,* p. [600].

19. About Capt. Partridge's academy: William A. Ellis, *Norwich University, 1819-1911* (Montpelier, Vt., 1911), v. 1, pp. 16-18, 60; *National Intelligencer,* advertisements of Dec. 31, 1823, and Jan. 6, 1824; John Pintard, *Letters to His Daughter,* v. 2, pp. 238-39.

20. Number of midshipmen in schools: Benjamin, *op. cit.,* p. 110. The two observers of schools at sea who reported favorably on them in their respective books were: Henry M. Brackenridge, *Voyage to South America* (Baltimore, 1819), v. 1, p. 110; and Levasseur, *loc. cit.*

21. About Darcy Lever's *Young Sea Officer's Sheet Anchor* (1819): RG 45(*1*), SN to Kearney, Feb. 5, 1827; (*213*), Jan. 14, 1825.

22. James M. Hoppin, *Life of Andrew Hull Foote, Rear-Admiral, USN.* (New York, 1874), p. 31; Charles H. Davis, Jr., *Life of Charles Henry Davis, Rear-Admiral, 1807-1877* (Boston, 1899), pp. 49-50, 223.

23. Howard Clayton, "The American College Library, 1800-1860," *Journal of Library History,* 3 (Apr., 1968), 120-37.

Chapter VII

Quotation at chapter head: Frederick Chamier, *The Life of a Sailor* (London, 1832), v. 1, p. v.

1. RG 45(*222*), Jan. 21, 1828. See note 2 of Chapter IV for an explanation of the notation used for citing National Archives record groups in this study.

2. Paulding: Ralph M. Aderman, ed., *The Letters of James Kirke Paulding* (Madison, 1962), pp. 95-97; RG 45(*6*); (*1*), May 16, 1828. Sloat: RG 45(*1*), to Tingey, Dec. 9, 1828; USNA-L, Sloat to Paulding, Dec. 17, 1828.

3. The *Constellation:* Enoch C. Wines, *Two Years and a Half in the Navy* (Philadelphia, 1832), v. 1, p. 23, v. 2, pp. 110-11; *Potomac* (1831-34): Reynolds, *Voyage of the U.S. Frigate Potomac,* p. 526; and Warriner, *Cruise of the U.S. Frigate Potomac Round the World,* p. 109; *Lexington:* McNally, *Evils and Abuses . . . Exposed,* pp. 160-61; *Guerriere:* Stewart, *A Visit to the South Seas,* v. 1, pp. 28-29; *Brandywine:* SM & NJ, 2 (Apr., 1830), 229; *Potomac* (1834-37): Rockwell, *Sketches of Foreign Travel,* p. 396; *Columbia:* Henshaw, *Around the World . . . ,* v. 2, p. 174; *Ontario:* Samuel E. Morison, *"Old Bruin," Commodore Matthew C. Perry, 1794-1858* (Boston, 1967), pp. 117-18. A photograph showing the location of a book cabinet in the wardroom of the restored frigate *Constitution* appears in Thomas P. Horgan's *Old Ironsides* (Boston, 1963), p. 99.

4. Aderman, *op. cit.,* pp. 126-27; RG 45(*6*), Dec. 29, 1832.

5. RG 45(*212*), Feb. 26, 1831, with endorsement for Cooper's *Naval History* added May 20, 1839; (*24*), Read, Dec. 10, 1837; Aderman, *op. cit.,* pp. 256-57, 478; Burr, *Education in the Early Navy,* pp. 174-75. The *Fulton:* RG 45(*1*), Sept. 29, 1837; (*24*), C. W. Skinner, July 5, 1838.

6. RG 45(*464*), Subject file NE—"Vessels Libraries, etc., Mar. 7, 1843."

7. U.S. Navy Dept., *Tables of Allowances of Equipment, Outfits, Stores, &c, &c, &c. for Each Class of Vessels in the Navy of the United States* (Washington, 1844); RG 45(*1*), Wyman, Aug. 14, 1843. About Brunet: Leo E. La Montagne, *American Library Classification* (Hamden, Conn., 1961), pp. 122-24, 127-32. The books contracted for by the Norfolk Navy Yard in 1845 were listed in *House Documents,* 29th Cong., 1st Sess., Doc. 94, pp. 4-9.

8. RG 45: *John Adams*—(*23*), W. J. McCluney, July 9, 1845; *Ohio*—(*1*), Parker, Dec. 21, 1846; *Raritan*—Parker, Apr. 24, 1849; SN to Bureau—(*13*), C. W. Skinner, Apr. 24, 1849; *Porpoise*—(*464*), Subject file NE —"List of Books Furnished U.S. Brig Porpoise, June, 1850."

9. RG 45(*32*), June 12, 13, 1852; *Michigan:* (*1*), Cdr. J. S. Nicholas, Apr. 4, 1854; *St. Mary's:* (*1*), Cdr. T. Bailey, Sept. 29, 1853; *Germantown:* (*23*), Cdr. W. F. Lynch, Nov. 15, 1853.

10. Two general accounts which survey the further development of libraries in the navy, with more emphasis on recent times, are: Louis N. Feipel, "The Rise and Development of Libraries on Board Vessels of the U.S. Navy," *Library Journal,* 44 (Oct., 1919), 638-44; and, Dorothy F. Deininger, "The Navy and Marine Corps System of Shipboard Libraries and General Libraries Ashore," in *Encyclopedia of Library and Information Science* (New York, 1968), v. 1, pp. 557-61.

11. *U.S. Statutes at Large,* v. 2, chapt. 28, pp. 536-37; v. 4, chapt. 43, pp. 20-21. Reports of expenditures for books: *House Documents,* 25th Cong., 2d Sess., Doc. 23, p. 2; 21st Cong., 1st Sess., Doc. 35, p. 5; 24th Cong., 2d Sess., Doc. 60, pp. 3, 24.

12. The *Decatur*: RG 45(*464*), Subject file NE—"Catalogue of Books Belonging to the Cabin Library of the U.S. Ship Decatur," and letter, Ogden to Morris, June 1, 1842; (*1*), Lt. H. Ingersol, Aug. 14, 1839; (*1*), Capt. W. B. Shubrick, Jan. 16, 1843.

13. The *Independence*: [Henry A. Wise], *Los Gringos, or An Inside View of Mexico and California* (New York, 1850), pp. 6-7, 24-25; *Powhattan*: Alan B. Cole, ed., *With Perry in Japan: the Diary of Edward York McCauley* (Princeton, 1942), pp. 112-13. About hospitals: Frank L. Pleadwell, "William Paul Crillon Barton," *Military Surgeon,* 46 (Mar., 1920), 273; RG 45(*1*), Asst. Surg. S. R. Swann, July 1, 1854.

14. [John S. Skinner], "Letter From a Friend to a Young Gentleman of Maryland, on His Entrance Into the Navy of the United States," *A & NC,* 12 (Nov. 4, 1841), 345-48; and another version in *A & NC & SR,* 2 (Dec. 7, 1843), 710-17.

15. RG 45(*213*), Dec. 15, 1831, and Nov. 1, 1834.

16. The *Delaware* (1834): RG 45(*464*), Subject file NE—"School Reports of Midshipmen, U.S.S. Delaware, 1834"; *Java*: Burr, *op. cit.,* p. 135; *Delaware* (1842): Peterson, *Journals of Daniel Noble Johnson,* pp. 37-39; *Vandalia*: Daniel Ammen, *The Old Navy and the New* (Philadelphia, 1893), p. 63; RG 45(*22*), W. M. Walker, June 8, 1833. The New York Navy Yard list is included among other library lists found in RG 45(*464*), Subject file NE; and the Norfolk list was sent by Capt. Shubrick to SN, Feb. 4, 1843 (*24*).

17. Burr, *op. cit.,* and Benjamin, *The U.S. Naval Academy,* provided background information about the Naval Asylum, along with Ammen, *op. cit.,* pp. 94-95, and Charles H. Stockton, *Origin, History, Laws and Regulations of the U.S. Naval Asylum* (Washington, 1886), pp. 18-23.

18. James R. Soley, *Historical Sketch of the United States Naval Academy* (Washington, 1876), pp. 27-31.

19. *House Documents,* 29th Cong., 2d Sess., Doc. 21, p. 4.

20. RG 181 (Boston Navy Yard), SN to Commo. F. A. Parker, May 19, 1846.

21. U.S. Naval Academy: Book purchases from New York and Philadelphia —RG 217, Fourth Auditor's Reports and Accounts, Alphabetical Series— Joseph White Vouchers, no. 108, Mar. 20, 1847; no. 143, Oct. 9, 1846; no. 120, Oct. 12, 1846. Growth of Library (1852): RG 45(*326*), "Books in the Library of the Naval Academy, Feb. 10, 1852." About Vattemare: Charlotte Fletcher, *Library Quarterly,* 27 (Apr., 1957), 95-99; RG 45(*326*), Jan. 12, and May 28, 1851. The academic board: *Ibid,* May 28, 1851.

22. About the 1860 catalog: Thomas G. Ford, Autobiography, 1st draft (MS at USNA-L). The "Synopsis of the Analytical Catalogue" of the Naval Academy Library of 1860 is reproduced and commented upon in LaMontagne, *op. cit.,* pp. 163-66. About the library at Newport: RG 405, Letters Received, 1845-1909, folder "Naval Academy Library, 1862-65," Librarian to Superintendent, Nov. 18, 1862, and July 28, 1865; Paymaster to Supt., March 5, 1863.

23. About Confederate States Navy: *Regulations for the Navy of the Confederate States* (Richmond, 1862), p. 110; *Regulations of the Confederate States School-Ship Patrick Henry* (Richmond, 1863), pp. 6, 26-27. Return of the Naval Academy to Annapolis: Benjamin, *op. cit.,* pp. 262-83.

Chapter VIII

Quotation at chapter head: Thomas Campbell, *The Pleasures of Hope,* 1799.

1. Most of the general background information about the navy and science,

and about early scientific institutions and expeditions in America used in this chapter was taken from A. Hunter Dupree, *Science in the Federal Government, a History of Policies and Activities to 1940* (Cambridge, Mass., 1957). "Museums" in sailors' taverns are commented upon in Stan Hugill's *Sailortown* (London, 1967), p. 88; and the instinct to collect is mentioned by Charles B. Davenport in relation to thalassophilia in his study, *Naval Officers, Their Heredity and Development,* Carnegie Institution Publication, no. 259 (Washington, 1919), p. 26. An enumeration of the various objects collected by one naval officer is appendad to a *Speech of Commodore Jesse Duncan Elliott, USN, Delivered at Hagerstown, Md., on 14th November, 1843* (Philadelphia, 1844), pp. 73-74.

    2. Maurice E. Phillips, "A Brief History of Academy Publications," *Proc. Academy of Natural Sciences of Philadelphia,* 100 (1948), ix. Commo. Downes's orders appeared in Reynolds, *Voyage of the Frigate Potomac,* p. 526. See note 2, Chapter IV for an explanation of the notation used for citing National Archives record groups in this study.

    3. Unless otherwise cited, the source for information on the Naval Lyceum used in this section is "Minutes of the U.S. Naval Lyceum, Nov. 27, 1833–Apr. 29, 1882" (MS. at USNA-M). About the lyceum movement: Carl Bode, *The American Lyceum, Town Meeting of the Mind* (New York, 1956); and Cecil B. Hayes, *The American Lyceum, Its History and Contribution to Education,* Office of Education Bull. no. 12 (Washington, 1932).

    4. *SM & NJ,* 6 (Jan., 1834), 145-46.

    5. [James H. West], *A Short History of the New York Navy Yard* (Brooklyn: U.S. Navy Yard, 1941), pp. 74-80.

    6. Rhees, *Manual of Public Libraries,* p. 240.

    7. USNA-M, Capt. Phythian to Capt. F. M. Ramsay, Chief of Bureau of Navigation, Nov. 25, 1890, and Ramsay to Phythian, Nov. 28; Correspondence of the U.S. Naval Lyceum, no. 274. As described by Alfred T. Mahan in his recollections, *From Sail to Steam* (New York, 1907, pp. 293, 303), the War College had a precarious existence during its early years. Although its library was thought to be fairly "respectable," Mahan likened some of its content to "Quaker guns," which "made a brave show if not too closely scrutinized."

    8. The history of the Naval Library and Institute is drawn from its two publications, *Statutes of the Naval Library and Institute . . . With an Account of Its Origin and Purpose* (Boston, 1867), and *Annual Report for the Year 1868* (Boston, 1868); and unless otherwise cited, all other information about the Naval Library was obtained from its Book of Minutes, kept from the inception of the organization until May 15, 1916 (MS at USNA-M).

    9. "Catalogue of Books at the Naval Library and Institute, 1875" (MS at USNA-M).

    10. "Log of the U.S. Naval Academy Library, 1917-1940" (MS at USNA-L). The disposition of the property of other small lyceums which existed in naval shore establishments between 1830 and 1910 is also mentioned in Harry A. Baldridge's article, "Naval Academy Museum—the First 100 Years," *Proc. USNI,* 71 (Sept., 1945), 1007-21.

    11. About the U.S. Naval Institute: Letters to the Boston Branch of the USNI, v. 3, Oct. 16, 1879 (MS at USNA-M). Roy C. Smith, "Fifty Years of Service," *Proc. USNI,* 49 (Oct., 1933), 1417-21.

    12. *American State Papers,* v. 3, pp. 309-10, 547.

    13. The letters were also published by Reynolds in his *Pacific and Indian Oceans, or The South Sea Surveying and Exploring Expedition, Its Inception, Progress and Objects* (New York, 1841).

14. The letters received by the secretary of the navy relating to the expedition, in addition to various journals and logs which were kept during its existence, have been collected in RG 37 of the National Archives. This material (chiefly vols. 1, 3, and 12 of the Records Relating to the U.S. Exploring Expedition), and other records contained in RG 45, *viz.* (*1, 3, 21, 22, 464*), are the sources for most of the references to the provision and disposition of the expedition's library, unless otherwise cited.

15. About the library on the *Vincennes*: Jared L. Elliott, "Journals Kept as Chaplain on the Wilkes Expedition, Aug. 3, 1838 to May 6, 1842" (MS at Library of Congress); Charles Wilkes, *Narrative of the U.S. Exploring Expedition, 1838-1842* (new ed. New York, 1851), v. 1, p. 381. Loss of the *Peacock: House Reports,* 28th Cong., 1st Sess., Rept. 427, pp. 13, 17.

16. The book items which the expedition sent to Washington were also listed by Dr. Pickering in a report of the holdings of the National Institute. See *Annual Report of the Smithsonian Institution, 1897: Report of the U.S. National Museum* (Washington, 1901), pt. 2, pp. 161-63.

17. Daniel C. Haskell, *The United States Exploring Expedition, 1838-1842 and Its Publications 1844-1874; A Bibliography* (New York, 1942), pp. 1-24. On the occasion of the "Centenary of the Wilkes Exploring Expedition, 1838-1842," several papers concerning the history and significance of the expedition were presented at a meeting of the American Philosophical Society on Feb. 23, 1940. See its *Proceedings,* 82 (June, 1940), 519-800.

18. About minor expeditions: William F. Lynch, *Narrative of the United States' Expedition to the River Jordan and the Dead Sea* (9th rev. ed. Philadelphia, 1854), p. 14; William L. Herndon, *Exploration of the Valley of the Amazon* (Washington, 1853-1854), v. 1, pp. 6, 24-26; James M. Gilliss, *The U.S. Naval Astronomical Expedition to the Southern Hemisphere During the Years 1849-52* (Washington, 1855), v. 1, pp. 401-2, 450; RG 45(*1*), T. J. Page, Dec. 7 and 13, 1842.

19. About the Japan expeditions: William E. Griffis, *Matthew Calbraith Perry, a Typical Naval Officer* (Boston, 1890), pp. 294-95; Morison, "*Old Bruin,*" *Commodore Matthew Calbraith Perry,* pp. 276-77; Alan B. Cole, *Yankee Surveyors in the Shogun's Seas* (Princeton, 1947), pp. 4-6; RG 45(*23*), Cdr. C. Ringgold, Dec. 16, 17, 1852; (*1*), same, Dec. 17, 1852.

20. Elisha K. Kane, *Arctic Explorations: The Second Grinnell Expedition . . .* (Philadelphia, 1856), v. 1, pp. 19-20, v. 2, pp. 196-97, 215-17; Joseph E. Nourse, *American Explorations in the Ice Zones* (Boston, 1884), pp. 68, 88.

21. Duty with the coast survey is commented upon in Benjamin Sands's *From Reefer to Rear-Admiral, Reminiscences . . . of Nearly Half a Century of Naval Life, 1827-1874* (New York, 1899), pp. 88-89, 120-21.

22. *Senate Documents,* 28th Cong., 2d Sess., Doc. 114, pp. 54-66; Marjorie S. Clopine, "United States Naval Observatory Library: Resources and Treasures," *Special Libraries,* 52 (Feb., 1961), pp. 78-81.

23. About the Nautical Almanac Office: Davis, *Life of Charles Henry Davis,* pp. 86-89; Simon Newcomb, *The Reminiscences of an Astronomer* (Boston, 1903), pp. 63-77. About Bowditch's library: Jewett, *Report on the Public Libraries of the U.S.,* pp. 30, 39-40; Margaret Munsterberg, "The Bowditch Collection in the Boston Public Library," *Isis,* 34 (Autumn, 1942), 140-42.

24. RG (*229*), Sept., 22, 1832, and Oct. 7, 1833.

25. Aderman, *Letters of James K. Paulding,* pp. 118, 134-45, 145-46; RG 45 (*6*), Nov. 20, 1833.

26. About *Annales maritimes*: RG 45(*464*), Subject file XS—New York navy agent to BNC, July 25, 1842. About Franck Taylor: *Ibid*, Subject file NE—Taylor to BNC, Aug. 12, 1842; (*3*), Taylor, Nov. 6, 1845. The Pacific Squadron: (*1*), F. A. Parker, July 17, 1846. About ship's library: (*6*), Seth Thomas, Storekeeper, Aug. 28, 1847.

27. About Bolton's loan: RG 45(*1*), Oct. 13, 1843; (*24*), Oct. 16, 1843. Perry's loan: RG 45(*214*), Apr. 6, 1839.

28. About the bureaus' libraries: RG 45(*464*), Subject file NE—Capt. W. N. Crane to SN, Oct. 21, 1843; *Paullin's History of Naval Administration,* 211-14; Jewett, *op. cit.,* p. 140.

29. Rhees, *Manual of Public Libraries,* pp. 78, 239-40, 514, 520-21.

30. James R. Masterson, comp., "Preliminary Checklist of the Naval Records Collection of the Office of Naval Records and Library, 1775-1910," (mimeographed, National Archives, Dec., 1945), pp. v-x.

Chapter IX

Quotation at chapter head: Frobisher's second voyage (1577), *in* Hakluyt's *Voyages* (facsimile ed., Cambridge, 1965), v. 2, p. 623.

1. About literacy: Sanford Winston, *Illiteracy in the United States* (Chapel Hill, 1930), pp. 3-6; U.S. Bureau of the Census, *Historical Statistics of the United States, Colonial Times to 1957* (Washington, 1960), pp. 9, 206.

2. Most of the authors mentioned specifically in the text of this chapter have already been cited in Chapter V in connection with seamen's libraries. The references previously given usually apply in this chapter also, and are not repeated here unless additional or different pages are cited. About the composition of the *Constitution's* crew: Benjamin F. Stevens, *A Cruise on the Constitution; Around the World in Old Ironsides, 1844-1847* (New York, 1904), pp. 41-42.

3. *Ibid.*

4. "The Pitcairn Bible," *Bull. New York Public Library,* 28 (June, 1924), 443-52. About Chaplain Colton: [Walter Colton], *Ship and Shore, or Leaves From the Journal of a Cruise to the Levant* (New York, 1835), p. 215; Van Denburgh, *My Voyage in the U.S. Frigate "Congress,"* p. 169.

5. William H. Meyers, *Journal of a Cruise . . . in the Sloop-of-War Cyane, 1841-1844* (San Francisco, 1955), p. 19. About forecastle etiquette: Charles Nordhoff, *Sailor Life on Man of War and Merchant Vessel* (New York, 1884), p. 347. Lending of personal books in the merchant marine: Marine Historical Association, *John T. Perkins' Journal at Sea, 1845* (Mystic, Conn., 1934), p. 126.

6. Three religious sailors' magazines provided the quoted passages, *viz: NSM,* 1 (May, 1821), 35; *CH & SM,* 10 (Dec. 20, 1823), 473-75; *SM & NJ,* 22 (Apr., 1850), 251, and 18 (Jan., 1846), 157, 18 (Oct., 1845), 47-48, respectively.

7. RG 45(*23*), Mackenzie to SN, May 13, 1842; (*1*), May 16, 1842.

8. Scott on the frontier: James D. Hart, *The Popular Book, a History of America's Literary Taste* (New York, 1950), p. 69. *Astoria,* etc., in California: Nunis, *Books in Their Sea Chests,* pp. 6-7, 15-17. *The Cabin Boy's Locker* was compiled in book form by John K. Davis.

9. Charles W. Parsons, *Memoir of Usher Parsons, M.D.* (Providence, 1870), p. 24. A discussion of manuals written for seamen is presented in Craig Hardin's article, "An Anchor to Windward: Manuals for Young Americans in Days of Sail," *American Neptune,* 30 (Jan., 1970), 40-45.

10. The contemporary writers, Torrey, Gould, Ames, Warriner, Mercier, Gragg (all cited in Chapter V), and Morison in "*Old Bruin*," as well as Kane and the Parrys all mention or describe shipboard theatricals in their works. *Troupes dramatiques* were referred to in Joseph G. Casy, *Organisation du personnel d'un vaisseau* (Paris, 1840), p. 222.

11. About crossing the line: Henning Henningsen, *Crossing the Equator, Sailors' Baptism and Other Rites* (Copenhagen, 1961), 52, 85, 92, 114-15, 291-99, 310; Harry M. Lydenberg, comp., *Crossing the Line, Tales of the Ceremony During Four Centuries* (New York, 1957), pp. 217-18; [Noah Jones], *Journals of Two Cruises Aboard the American Privateer Yankee* (New York, 1967), pp. 83-86.

12. Magic lantern shows were mentioned in Edward Parry, *Memoirs of Rear-Admiral Sir W. Edward Parry*, p. 137, and ship models in Cobb, *A Green Hand's First Cruise*, v. 2, pp. 161-62. About the value of recreation: William P. C. Barton, *A Treatise Containing a Plan for the Internal Organization and Government of Marine Hospitals in the United States* (Philadelphia, 1814), p. 240.

13. George Bayly, *Sea-Life Sixty Years Ago* (London, 1885), pp. 112-13.

14. [Daniel Defoe], *A New Voyage Round the World By a Course Never Sailed Before* (London, 1725), p. 1.

15. The *North Georgia Gazette* was also reproduced as an appendix in an American edition of William E. Parry's *Journal of a Voyage for the Discovery of a North-West Passage* (Philadelphia, 1824). W. E. Parry commented upon the *Gazette* in his journal, as did his son Edward in his biography, *Memoirs of Rear-Admiral Sir W. Edward Parry*, pp. 104-5. About the *Constellation's* "Gazette": Pintard, *Letters to His Daughter*, v. 2, pp. 55-56. *The White Star Journal; Published Weekly on Board the Clipper Ship White Star . . . in the Year 1855* was reprinted by the Marine Historical Association of Mystic, Conn., in 1951.

16. Walter H. Blumenthal, *Bookmen's Bedlam, an Olio of Literary Oddities* (New Brunswick, N.J., 1955), pp. 58-60.

17. About Colton as *alcalde* and journalist: Walter Colton, *Three Years in California* (New York, 1852), 13-19, 32-33, 174, 230-31; Clifford M. Drury, "Walter Colton, Chaplain and Alcalde," *California Historical Society Quarterly*, 35 (June, 1952), 102-6; John T. Winterich, *Early American Books and Printing* (Boston, 1935), pp. 207-8.

Appendixes

Naval storekeeper's inventory— ⎱
Library of the York Navy Yard— ⎰   These two book lists comprise one document, *viz.*, RG 45(*464*), Subject file NE—"List of Books, the property of the United States, in the Commandant's Office at the Navy Yard, New York, composing the Library of the Yard on the 6 April 1846," [and] "List of Books, the property of the U.S. Navy Department, in charge of the Naval Storekeeper, [a] For Libraries of Ships, [b] Libraries for Seamen, [c] School Books, April 10th 1846."

1827 List of books for navy yards—RG 45(*212*), BNC to Commandants, May 3, 1827.

1845 List of books contracted for by the Norfolk Navy Yard—*House Documents*, 29th Cong., 1st Sess., Doc. 94, pp. 4-9.

Karpinski—Louis C. Karpinski, *Bibliography of Mathematical Works Printed*

in America Through 1850 (Ann Arbor, 1940).
Sabin—Joseph Sabin, *Bibliotheca Americana; A Dictionary of Books Relating to America From Its Discovery to the Present Time* (New York, 1868-1936).

Index

Book titles mentioned in the text and also included in the Appendixes are listed in the Index by appendix letter and entry number: *e.g.*, E12 means Appendix E, entry [12]. Where the same title occurs in more than one appendix, only the last appendix reference is given.

Wise, Sailing Master Henry A., 155

Wood, William, 173; and library of *Franklin*, 50, 65-76 *passim*, 179; mechanics' and apprentices' libraries, 50, 52-53, 55, 56; philanthropy of, 50-52, 57-58; role in naval libraries evaluated, 50, 54, 56-57, 91-92; seamen's libraries and, 56-57, 67, 68, 79; subscription libraries, shipboard, 79, 81, 82, 91, 130

Wood, William (zoologist), 52

Woodall, John, 13

Woodbury, Secy. Navy Levi, 72, 73, 74, 138, 140, 141-42, 169-70, 172, 198

Woodward, Josiah, 19, 210

Writing, by sailors. *See* Seamen

Wyman, Capt. Thomas W., 146, 200

Yale College, 131, 204

Yankee, privateer, 214

York, packet, 48

Young Men's Christian Association, 104

"Youth's Christian Library," (ATS), 100

Zebulon (Harris), 107, B50

Zebulun, the Mariner's Tribe, 21